Miceal Woakle

Not all the King's Men

CHANGE AND CONTINUITY IN AFRICA

MOUTON PUBLISHERS · THE HAGUE · PARIS · NEW YORK

MARTIN R. DOORNBOS

Institute of Social Studies, The Hague

Not all the King's Men

Inequality as a Political Instrument in Ankole, Uganda

MOUTON PUBLISHERS · THE HAGUE · PARIS · NEW YORK

ISBN: 90–279–7707–0

Cover design by Jurriaan Schrofer

© 1978, Mouton Publishers, The Hague

🔲 *Typeset and printed in Great Britain by H Charlesworth & Co Ltd*

Preface

Analyses of development and change in Africa have frequently focused on colonial intervention as the major catalyst of structural transformation, first describing the precolonial situation, then contrasting it with subsequent developments. All too often, however, these efforts have been limited to one of two purposes. One considered the distinctive characteristics or cultural attributes of a particular society, supposedly rooted in tradition, which the researcher traces through the colonial period and beyond in order to document how 'change' had been 'mediated' and accommodated' in that particular case. 'Continuity of culture' has long been a pervasive theme in anthropological and historical literature on single African societies that were incorporated into colonial frameworks.

The other perspective is different and disregards much of the detail. Colonial intervention again is treated as a major watershed, but here African societies are seen as moulded to the image, or shaped by the intention, of the colonizing power into either 'modernizing' entities or exploited reservoirs of human and material resources. The stress is on the forces and consequences of colonialism rather than on what is distinctive or culturally specific. 'Tradition' becomes a residual category. Detailed socio-political features of a particular society may scarcely figure in the analysis of colonial transformation, or may be considered separately from external influences, leaving ambiguous how exactly colonial processes impinged upon and transformed social structures.

These differences are matters of emphasis, related in part to disciplinary traditions, in part to other kinds of preferences. But as points of view they can illuminate one set of conditions and eclipse another. While the present study also tries to understand incorporation processes, my main interest is to grasp the effects of colonialism on the formation of socio-political groups and structures in a particular society, that of Ankole in western Uganda. I am therefore concerned with 'change' rather than 'continuity', and with examining its specific repercussions within the Ankole socio-political context, hopefully without losing sight of the 'general' effects of colonial incorporation.

The focus is thus on the impact and continued effects of British colonialism in Ankole, in terms of shifting patterns of socio-political power relationships – expressed mainly in the dynamics of inequality and in ethnic-religious factionalism. The thesis of this study is that these patterns have been structurally determined; put differently, that the socio-political order and inequality which emerged in Ankole were fundamentally congruent with the format and objectives of the colonial state.

At this point, it is pertinent to introduce a few salient features of the historic Nkore system, the pre-colonial precursor of Ankole. These include a basic social and economic separateness of two major population groups, Bairu peasants and Bahima herdsmen; a certain power advantage held by the Bahima in their contacts with the Bairu; and an institution of kingship whose incumbent acted largely as *primus inter pares* among the Bahima political elite. Colonial rule affected these arrangements most profoundly. Its different and externally de-termined modes of political control, the introduction of a market mechanism, the redirection of production processes, and its other impacts on social relationships, were among the major departures which, in Ankole as elsewhere, began to generate a new species of society: dependent and ruled largely on a basis of peasant production plus law and order. These effects, to be sure, were fundamentally 'general', as was the corollary emergence of class society with which we are also concerned. But in a society that had its own specific pattern of ethnic cum occupational groupings and a distinctive institutional structure, these general effects could only manifest themselves in a similarly specific way, producing new cleavages and frictions that also need to be understood against the dynamics and forces which distinguished the context.

Our argument thus runs roughly as follows. Notwithstanding a semblance of 'indirect rule' and institutional continuity, colonial incorporation in the case of Ankole, and elsewhere in Uganda, meant the establishment of a colonial administrative state. This in turn implied the creation of a new chiefly elite, whose socio-political status was derived from, and defined by, the colonial framework. By virtue of the 'franchise' and benefits granted to them, and in the absence of alternative powerful ranking criteria, this elite's strategic position turned it into a privileged class and a local ruling stratum. These arrangements caused two peculiar constellations. First, whether as a matter of historical misconception or of deliberate strategy, the Bahima were recruited in disproportionately large numbers into the senior ranks of the new chiefly class. This practice entailed a self-implementing but erroneous hypothesis: that historical Nkore had been based on an ethnic hierarchy, with Bahima on top and Bairu at the bottom. It also entailed inbuilt ethnic friction, as Bairu in due course began to question and to challenge the basis on which political privileges were allocated. The second peculiarity pertained to the role of kingship. Nominally this was posited as a kind of mythical umbrella under which colonial transformations took shape, but in reality it was used as an instrument of colonial rule. Due partly to colonial lack of appreciation of the historical role of kingship, however, the institution was ineffective at its new task; moreover, its ineptness was made even more equivocal due to the Bairu-Bahima division.

The study is concerned with these two sets of problems. It covers three broad historical periods, i.e. pre-colonial, early colonial, and late colonial and post-colonial, so as to get a better grasp of the processes of transformation in Ankole society. Thus, while Chapter 1 gives a background to the Uganda context, particularly its local politics, the study is first concerned, in Chapter 2, with a reinterpretation of political relationships in pre-colonial Nkore. This is focused on the nature of the relationships between the major socio-economic groups, the Bairu and the Bahima, as well as on the institutional framework, specifically the historical role of kingship.

Chapter 3 traces the major impacts of the new colonial arrangements on the society, particularly as they affected the nature of socio-political relationships and institutional arrangements in Ankole. The chapter shows how, beginning during the early colonial period, major transformations of the socio-political framework inaugurated drastically redefined group and institutional relationships in the society. Ethnic divisiveness and growing social inequality, the evidence suggests, were hardly accidental by-products of this transformation: the hierarchy and subordination of which they were a function were basic to the maintenance of the colonial state. Chapter 4 is concerned with the late colonial and early post-colonial period in Ankole, and attempts to identify the major continuities and changes that occurred in the patterns of socio-political relationships. Ethnic hierarchy, compounded by religious divisions, provoked ethnic protest but in the end lost its sharpness in Ankole. Less variable, it turned out, were the dynamics of social inequality. Though its basis had been shifting – from one that was largely 'ascriptive' and more ethnically exclusive to one that increasingly stressed criteria of wealth and power, stratified privilege had clearly come to stay. Connected with this has been the role and position of the bureaucracy, making for a sharp line of differentiation separating those within from those outside the area of government employment. Moreover, the increasing redundancy of the Ankole kingship is documented here. During the late colonial period and beyond, however, the framework showed signs of stress and overburdening. Chapter 4 is largely concerned with these strains and breakdowns which began to occur once the structure's linchpin, that of ultimate colonial control, was withdrawn. In conclusion, Chapter 5 is in part retrospective, in part more generalised: on the basis of the Ankole experience, it reconsiders the role and weight of ethnicity as a variable, and juxtaposes it with the effects of structural arrangements. Lastly, the impacts and repercussions of the colonial framework in Ankole society are shown to be reflected in the fortunes of the kingship: redefined in terms of that framework, its staying power was seriously reduced and its eventual eclipse proved to be a cause of little consternation.

The trend of developments in Ankole is followed in this study up to the early years of the Amin regime. Since 1973, in particular, a whole range of confrontations and measures have begun drastically to alter and obliterate many of the patterns and dynamics which had earlier been dominant. Among other things, Ankole suffered more than its share of victimization as a result of army brutality, and in 1974 provided the sorry scene for the abortive Obote invasion from Tanzania. Like the rest of Uganda, the larger part of Ankole's administrative cadre at all levels was pushed out and replaced under military control, thus throwing out of balance the particular power hierarchy and the pattern of group interactions which had been developing since its creation as a colonial sub-unit. Finally, Ankole formally ceased to exist as a sub-unit when the district was subdivided and the new parts incorporated into one of Uganda's new provinces. As it happens, therefore, this study is first focused on the establishment of Ankole as part of the process of colonial incorporation, then covers the period of its existence as a distinct, though dependent political arena, and concludes at the point of its dismantlement. Needless to say, this was hardly a matter of research 'design'.

The study is based on interviews, analyses of archive materials, correspondence and the relevant literature, first started in 1965–67 when I was a Research Fellow of the Makerere Institute of Social Research, and prepared for a Ph.D. at the University of California, Berkeley. This was supplemented by several additional visits to Uganda and Ankole up to 1973. In earlier publications I have reported on a number of specific questions raised during this research – issues of ethnic inequality and protest, the role of kingship, the land factor, and the nature of the political arena. Substantial parts of this material have been integrated, after revision, into the more general and detailed account of Ankole's experience with the politics of incorporation presented here. Permission to reproduce is acknowledledged for sections from:

'Kumanyana and Rwenzururu: Two Responses to Ethnic Inequality', in Robert I. Rotberg and Ali A. Mazrui (eds.), *Protest and Power in Black Africa,* Oxford University Press, New York, 1970; 'Some Conceptual Problems Concerning Ethnicity in Integration Analysis', *Civilisations,* XXII, 2, 1972; 'Images and Reality of Stratification in Pre-Colonial Nkore', *Canadian Journal of African Studies,* VII, 2, 1973; 'Some Aspects of Regional Government in Uganda and Ghana', *Journal of Administration Overseas,* XII, 2, 1973; *Regalia Galore: the decline and eclipse of Ankole kingship,* East African Literature Bureau, Nairobi, 1975; 'Land Tenure and Political Conflict in Ankole, Uganda', *Journal of Development Studies,* vol. 12, no. 1, 1975; 'Ethnicity, Christianity and the Development of Social Stratification in Colonial Ankole, Uganda', *International Journal of African Historical Studies,* vol. 9, no. 4, 1976; 'Ankole'. in René Lemarchand (ed.), *African Kingships in Perspective,* Frank Cass & Co. Ltd., London, 1977.

The research has been supported, at different times and in different ways, by the Makerere Institute of Social Research, the Institute of Social Studies at The Hague, and the African Studies Centre, Leiden. The Uganda Ministry of Regional Administration, the District Commissioner's Office, Ankole, and the Ankole Kingdom

Government extended their collaboration in the execution of the research. To all these institutions, I acknowledge my appreciation for the support received.

Many individuals have, directly or indirectly, contributed to the work presented here. While some have never been to Ankole, others cannot now leave, or return to Ankole. Some have died as victims of the spiralling conflicts in the district of recent years, especially those caused by external intervention. They and many other people in Ankole generously shared their insights with me, which I have tried to convey as accurately as possible.

While a particular word of thanks is due to several Ugandans and non-Ugandans for their support, present conditions dictate that the Ugandans concerned must remain nameless. For this reason I feel it is more appropriate to make no acknowledgements at all. I should add that responsibility for any deficiencies is my own.

Contents

Map 1.   *Uganda until 1973*

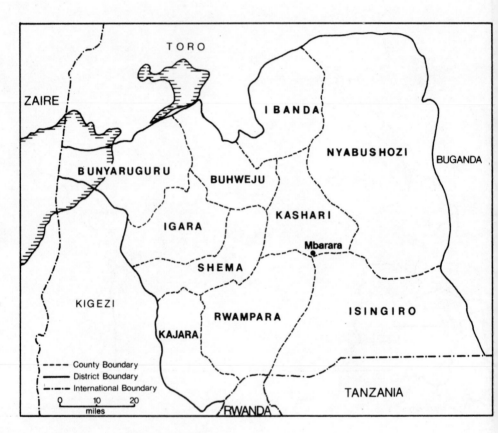

Map 2. *Ankole until 1973*

A Note on Orthography

In this book the spelling of names of population groups, areas, etc., is generally based on the orthography used in Runyankore, i.e. the language of Ankole. In quotations and other references I have maintained the spelling as used in the original documents. Readers may find it helpful to bear in mind some basic rules on the use of prefixes in Runyankore, which includes a few variations on the general pattern of prefixes in the interlacustrine Bantu languages. The prefix *Mu-* (as in *Muhima, Muganda*) or *Mw-* (as in *Mwiru*) designates a single person, while *Ba-* (as in *Bahima, Baganda, Bairu*) signifies the plural. In older spellings and in official names, however, an *O* is often added before the singular form (as in *Omugabe* = king) and an *A* before the plural (as in *Abagabe* = kings). Also, many names for population groups have the prefixes *Munya-* and *Banya-* (rather than *Mu-* and *Ba-*) for the single and plural respectively (for example *Munyankore* or *Banyankore* for a person or people from/of *Ankole*). Again, *Ru-* or *Runya-* (as in *Rutoro, Runyankore*) identifies the language (of *Toro* and *Ankole* respectively). This contrasts with the *Lu-* used in *Luganda* (the language of *Buganda*), in the spelling of which the *L* generally takes the place of the *R* used in Runyankore. Finally, *Ki-* and *Kinya-* designate adjectives (as in *Kiganda* and *Kinyankore*).

1. Local Politics in Uganda
A Background

Two characteristics of Uganda society have long fascinated its observers. One was the existence of several semi-traditional states (Buganda, Ankole, Toro, Bunyoro) within the country, which were incorporated into the colonial framework and continued through the first five years of Uganda as an independent state. These kingdoms, especially Buganda, featured elaborate institutional structures and cultural heritages and often appeared to exhibit a strong sense of solidarity. The other characteristic has been the juxtaposition of a wide variety of ethnic groups within Uganda's socio-political context. These two features have perhaps not been unrelated, although their precise bearings upon each other raise various questions. The strength of traditional authority, for instance, might have been enhanced within specific ethnocultural settings, while in turn ethnic solidarities might have been reinforced through traditional state structures. Also, coexistence within a single framework of semi-traditional states together with other, 'non-state' societies, in some sense may have influenced reciprocal perspectives and the nature of contact between these units. In either case, ethnic factors and traditional authority patterns were long markedly visible in Uganda.

The purpose of this chapter is to provide some background to the Uganda context of which Ankole formed part, particularly to identify some aspects of the district-based politics which for a long time appeared so characteristic of Uganda. Issues of ethnic heterogeneity, whether or not enhanced by traditional authority structures, necessarily stand central in this discussion.

Yet, two caveats must be noted. One is that, ethnicity being a rather elusive concept, almost no classification or even discussion of ethnic groups can avoid arbitrariness. In the end, the number of categories established in any classification depends on the criteria employed, whether language, kinship, political unity, region, custom, or some other. That procedure, already, is not without problems. But a recurrent difficulty is that several criteria may at once underly an inventory – perhaps reflecting that ethnic groups in reality are never neatly patterned and may stress as their basis of solidarity regionalism in one case and language in another. Uganda's population groups provide ample evidence to corroborate this complexity.

Neither is the concept of 'tribe' particularly illuminating.[1] Not only does it lack an equivalent in several Ugandan languages, including Runyankore, but people may be distinguished – and distinguish themselves – from others without identifying themselves as a 'tribe' or any other kind of collectivity. The Bakiga in Kigezi District, for example, have only in recent times exhibited some sense of common identity, which perhaps was related to their juxtaposition with other groups in the district.[2] Uganda has various other examples of such 'ethnicity' where previously there was none, suggesting that, whatever else it is, it is a variable, if not manipulable property.

The second point is closely related, namely that during colonial times in Uganda tribes or ethnic groups were often 'manufactured'.[3] In regard to several of the interlacustrine kingdoms, British rule did much to sustain, and to strengthen, the cohesiveness of these states. In other, rather more heterogeneous districts such as Bukedi, Kigezi, Teso or Toro, efforts were made to make boundaries of counties or sub-counties correspond to lines of ethnic divisions. Again, in other cases, such as Busoga, Acholi or Lango, there were previously no common centralised authority structures, but the colonial administration grouped together various clan units whose linguistic or other affiliations might facilitate the development and assertion of common political orientations and processes – notwithstanding the internal factionalism which was usually also exacerbated. None of these measures could ever fully reflect the subtle shades of ethnic differentiation, either within or across areas, nor, for that matter, the complexity of criteria involved. Their effect – if not the intent – primarily seems to have been a freezing and formalisation of certain levels of ethnic differentiation, solidifying them at the expense of others. Thus, while administrative subdivisions in some parts of Uganda tended to be projected along lines of ethnic cleavage, in other cases ethnic units seem rather to have been projected on the basis of administrative divisions; yet even the distinction between these two processes was often only a narrow one. In either case, and no matter how variedly defined the ethnic component, these policies contributed greatly to the apparent salience of ethnic groups in Uganda.

With these qualifications in mind, it may be noted that some thirty-one sub-groups have officially been distinguished.[4] In the anthropological literature these have in turn been subsumed into larger categories as Bantu, Nilotic, Nilo-Hamitic and Sudanic people. Numerically the two main clusters are Bantu and Nilotic, situated in the southern and northern parts of Uganda respectively. They are distinguished from one another by many characteristics and customs which anthropologists define as traditional culture, as well as by manifold specific differences: in diet (plantains not sorghum), cash crops cultivated (coffee and tea against cotton), physical features (short stature and light complexions among the Bantu; taller darker Nilotics), traditional social organisation (more extensive and formalised socio-political structures as opposed to small-scale kinship groupings).

These differences are further reflected in the linguistic diversity. This is particularly pronounced as Uganda lies on the cross-roads of several main language groups in Africa. The South and West (comprising Buganda as well as Ankole, Kigezi, Toro and Bunyoro) and parts of the eastern region of Uganda (Busoga, Bugisu and some parts of Bukedi) have been defined as Bantu-speaking areas, while Nilotic languages are predominant in Lango, Acholi and parts of West Nile. In the north of West Nile and the Madi District the Lugbara, Madi, Kakwa and Kuku people again speak different languages. Finally, the Karamojong, Iteso and Sebei belong to a separate linguistic category, although the label 'Nilo-Hamitic' is not based on a linguistic criterion but on a probably misconceived notion of ethnic origin.[5]

Still, the linguistic pattern can be more fully appreciated from the fact that more than 15 languages have been spoken on Radio Uganda and about 20 newspapers printed in some eight languages.[6] These figures varied over time with the introduction and termination of programmes and news media. There is also variation with respect to the numbers of people for which Uganda languages serve as vehicles of communication. Luganda is the most widely spoken language (1.100.000 people), followed closely by Runyankore-Rukiga (980.000), and Ateso (600.000).[7] On the other hand, there are some languages which are limited to only a few thousand people, while in certain cases, such as Bukedi District or Bwamba county in Toro, an extraordinary complexity obtains with three or four highly distinct languages spoken within a small area, several of which are never used in any mass media.

Obviously, then, Uganda's linguistic mosaic, merely one dimension of its ethnic diversity, does not provide a ready basis for communication across the country. Inordinate problems result from Uganda's multiplicity of languages, not least the excessive cost and duplication of administration, burdensome for a country with limited resources: any document that needs to be read throughout the country must be translated into as many as ten main languages. Politically, the effect is that language areas remain strongly centripetal; the possibility of transferring personnel from one area to another is severely reduced.

English has served as Uganda's official language not least to provide for convenient international – and internal – contact. However, it will not in the foreseeable future be spoken by a vast majority, since even the lower primary grades, conducted in vernacular, only 50% of Uganda's school-age children are eligible to enter. As a result, sufficient command of English is restricted to those categories who have education beyond the primary level, tending to turn it into an elite language.[8] This possibility has been recognised by successive governments,[9] though announced policies have hardly been likely to reduce the adverse implications. On the contrary, one may fairly predict a highly explosive issue to arise if, as has sometimes been contemplated, one of Uganda's languages were selected as the national vehicle of communication.

Linguistically, Uganda's conditions compare unfavourably with Tanzania or even Kenya, where Swahili is at least understood in most parts of the country. Past attempts to raise Swahili to the status of a *lingua franca* for Uganda appear to have failed, partly due to the command which Luganda enjoyed in a large part of the country.[10] Today, its introduction might be negatively affected by the low regard in many areas for the armed forces who, due to historical reasons, happen to be the main carriers of Swahili. Also, to promote Swahili as a national vehicle would yield limited benefits in the Uganda context; in many areas it would be another alien language, one moreover with reduced facility for international communication.[11]

Similar to the linguistic pattern, other aspects of Uganda's ethnic heterogeneity can also be considered in terms of their implications for cross-national interaction. One would find considerable diversity, particularly in economic patterns, and the welter of differences might easily seem to provide a basis for the perpetuation of sectional interests and attachments. At least, it might be deduced that these differences can hardly be seen as particularly conducive to social and political integration. However, it does *not* immediately follow that they possess unusual potential for fragmentation. We will return to this argument later. Instead, it will be more important to look at the processes of social and economic differentiation that were first initiated in the wake of colonial rule, which had profound effects in exacerbating differences in economic opportunities as well as in social and political influence – both within and among Uganda's various population groups. In Ankole, for example, these processes were to imply serious conflict between Bairu and Bahima.

UNEVEN COLONIAL DEVELOPMENT: BUGANDA AND THE REST

Uganda has not avoided problems caused by uneven development within one country. Beyond the historical differences in organisation and ways of life of Uganda's population groups, social and economic changes and new organisational forms developed during colonial and post-colonial times profoundly affected orientations and created new arenas for social and political action. But they had a differential impact. Often this originated in historical accident, namely the fact that certain crucial changes happened to start in one place rather than another, and initiated transformations which increasingly differentiated one area from the next. As some Ugandans put it, 'this country would have become a very different one if the British had landed on, say, Mount Elgon rather than in Buganda'.

As it happened, Uganda's history has in a fundamental sense centered upon Buganda. Even the country's name is derived from that of the kingdom of Buganda, which has been a focus of attention ever since Speke in the 19th century traversed it while searching for the sources of the Nile.[12] Missionaries and traders who arrived on the scene later made Buganda their basis of operations. Towards the close of the century, the British set up colonial administration in the area as a whole, rule that was extended outward from Buganda and established with the assistance of Baganda agents. Thus, at the end of the first world war, when the demarcation of the south-west border completed Uganda's external boundaries, they assumed their present shape of a broad half circle around Buganda, in the heart of the country. Among other things, these conditions soon gave Buganda a lead in areas like education and cash-crop cultivation, and in turn created early Baganda ascendancy in administration and economic status. As we will see, the discrepancies with other areas which followed created a sense of pride on the one hand, a mixture of jealousy and admiration on the other, about Buganda's achievements.[13] The substantial autonomy Buganda enjoyed in running its own affairs for prolonged periods, and the role and position of its Kabaka, summarises one dimension of Uganda's problems in achieving national unity.

Historically, the fourteen kingdoms and districts other than Buganda which existed in Uganda developed separately over half a century or more, although along roughly similar lines. This was an important factor in the growth of district-orientations and in the end of district-centered politics in Uganda. Even though central policy directives were transmitted through the Commissioners for the Western, Eastern and Northern Provinces (who stood on a par with the Resident in Buganda), at the level of the District Commissioners government influence was exercised most forcefully. It was here that chiefs were appointed, taxes collected, judiciary powers exercised, and many measures introduced to ensure workable units of colonial government. As already noted, to a significant extent the kingdoms and districts were also pushed forward as symbols of identification; in the early part of the century, for instance, it was not uncommon for District Commissioners to report on their 'countries'. In several areas, such as Teso and Busoga, these efforts met with considerable response, as evidenced by the fact that some people began to consider themselves as belonging to one society, or one 'tribe', where previously a series of smaller groups had existed.[14] But also in areas where marked ethnic cleavages persisted, such as in Ankole, Kigezi and Toro, strong pulls for re-alignment emanated from the new district contexts. The crystallisation of factions and redefinition of membership groups on the basis of ethnicity, region, clan or other criteria, largely derived their significance from the district arenas in which coalitions seemed called for; in turn these developments gave new meaning to these splits. Thus, when Protectorate officials in the 1940s initiated a step-by-step devolution of authority to local bodies and increased the representative element in local assemblies, in most areas these measures found a fertile soil because social frameworks had already begun to be oriented to the district units. At the same time, the effect was to further enhance the districts as focal points for alignments. But when, in the 1950s, experiments were made with Provincial Councils in an attempt to create new levels for alignments, these bodies proved by and large devoid of meaning and in the end were abandoned. District politics, therefore, did long command greater involvement than regional or even national questions. Around 1960 the casual observer might well have called the Ugandan state a sort of supranational framework for its heterogeneous components.

The development of Ugandan district government during the colonial period cannot be seen in isolation from the policies pursued in regard to Buganda. In more than one way the two appear to have been significantly related, even though government policies toward Buganda have varied considerably over time. Significantly, changes in these policies appear to have correlated with variations in the attitudes of other areas towards Buganda.

First, early in the century, Buganda was treated as a special unit, accorded privileges and opportunities not available to other parts of the country. The basis for this was laid by the Uganda Agreement of 1900, which entrenched powers then held by the Kabaka and the senior chiefs and, among other things, provided for the distribution of vast stretches of freehold land among them.[15] These measures had far-reaching consequences, especially in terms of social stratification, for they contributed greatly to the formation of a powerful new Buganda elite. The privileges and sinecures granted to them functioned essentially as rewards, for the British expected to rule Buganda through this class and with their assistance to strengthen the imperial hold on other areas. Not the least effect of this was to raise the political standing of Buganda as a unit within the Protectorate. Within Buganda, the neo-traditional establishment enjoyed important reserved powers. Elsewhere Baganda agents were employed as administrators, Baganda traders set up the first marketing arrangements in other districts, and Baganda catechists were recruited to other areas for missionary purposes; all usually maintained close links to Buganda. Much of this activity could thus be seen as a sort of Buganda imperialist expansion throughout the Protectorate, although masked as colonial penetration. Since Buganda was considered more wealthy, advanced and prestigious relative to other areas, it is not surprising that Kiganda (the adjective of Ganda) ways, dress and speech were being assimilated by people in other districts during this early period, particularly by those who aspired to play a part in the framework. As a colonial state, the rest of Uganda was almost literally an extension of Buganda, a situation which obtained at least until the 1920s.

Policies and attitudes towards Buganda changed markedly once the colonial framework had become more firmly established. During the decade or two before the end of the second world war, Buganda was administered much as were other parts of the country. The kingdom was divided into four districts: notwithstanding the role of the Kabaka and his senior officials, District Commissioners and other officers performed similar functions to those of colonial administrators in other districts. At the same time the envy of Buganda's affluence took different expressions. In several areas a reaction grew to the adoption of Luganda for various purposes and it was insisted that local vernaculars be used instead.[16] In a number of districts fierce opposition arose to the Baganda chiefs whose administration was felt to be ruthless and capricious.[17] In the mid-thirties a policy of replacement of these chiefs was carried out, followed also by the substitution of Kiganda chiefly titles by local equivalents. Straightforward district administration throughout the country became the general model.

It is interesting to speculate as to what might have evolved had this pattern been continued. A uniform local administration underlying the immediate pre-war framework, if allowed to develop, might have provided a basis for a more 'equitable' government framework. However, the end of World War II brought new approaches to the structure of government in Uganda. A new concern that existing institutional forms be adapted so as to prepare the ground for self-government pervaded administrative thinking and was made explicit in the Colonial Office's well-known Creech-Jones policy directives. In Uganda this new departure was taken to mean that those structures which could readily be developed into local and regional government units should be strengthened and allowed to undertake more tasks. The unit which fulfilled these requirements was Buganda; in the immediate post-war years, therefore, Governor Dundas initiated farreaching reforms for devolution of administrative jurisdiction to the

Kabaka's government.[18] Thus Buganda was again treated as a single unit, administratively developed along separate lines from the rest of the country. It was apparently theorised that Buganda would set an example of administrative proficiency and that the other regions of Uganda would in time come to emulate.

As a matter of fact, Buganda did constitute an example, although perhaps not quite of the kind anticipated in the blueprints for constitutional government entertained in the late 1940s. Political elites in neighbouring districts began to express their interest in receiving similar prerogatives as those enjoyed by the Buganda government and felt encouraged to put forward demands to that effect as a result of the general government policy to develop the local authorities. Thus, an interesting change of attitude occurred. The earlier aspirations to become like Baganda (the people) had by this time been largely abandoned; now the preference was to become like Buganda (the region). The basic motive was essentially the same, namely an interest in positions of influence in the administrative framework of the time. Whereas earlier the positions that seemed within reach were those of Baganda agents, later a bid appeared possible for local governments on the Buganda model. While the interest to emulate Buganda thus took on quite different forms, so one of its effects definitely was a growing sense of ethnocentrism in various areas.

In Buganda itself the effect of post-war policies appears to have been a solidifying of its political structure and hence a considerable strengthening of the position of the Buganda government. In the pre-independence decade Buganda began to loom large in the country as a whole, giving reason to believe that the policy of promoting regional government had actually overshot its aims. Thus, the assumption that the roots of the 'Buganda problem' lay in its historical authority and value structure should at least be qualified by consideration of the government measures that promoted Buganda's political standing.

The measures designed to induce other areas to follow Buganda as an administrative model eventually became a means of countering Buganda. Indeed, probably the most decisive reason for strengthening district government in the 1950s and early 1960s was to counteract the strong political position of Buganda. Before and immediately after independence the reasoning appears to have been that Buganda's weight might be offset by a policy of devolution of government functions elsewhere in the country. Eventually, then, the theory was, Buganda might become encapsulated as simply one among many government units.

Thus, the development of district government, and also, in the early independence period, the renewed, explicit recognition of Ankole, Toro and Bunyoro as 'kingdoms' and the parallel policy of permitting other districts to adopt quasi-monarchical constitutional heads, may be seen as attempts to create a multitude of small Bugandas which would reduce the visibility of the bigger one.[19] As a result, protectorate and early post-colonial policies coincided with the aspirations of the elites in the smaller kingdoms and districts. Significantly, however, the political framework of Uganda prompted the latter to press for expanded autonomy largely on an individual basis, if necessary in competition with one another. The dominant position of Buganda, therefore, did not provoke political groups of other districts to unite in opposition to it, but as a model for emulation Buganda contributed greatly to the district-basis of politics in Uganda.

The district-centred nature of Uganda politics manifested itself in the kind of conflicts which became major. Issues attaining national significance in the years immediately before and after independence mainly involved Buganda's relationships to the centre, the 'lost counties' dispute between Bunyoro and Buganda (involving the return to Bunyoro of two counties which, with British consent, had been incorporated into Buganda at the establishment of colonial rule), and the Rwenzururu secessionist movement in Toro, which emerged among Bakonzo and Baamba in reaction to Batoro domination.[20] Each of these questions was rooted in sectional disputes and thus not only confirmed but also continued the subnational basis of politics. This pattern was further strengthened by other factors. The rural basis and occupation of the vast majority of the population, and the relative absence of countrywide issues for which people from all quarters could be mobilised, prevented the emergence of strong national alignments. No problem of the magnitude of a white settlers' presence, for instance, which might have served as a unifying mechanism, complicated Uganda's road to independence.[21] Thus chances of the growth of over-arching solidarities remained inversely correlated to the powerful position of Buganda and the lesser extent to which other areas, particularly the Western kingdoms of Ankole, Toro and Bunyoro, acted as centripetal nuclei. Against this background, Uganda's 1962 independence was engineered on the basis of an unusually complex formula: a constitution which provided for the existence of four kingdoms within an independent state, one of which (Buganda) was to enjoy a federal relationship to the central government, the three others to have quasi-federal powers, while the rest of the country was to be administered through a form of district government which left a fair amount of discretion to the local administration.[22] The delicate nature of this arrangement was indirectly suggested by the token declaration of independence by the Kingdom of Buganda on the eve of Uganda's independence. Later events were to prove the fragility of the formula.

POLITICS OF STATUS AND PRIVILEGE

The effects upon local politics of the arrangements introduced during the terminal period of colonial rule can be more properly understood and the course of pre-independence Uganda politics grasped in the context of the opportunities and restrictions for profitable action created by Protectorate rulings. During the 1950s and early 1960s, pervasive activity took place in the political field. To clear the ground for independence it had become necessary to redefine the relationship between constituent units. A whole series of government measures were prepared to this effect, of which new frameworks for district government, reports on constitutional relationships, local and national elections, and a final independence conference were the more obvious landmarks.[23] While many steps were thus taken to establish new political forms and procedures, at the same time a heightened political awareness spread through the country, stimulating demands for participation at many levels. This interaction created not only the format, but also many of the problems, of the new state.

At the national and district level more elaborate institutions were established than had existed during the earlier authoritarian days of colonial rule. These bodies were invested with increased powers and duties and were gradually made more answerable to popular representation. Elections made their entry and political parties mobilised people around various issues, often capitalising on existing social cleavages. After a number of splits and mergers, the major parties which emerged were the Democratic Party (1954-56), with a predominantly Roman Catholic following, and the Uganda

People's Congress (1958), supported mainly by non-Catholics; they were later (in 1961) joined by Kabaka Yekka, the movement party which stood solely for Buganda interests.[24] During this process relationships between various groups and strata of the population were infused with a new political quality and often with increased sensitivity. Longstanding grievances between rival parties could be transposed into new political terms and expressed through new means of communication. In addition political units which had formerly been in a non-competitive relationship found themselves competing for influence and benefits, or concluding new alliances.

However, when political parties appeared on the scene, they came to reflect the distribution of power characteristic of Uganda society. Aside from Kabaka Yekka, whose social basis was the neo-traditionalist sub-stratum in Buganda, both the Uganda People's Congress and the Democratic Party characteristically featured an amalgam of local caucuses rather than a strong national leadership which would try to branch out into the districts. This pattern was particularly pronounced in the case of the UPC, for Protestant elites had for long enjoyed a semi-establishment position in most districts of Uganda. Nonetheless, in various districts the two parties came to reflect other social cleavages in addition to the religious one, and in several cases, including Ankole, this gave rise to deviations from the general Protestant versus Catholic pattern of division between UPC and DP. (Later, in the mid-1960s, the two major parties no longer had the pronounced religious basis they started out with, although in some UPC quarters there has been a tendency to regard lateral entrants who crossed from the DP as 'still DP in spirit'.)

Clearly, therefore, a much more complex interplay of interests ensued in the formative stages of the Uganda political framework than merely a dialogue between nationalist leaders and colonial authorities. Many district factions, whether with an ethnic, regional, religious or other basis of support, had definite interests in the future distribution of power. These factions became crucial factors in the political bargaining on the eve of independence. While the timing of independence resulted from nationalist interest to assume power and British willingness (not to speak of interest) to withdraw, it was the juxtaposition of political demands at all levels which produced the distinctive features with which Uganda assumed independence. One of the characteristics of Uganda politics in the terminal colonial period was thus the articulation of two levels of response to the advent of independence. Nationalist politicians uniformly expressed interest in the control of government, while at the same time concern was voiced in many quarters over the status and interests of sub-groups in the future state.

The climate of the time encouraged belief that the framework under construction was to be final, and the possibilities for arbitration terminated with the colonial departure. A related assumption was that amendments to the projected structure must be made before the transfer of power. Hence, as independence drew nearer, several issues came to a climax. Serious friction marked Buganda's claims for full federal powers and also Bunyoro's wishes to recover the counties it had lost to Buganda at the establishment of British rule. Meanwhile, the kingdoms of Western Uganda, Ankole, Bunyoro, and Toro, keenly expressed their interests in a status similar to Buganda, and the district of Busoga campaigned for inclusion among these lesser kingdoms. (In the end this was granted with the status of 'Territory' and its Kyabazinga on a par with the hereditary rulers of the kingdoms.) Most of the non-kingdom districts, as already noted, similarly aspired to have their position elevated to that of the more prestigious monarchies, and in the end all but two (Teso and Karamoja) chose to have a Constitutional Head who could perform essentially the same ceremonial functions for them that the rulers of the kingdoms did.[25] Except for the Buganda issue, however, none of these questions implied a conflict between a desire for Uganda independence and the determination to seek safeguards or greater status for specific groups. Even the Rwenzururu movement, which later sought to secede from the country, had hoped to achieve its objectives within an independent Uganda. Clearly, the expression of minority demands was a corollary of the move to independent statehood.

It was equally plain that intra-district (as opposed to inter-district) dissension and disputes would increase during this process. Sub-groups in several kingdoms and districts of Uganda became alerted to the relative gains and losses in political influence which wider local powers, increased representation and redefinition of relationships might entail for them. Many were anxious to secure a position which would give them enhanced influence in government. Some were mainly interested in retaining the privileged position they had enjoyed, while others tried to seize what appeared the last opportunity to redress their subordinate status. Conflict thus mounted among the Sebei and Bagisu in Bugisu district, between the people of East and West Acholi, among the amalgam of ethnic groups in Bukedi, between Bakonzo and Baamba and Batoro in Toro, and not least between Bairu and Bahima in Ankole.[26] Strong protests and claims were character-istic of the period. As political benefits for one group could only be obtained at the expense of others, the relationships which were being established among them in many instances became a matter of intense political controversy.

Potentially, this process had important implications for the socio-political hierarchies which existed in various parts of Uganda. Efforts to draw sub-groups more closely together were largely expected to create greater equity. Egalitarian values were also attributed to the political parties. Policies and expectations could thus easily lead to clashes with historically entrenched positions of privilege in particular areas. The introduction of universal suffrage into the ethnically stratified societies of Western Uganda, for instance, might help to significantly reverse the political hierarchy.[27] A redrawing of the boundaries of Toro or Sebei would be an alternative way of promoting the subordinate categories to an equal rank with the hitherto dominant elites.[28] Conflict about these matters was intensified by the common expectation that as soon as changes were made, a host of additional gains would fall to the rewarded groups. Besides, as for the question of district boundary rearrangements, by the time the independence constitution was in the making it may have been clear to some of the groups concerned that one of the most heavily entrenched clauses would be that regarding the permanence of inter-district boundaries. Not without tragedy, others such as those in the Rwenzururu movement would only come to find out later.

These issues about redefinition of relationships tended to become even more sensitive as a result of economic and educational developments in the preceding decades. In many areas income differentiation had followed the cultivation of cash-crops such as coffee and cotton. Expanded school enrolment in many districts had instilled new orientations and expectations, and widened the social basis for administrative recruitment. Thus, various categories had begun to expect social opportunities which previously accrued to a small dominating class. Such developments were accompanied by increased self-awareness and a desire for more general equality on the part of the under-privileged categories. By the end of the colonial era these developments had often been profound enough to leave their marks on the socio-economic structure. However, political emancipation had not necessarily kept pace with these changes; it was often seen to be halted by established elites. Hence, the measures introduced in preparation for independence were viewed by many groups as providing a major chance to raise their political influence. Indeed, sub-group interest in a strengthened position was often of more immediate concern than the notion of independence as such. Insofar as these conflicts were between 'ethnic' groups, it also suggests that their roots should not so much be sought in their 'ethnicity', but rather in the differential advantages which the system had allowed to different categories.

2. State and Society in Pre-Colonial Nkore

This chapter tries to provide an understanding of socio-political relationships in pre-colonial Nkore society, the precursor and core of the Ankole District of Uganda.[1] We shall need to be particularly concerned with the social basis of power and the manner in which the functions of the state, here those of a traditional African kingdom, were structured and discharged. Against this background we shall be better able to evaluate the changes that were brought to bear upon this society as a result of colonialism.

In the case of Nkore, two aspects of its political organisation deserve special attention, namely those concerned with the relationships of the two main population groups, the Bairu and the Bahima, and the structuring of monarchical institutions. The Nkore situation is particularly intriguing as a case of historical political analysis because it confronts us with two *prima facie* contradictory images of socio-political organisation. While one suggests a pattern of coexistence and symbiosis between two separate communities, the other conveys a picture of basic inequality and subordination between them. To reassess and, to the extent possible, try to reconcile these two images is the primary function of this chapter. In particular, this raises the question as to what extent Nkore society was based upon a single system of social and economic production, or, if not, how the pattern of power relationships related to the two main population groups. Related to this, the identification of the pattern of socio-political stratification characteristic of Nkore raises special problems. For a better perspective on these questions, however, we should first turn to the wider political and cultural setting of which Nkore formed part.

NKORE AND THE INTERLACUSTRINE AREA

For many centuries prior to British rule, the Ankole area had been politically and culturally related to various other societies in the interlacustrine region of Eastern Africa. The kingdom of Nkore, which was the nucleus around which the Ankole district was formed at the beginning of the colonial period, was centrally situated within this large region: its most important neighbours were Bunyoro-Kitara to the north, Karagwe and Buhaya to the south, Mpororo and Rwanda to the southwest, and Buganda to the east.[2] In a narrow circle around Nkore lay a string of smaller kingships, including Koki, Buzimba, Buhweju, Igara.

Some key trade routes, travelled by Arabs and others (especially to the Katwe market and salt deposits), passed through the area.[3] Other contacts, notably political relationships, were maintained over long distances. Pastoralists on trek covered wide circles; warfare, droughts and epidemics at times caused groups to move and resettle within the region at large, or even further away. For these reasons, already, the interlacustrine region featured a certain unity and distinctiveness, some characteristics of which are still found today in Ankole and elsewhere.

Politically, the region constituted a kind of international arena *avant la lettre*. Within this area several distinct polities – some that would be called states (if not empires), others proto-states, some independent, others semi-independent by today's terminology – exercised powers and engaged in inter-state relationships. Reflected in shifting coalitions, tribute relationships and lines of conflict, their respective influence now grew, then subsided, to continuously form new balances of power.

For centuries the major axis along which power extended and contracted lay roughly north-south between Bunyoro-Kitara based Babito ruling groups, on the one hand, and Bahinda (Bagyesera) originating from Gisaka, on the other. At its zenith, Bunyoro-Kitara's suzerainty was claimed to reach far into the area that is today the Bukoba region of north-west Tanzania. Until well into the nineteenth century, the basic trend was for the Bahinda to gradually extend their control northwards into areas which had for long been subject to Babito overrule. Paralleling the decline of Bunyoro-Kitara's power as a result of these Bahinda encroachments, a third party ascendancy and expansion of Buganda was made possible towards the middle and latter parts of the nineteenth century.[4]

Thus in the specific case of Nkore, its relative standing within this pattern was strongly dependent upon the role and pursuits of its more powerful neighbours and suzerains – Bunyoro-Kitara, Gisaka and, less directly, Buganda. Roughly until the early part of the nineteenth century Nkore, though one of the Bahinda states, had been weaker than, if not actually dependent upon, Bunyoro-Kitara. With Bunyoro-Kitara's decline Nkore's political position gradually became stronger. Several smaller neighbouring states, such as Igara, Buhweju and Buzimba, that had earlier been subject to Babito overrule, first became 'independent' (most notably in the case of Buhweju) and eventually were made to acknowledge Nkore's paramountcy, expressed through the tribute they paid to its ruler. Nkore's 'imperialism' finally reached a peak during the rule of Ntare V, shortly before the British arrived on the scene.

Culturally, manifold areas of overlap existed between the societies of the interlacustrine region.[5] With few exceptions their languages were all patterned on the basic Bantu structure. On top of this several languages were especially closely related and in some instances two or more societies virtually shared a linguistic identity. Runyankore, for example, was basically identical to the Rukiga spoken by the Bakiga (in the present Kigezi district of Uganda), so that in the present century a common orthography could be developed for the two languages.[6] While Runyankore was less close to Luganda, its linguistic affinities with, among others, Karagwe and Bunyoro-Kitara (and the latter's nineteenth-century offshoot Toro) easily allowed two-way communication with these societies. Pockets of linguistically distinct sub-areas nonetheless persisted in various parts, such as Bunyaruguru in the present Ankole area or the Bakonzo and Baamba parts of the Ruwenzori region. But even in such instances what appeared to underscore the cultural ties within much of the interlacustrine region was the tendency for a certain give and take – of vocabulary if not of grammar – to permit a fair amount of linguistic assimilation – probably more than occurred later after the languages were codified.

Similar overlaps were salient in regard to other aspects of culture. Various interlacustrine societies, especially the Bahinda-ruled areas, had basically similar myths of origin, the common mythology being the presumed sojourn in the region of the semi-legendary Bacwezi.[7]

Subsequent to that era, Bahinda rule itself became mythologised, though most groups nonetheless gave these myths their own, slightly different but yet unique, interpretation. One such local adaptation was the mythical charter predominant in the Ankole area. According to this Ruhanga, the Creator, once put his three sons, Kakama, Kahima and Kairu, to a competitive test, on the basis of which he then entrusted each of them with a different task. The test involved keeping a milkpot filled for one whole night. Kakama won and was charged with the rule of the country. Kahima, who had given some milk to Kakama, was made to look after the cattle, while Kairu, who had spilled his milk, was told to till the soil.[8]

More prosaically, other similarities pertained to modes of existence and social relationships. Throughout most of the interlacustrine region subsistence was based on one or another of a few main poles: agriculture, cattle-raising, some fishing – agriculture being mainly concentrated on beans, millet, casava, plantains, or some combination of these.[9] (In Ankole millet and beans were historically the main crops; plantains were introduced by the first Baganda agents.[10]) Additional economic goods characteristic of the region included iron implements (e.g. spear heads, hoes, axes), salt, barkcloth, pots, baskets and wooden vessels, augmented in the second half of the nineteenth century by ivory, arms and slaves.[11]

Again, social organisation followed a few basic patterns, its diversity being largely a question of variations on a theme. Residence patterns were generally based on scattered homesteads, not villages, a fact with far-reaching implications in terms of the kind of socio-political frameworks that evolved. Over and beyond the immediate extended family, clan membership – of either a corporate group or a reference category – was common throughout and of major importance. For purposes of land utilization and security, if for no other, it appears that clans used to be territorially more concentrated than they are at present. Today, in not a few instances only a historic place name identifies a clan with a particular locality. Mostly patrilinial and exogamous, as in Ankole,[12] though varying as to the criteria and nomenclature of identification (e.g. totem avoidance as a principle as opposed to, or in conjunction with, accepted area of origin), it was also common for clans to be ranked in terms of higher or lower status and for some of them – as clans – to demonstrate over time some measure of vertical social mobility.[13]

Status differentials in other than clan terms were similarly pervasive in many parts of the region. Institutionalised in greater or lesser formal fashion, though with variations as to the exact behaviour expressive of hierarchical social relationships, in various areas inequality of status was particularly pronounced – socially, politically, economically. Among other things, these inequalities were closely related to patronage relationships, and to an occupational structure in which, for example, some people were cattle-keepers, others cultivators, blacksmiths, woodcarvers, potters and musicians.

Over and beyond these various political and cultural connections, two characteristics made the interlacustrine region particularly distinctive. One was the co-existence in many, though by no means all parts of the area, of two or more different ethnic groups, often in positions of unequal status *vis-à-vis* one another.[14] The other was the existence of institutions of kingship in various – again not all – societies within the region. The exact pattern of ethnic relationships and monarchial powers varied from case to case. As regards ethnic relationships variations depended, among other things, on the extent of social distance between the groups concerned, the occurrence and frequency of intermarriage among them, the extent to which they were politically autonomous within the system as a whole, and the extent of their relatedness to and involvement in an integrated system of economic relationships as opposed to the pursuit of separate economic activities. As to the pattern of monarchical powers, variations corresponded with the degree of centralisation of the system, (in turn with) the weight of appointive as opposed to hereditary criteria of chiefly recruitments, and the existence or absence of a central administrative machinery as against sub-unit structures of authority.

In each case it was therefore the particular combination of these two patterns, of ethnic status designations and the institutions of kingship, which defined the specific nature of political relationships in the interlacustrine society concerned. In Rwanda, for example, politically superior Batusi and subordinate Bahutu were further integrated, through a system of clientship arrangements, into a unified political and economic system, than had evolved in various neighbouring societies. Intermarriage took place here, though not to the extent that it obliterated ethnic distinctions between the two groups or replaced these by status distinctions only. In Rwanda as elsewhere the kingship stood at the pinnacle of this pyramidal web of relationships.[15] In

Bunyoro-Kitara and Toro, by contrast, assimilation between high-status Babito and Bahuma and low-status Bairu (of which the latter two were historically related to Nkore's Bahima and Bairu) had taken place to a degree where the respective terms had basically come to denote status, rather than ethnic distinctions. Politically and economically, these systems had also become more vertically integrated, though generally with Babito, Bahuma and Bairu clans in a descending order of prominence and also – in the nineteenth century – due to the absence of strong central bureaucratic structures, with a high potential for horizontal fragmentation based on sub-unit 'separatism'.[16]

Notwithstanding general similarities on account of the existence of kingship in conjunction with ethnic stratification (not to speak of other cultural ties), pre-colonial political relationships in Nkore differed in some significant respects from the patterns in both Rwanda and Bunyoro-Kitara and other interlacustrine societies. The Bairu-Bahima division, which in social stratification terms bears a certain, though not too close, resemblance to that between Batusi and Bahutu in Rwanda, existed also in neighbouring systems such as Karagwe and Buhaya, but in few places had it remained as clearcut as in the case of Nkore. Briefly, Bairu and Bahima were both members of the same general society of Nkore, though in various ways Bahima enjoyed more powers than did Bairu. The two groups were involved in a variety of social, political and economic contacts, and some flexibility in the general, somewhat diffuse, status hierarchy appears to have allowed a limited possibility of social mobility and in the long run even some minimal assimilation. Nonetheless, Bairu and Bahima by and large remained more distinct, ethnically as well as socially, and kept more exclusively engaged in different bases of subsistence than was true for most adjacent areas. Whereas their distinct modes of life and patterns of social interaction were comprised within a general common context, there was a Bahima-oriented – and dominated – political system which, as reflected in its kingship, lacked not only the structure but in a sense also the focus and 'interest' to sustain a pervasive downward control. Thus, Nkore's complex political framework was characterised not only by separate economic pursuits of its ethnic groups, which were combined with a pattern of limited if unequal exchange, but also by two 'levels' of state functions – differing in intensity, purposes and the nature of rewards and sanctions passed in relation to the two groups.

Other lines of differentiation and authority qualify this pattern further. To see this, we will below first consider the ethnic relationships in Nkore, then the institution of kingship.

A few reservations must however be mentioned. One is that our discussion will primarily concern Nkore, not the expanded Ankole region. This is mainly because more extensive information is available on pre-colonial Nkore than on some of the other areas incorporated into Ankole.[17] Nkore constituted the largest and politically the most important society among those which made up the new district. But although it is the case that roughly similar patterns existed in some of the annexed areas, especially those obtained from Mpororo, demographic and political changes which followed the redefinition of Ankole society at the beginning of colonial rule still do not permit a direct juxtaposition of socio-political patterns in pre-colonial Nkore with those in the new district.

Timewise, a second reservation is necessary. Our discussion will be partly based on oral evidence and on sources written in the early part of the present century, both of which presumably refer primarily to the immediately preceding period, i.e. the latter part of the nineteenth century.[18] A relative lack of evidence on *historic processes* makes it difficult to distinguish between the Nkore political system of one period and another; to do that would in any case lie outside the scope of this study.[19] Thus our references to the pre-colonial period pretend to refer mainly to the latter part of the nineteenth century and do neither imply that this period was in any way 'typical'. (In fact there are reasons to assume that this period was not typical: that while Nkore was aggrandising, its potential for internal fissure became strongly enhanced; and that the prominence it nonetheless received as a nucleus for colonial state formation was largely due to the British' earlier experience with the centralised system in Buganda and their belief that a similarly strong state organisation obtained in Nkore.)

Closely connected is a third and final caveat which, though in principle pertinent to most historical analysis, is certainly in order in the present case. In the virtual absence of first-hand, written information on pre-colonial Nkore, available evidence is largely confined to secondary source materials and the oral traditions and memories of elderly members of Ankole society. Both frequently pose similar problems of analysis – a certain inexplicitness on key questions, contradictory accounts and, at times, rather *a priori* interpretations which may be instigated by the present perspectives, political or otherwise, of observers or participants. One major, if not entirely foolproof, rule of thumb that can be employed in regard to any such ambiguities, is a cross-checking and critical re-analysis of the available data – a method on which the present chapter is largely based.

BAIRU-BAHIMA RELATIONSHIPS: A BACKGROUND

Mbarara, the central town of Ankole, is a colonial creation. At its entrance stands a statue of a cow's head, which serves as a reminder of the district's fame as cattle country. Ankole's pastoral reputation is an old one; cattle-raising distinguishes the region even today. Sizable herds of long-horn cattle are often encountered, commonly guarded by a herdsman in colourful cloth, and ever in search of good pasturage and water. Yet, despite the salient role of cattle in Ankole's mythology and life patterns, the area has never been mainly pastoral. In the past as well as the present, the predominant economic activity has been the cultivation of foodcrops. At least as characteristic as its cattle – if less conspicuous – are the areas of Ankole which have been given over to farming. To date, cattle raising and cultivation have generally occurred in different sections of Ankole. Although cattle have been found in most parts of the region, they have always been particularly plentiful in Nyabushozi, Kashari, Mitoma and Kajara – the two former areas of which, together with Isingero, historically formed the core of the Nkore kingdom. These areas consist largely of plains and gently rolling grassland, with only thornbush and an occasional flametree standing out. Well suited for grazing (but for the perennial problem of tsetse infestation, which has been particularly troublesome throughout the present century), concentrations of herds of as many as several hundred head have always been found here, laying the basis of a semi-nomadic, subsistence mode of existence. In contrast, the cultivation of foodcrops has historically been the main form of production towards the west, north and south of the pastoral areas: Isingero, parts of Kashari, and the sections of Rwampara and Shema that formed part of the Nkore kingdom immediately before the colonial period, continue to be distinguished from the plains by their more abundant vegetation. Also, the land here is generally more hilly.

Cattle and crops, the two mainstays of Ankole's economy, have been traditionally related to the population's division into two main groups. Historically the possession of cattle, especially breeding cattle, was limited to the Bahima who numerically formed a minority. Bahima life was very much centered around their famed long-horn cattle, which for them were not only a means of subsistence, but a symbol of wealth, power and prestige. The usual assumption has been that Bairu were not allowed to have cattle.[20] Whether or not this has been the case, a more direct and simpler explanation appears to be that economically Bairu were not in a position, ordinarily, to obtain cattle, basically for lack of equivalent exchange value. The Bairu majority have traditionally been mainly engaged in agriculture. This historical division of labour still has contemporary relevance: at present most Bairu, even those who own cattle,[21] are primarily engaged in agriculture, whereas the majority of Bahima continue to be mainly occupied in cattle-rearing. It is not known exactly what proportions Bahima and Bairu represented within the population of pre-colonial Nkore. Nonetheless, it is beyond doubt that the number of Bahima was substantially larger than the 5–10% which it is assumed they constitute in the present Ankole district.[22] One explanation for this relative decrease of the Bahima population in Ankole, as compared to Nkore, is that most areas incorporated into what became Ankole district were more predominantly Bairu populated than was Nkore. Moreover, roughly parallel to this incorporation in the latter part of the nineteenth century and the beginning of the twentieth, rinderpest, other epidemics, and political conflict caused many Bahima to move away, into Buganda and further east, thus leading also to an absolute decrease of the Bahima population. It has been locally estimated that the Bahima constituted as much as 40–60% of the population of pre-colonial Nkore – a figure which may well be somewhat inflated.[23] However, while it is difficult to establish the proportions of Bahima and Bairu which obtained in Nkore with any great degree of accuracy, for an understanding of political power relationships in the pre-colonial society it must be kept in mind that the Bahima component was in any case considerably larger than it is at present.

According to a rather widely held assumption the Bahima migrated into the present Ankole area some four or five centuries ago, and set up the state structures which have been handed down through time. This 'Hamitic myth' has been a dominant theme in explanations of the origins of the interlacustrine states virtually since Speke's account of his first explorations in the areas.[24]

Debates around this theme continue today, with archaeologists, historians, and biochemists among the interested parties.[25] The conquest theories of state origins have recently been criticised as being based on prejudice. In the summary of C. P. Kottak, '(t)here has been a regrettable tendency ... to assume that wherever sophisticated political developments have occurred in East Africa, they could not possibly have developed internally. They must either have been borrowed from some "superior" group or have been imposed by conquerors of some sort. Whether Nilotes or "Nilo-Hamites" conquering Bantu, or Cushites or Hamites conquering some indigenous population, the resulting picture has been the same – a dominant ruling class or caste of ultimately foreign origin, which somehow managed to form a state out of something that was not a state before.'[26] Certainly, even if the Bahima came in from elsewhere – as still may well have been the case – to connect the establishment of state structures with the arrival of the Bahima essentially amounts to a twofold hypothesis, one for which the necessary evidence is lacking. On the contrary, while there would seem to be no *a priori* reason why two such developments should have coincided in the first place, the inauguration rites of the Omugabe (king) of Nkore used to include some rather un-pastoral ceremonies, such as the planting of millet seed, which might indicate the existence of kingship in an era before the Bahima gained political control.[27] It seems possible, therefore, that what long used to be a Bahima-dominated state structure has been projected back into history to establish a claim on its origin. On a mythological plane (as opposed to historical speculation), meanwhile, the royal clan of Nkore, the Bahinda, supposedly had an origin which was distinct from that of both Bahima and Bairu.[28] But this again did not alter the fact that in known history the Bahinda led essentially the same type of life as Bahima and have generally identified themselves with Bahima interests. The Bahinda have also normally been considered a Bahima clan, although a somewhat special one. Nkore might well therefore be called a Bahima-state,[29] notwithstanding the references to the myth of origin which Bahinda and other Bahima often made (and make). The function of this myth was basically a legitimising one, as it purported to establish a statutory equality between Bahima and Bairu and might thus conceal the social distance between the latter two groups – even if (but precisely because) it recognised the supremacy of one section of the Bahima, the Bahinda.

Bairu and Bahima speak the same language, Runyankore, although with different accents and often with such (skilled) use of different expressions and metaphors as to make many a conversation among Bairu or among Bahima unintelligible to members of the opposite group. The two groups are also linked through a common clan system, that is, Bairu and Bahima members of a clan recognise a common avoidance totem.[30] But their common clans are differently named by the Bairu and the Bahima segments and the rules of clan-exogamy adhered to by Bairu are not followed by Bahima.[31] Some clans have a more predominantly Bairu, others a more predominantly Bahima membership. But Kinyankore clans are essentially reference, not corporate groups, so that members normally do not know each other. Intermarriage between members of the two groups has been rare; in the past, according to recollections by Banyankore, the main – though limited – contact appears to have been that of Bahima taking Bairu 'concubines'.[32]

IMAGES OF NKORE:
COEXISTENCE VERSUS SUBJUGATION, CLASS VERSUS CASTE

The division between Bairu and Bahima doubtless constituted the single most important feature of the socio-political structure of Nkore. Put in its briefest form, the division basically rested on three overlapping criteria, differential occupation, status and ethnicity. The Nkore political elite was drawn almost exclusively from the Bahima segment of the population, whereas the Bairu stood largely outside direct political involvements in the state system and in a variety of areas enjoyed lesser rights and privileges in their contacts with the Bahima. But even then, these relationships were mediated and mitigated in a variety of ways that gave the Nkore political system its special complexity, also causing many questions to be endlessly debated among anthropologists and historians.

The central question concerning political relationships in Nkore is how to reconcile the existence of distinct Bairu and Bahima life patterns and modes of subsistence on the one hand with a pattern of inequality between the two groups on the other. The question arises for, if indeed, or insofar as, Bairu and Bahima were distinct groups, in terms of economic production, social organisation and ethnicity, how was there inequality between them?; or, *vice versa,* insofar as their relationships were based on inequality, how could they nonetheless be seen as distinct, differently oriented communities? Evidently, our understanding of the Nkore political system depends largely on how this paradox is resolved; we must therefore consider it more closely.

There are two interpretations of Nkore society which have a bearing upon this question, though in at least one important sense they convey directly opposite conceptions of the traditional Nkore system. Neither perspective, however, appears fully adequate to resolve the paradox. One, a dominant viewpoint in accounts of Nkore, suggests a pervasive, institutionalised, inevitably also a rather inflexible pattern of ethnic inequality between Bahima and Bairu. As Oberg has formulated it:

'from the standpoint of political and legal status the members of the Banyankole [*sic*] kingdom did not form a homogeneous mass, but were distinguished by a wide range of rights and prohibitions, resulting in a stratification of society into classes. At the top was the Bahima State with its governing nucleus centring around the Mugabe. Below were the subject classes of the Bairu ... The caste nature of this stratification was pronounced, resting ultimately on racial and economic differences.'[33]

Thus also, states Oberg, '[to] the Bahima, the word "Bairu" signifies serfdom, a legal status inferior to that existing between themselves'.[34] In other words, ethnicity ("race") is here seen as the basic principle underlying a division which relegated all Bairu to a subordinate position – socially, politically, economically – subject therefore in all respects to control by Bahima, and presumably "all" Bahima. In a similarly generalised fashion, the point has been echoed many times. Stenning, for example, concluded: 'In general terms, the traditional pattern of administrative authority in Ankole was that of a ruling pastoral "caste", the Hima, set in both local and central adminis-tration over an inferior "caste", the Iru'.[35]

The opposite view holds instead that Bairu and Bahima were both enveloped and economically interdependent within a common and open class system, which, though it knew higher and lower statuses, allowed any of its members to rise or fall on the social ladder and therefore could not be held to have had anything like a basic inbuilt premise of ethnic inequality: 'The one essential factor which is the key to the understanding of Nkore's class structure ... is that the class system was an open one.'[36] Karugire, a Munyankore historian and the principal proponent of this argument, speaks of the economic activities of Bairu and Bahima as complementary and as based on interdependence through a pattern of mutual exchange.[37] According to him 'Nkore was a capitalist society and the form of capital was cattle ... '.[38] This thesis, whose virtue is to place some weight on the economic basis of political relationships in Nkore, unfortunately leaves some key empirical questions unanswered, in particular on the point of class composition and mobility.[39] Nonetheless, for the central argument of an 'open class system' to be possible and valid in the first place, logic demands that there must not only be a certain basis of economic interaction and integration but also a demonstrable extent of 'open' status mobility. Notwithstanding some contrary evidence which he cites, it seems that Karugire would indeed accept that these criteria were fulfilled in Nkore.

Normally, when presented with a choice between two such alternative interpretations of a society, either as a caste or as a class system, one would want to check and decide which version to give greater weight. In the present case this would not resolve the issue, but instead another step is necessary first. For what relates the two positions is an assumption – which they both leave unexplored at the point of defining the specific type of society that Nkore constituted – of relatively close and continuous socio-economic and political interaction between Bairu and Bahima, thus either in a 'caste' or in a 'class' structure. Yet the nature, extensiveness and frequency of these contacts, in the economic as well as the social and political spheres, is surely the basic factor which must be considered when trying to determine a political system such as Nkore's; it may well drastically change the picture one would otherwise obtain.

Let us raise, therefore, a purposely elementary question and ask to what extent one could speak of 'one' society, or of 'two', in reference to Nkore.[40] I prefer provisionally to use a crude term such as 'society', with all its obvious limitations, rather than more specific and technically more sophisticated concepts such as 'arena' or 'political field',[41] because the latter, though offering greater precision when delineating networks of socio-political relationships between sets of actors, appear less adequate aids in identifying the totality of relationships between such large inclusive groups as the Bairu and Bahima of Nkore.[42]

To establish whether Nkore was 'one' society or not remains all the same an empirical task; but it requires circumnavigating some further conceptual issues. A 'one society' pattern commonly pre-supposes a single system of social and political stratification, whether drawn along ethnic or other lines.[43] The notions of 'class', 'caste', or 'feudal' society then denote major concepts with which the particular type of stratified society can be designated in a specific case. All their important differences (and the terminological controversies around each of them[44]) notwithstanding, as contrasted to a 'two societies' situation these concepts are essentially addressed to a single, 'shared' system of economic production and distribution; a system therefore which links the various social groups together, though in differential ways and often asymmetrically, and through which their unequal roles, statuses and rewards are largely allocated. In any such instance, and again in contrast to a 'two societies' pattern, manifestations of inequality are likely to be pervasive and enduring, and possibly intensive – rather than partial and intermittent. Any measure of openness within the system, allowing upward and downward mobility, does not alter this picture, but instead supports it.

In Nkore, the extent to which there was 'one' society – and thus a 'shared' socio-economic system as well as, in turn, a greater or lesser pervasiveness of institutionalised socio-political subordination – appears to have been limited; its complex configuration in any event precludes unqualified adoption of such terms as 'class' or 'caste' to characterise its specific pattern of stratification. Whereas there was a general societal context in which Bairu and Bahima subsisted, there was greater distinctiveness of modes of life and production patterns than would normally be associated with a single inclusive social system and a shared ranking pattern. We can begin to deduce this through a somewhat indirect procedure, namely by reviewing some concepts and images of Nkore that convey how the society was historically perceived, and which we can then relate to patterns of subsistence.

We might first note a few terms which seemed indicative of 'one society' existing in Nkore. For example, the Kinyankore concept of 'ihanga' roughly corresponded to 'nation' and as such presumably referred to the people – Bairu and Bahima – the land and the social orientations and relationships particular to Nkore society. This concept of 'ihanga' in turn overlapped with 'obugabe', connoting the kingship and kingdom. Yet an alternative concept of 'nation' – again presumably referring to *all* the people – was implied in the word 'engoma' or drum. Just as the term 'Nkore' itself, its derivative 'Banyankore' (the people of Nkore), or its affective equivalent 'Kaaro-karungi',[45] these concepts found their basis in the web of social and political relationships that involved 'all' the people and *prima facie* appear to have underscored a notion of Nkore as one society. Nkore's legitimising myth, as noted, meant to convey a similar image. None of this would seem particularly surprising, for in situations in which various subgroups – ethnic, regional or otherwise – have historically been in more or less regular interaction with one another, this interaction might well in a sense define 'society'. And, of course, notions such as the above are in any case only surface examples of many more interactive concepts in Nkore.

Nonetheless, in the past (as well as present) the major sub-groups, Bairu and Bahima, have often also themselves been considered – and considered themselves – the basic social units.[46] Until today, Bahima frequently refer to the distinctiveness of their culture and traditions and appear acutely aware of themselves as a 'people' different from others in the area. Bairu, in retrospect, similarly emphasise their own background and way of life in pre-colonial times as distinctive, also as one that formed the basis of their social organisation. Indeed Bairu and Bahima have often regarded the opposite group as another entity altogether. Various behavioural trends, many of them still valid today, appear to have confirmed these perceptions: the infrequency of intermarriage and friendship ties across the Bairu-Bahima division; the predominant interaction between Bairu and Bahima in 'market' situations, outside of their respective immediate circles; the numerous expressions, often derogatory, which continue to convey reciprocal stereotypes of the opposite group as 'different'. (Among the latter one frequently used among Bairu suggests that if indeed the Bahima were 'Hamites' who invaded the Ankole area some long time ago then they should go back where they came from – which surely is ironically 'real' evidence for what started as anthropological speculation.)

Intriguingly some early European travellers did not so much see Bairu and Bahima as distinct groups, but actually seemed only to note or consider the Bahima as the population of Ankole. In 1901, for example, a missionary, the later bishop Willis, who was about to spend two years in Ankole, noted in his diary: 'We are now close to the borders of Ankole and the people here are Bahima and speak Luhima –

the language of Ankole'.[47] It is unknown what Willis' sources were for this piece of information – possibly colleagues, Baganda or others. But rather than just conclude that he was uninformed, we should note that many Baganda to this day have a way of referring to the people of Ankole as 'Balalo', the people of the (cattle) kraal, who are basically Bahima, even though they are no doubt well aware that this does not exhaust Ankole's population groups. Also, by about 1898 the first Bahima students had been enrolled at the Protestant Mengo High School, which might provide an additional explanation for Willis' impression.[48] More surprising is to see how long it would take Willis to acknowledge the existence of others than Bahima in Ankole in his two-year diary, and that even then his journal shows few comments on different groups and group relationships in Ankole: his later references to the 'Banyankore' remain unclear and seem mostly to imply that these were essentially Bahima. Even more remarkable is that a similar perception underlaid the first book on Ankole, by Roscoe,[49] in which the Bairu were largely ignored. Roscoe consistently wrote of the people of Ankole as a pastoral or a Bahima 'tribe'; others were mentioned only in occasional references (to 'serfs' and 'peasants' mainly), apparently not to be counted as part of the society he was concerned with. The one pertinent reference, to 'Mwiru', which the book contains is in fact significant not only because – in regard to the majority of the population – it mistakes the singular for the plural and thus appears to reveal a wider lack of insight, but also because the reference occurs in the context of a listing of different positions of subservience which various categories filled in Nkore.[50] There are thus good reasons to assume that Roscoe meant to refer here primarily to those Bairu who were more closely attached to, or in the immediate retinue of, Bahima lords, not to the larger Bairu community which was less frequently involved in contacts with Bahima. It is quite possible that Roscoe's contacts with the Bahima ruling stratum, based as they may have been on a reciprocal 'aristocratic bias', have influenced these perceptions, including a tendency to leave out those members of the society who 'did not matter'. Nonetheless, the absence of a general discussion of the Bairu majority in the book is so striking that one must seriously consider whether Roscoe, quite simply, did not mean to just write about Bahima *society* – on the understanding that Nkore was that. (And, in that case, the rare attention paid to the 'Mwiru' can be (mis-)interpreted as supportive of pervasive subordination in the society at large, especially if its implications are extended to all Bairu).

Against these images it is no less noteworthy that Bairu and Bahima today may convey a picture of historical relationships in Nkore that, *prima facie*, seems contradictory. They may (and do) *either* advance the view that Bairu and Bahima led separate existences, each group arranging its own affairs, *or* indicate a pattern of inequality and subordination between them, *or* else both. As always, such seemingly conflicting notions may in part derive from contemporary perspectives on past relationships – allowing the latter insufficient appreciation in their own right. In part also, they may implicitly refer to different regions within Nkore – in some of which ethnic proximity and subordination was more pronounced, while in others ethnic autonomy was more salient. Nonetheless, the fact remains that these different perceptions exist, and coexist. Rather than dismissing them on the ground that they must be 'wrong', let us therefore consider another, probably more crucial explanation, which is that coexistence of such different perceptions of political relationships should probably be taken to reflect just what it conveys, namely that these opposites were somehow reconciled within the framework of Nkore society and that therefore also the apparent contradiction – of 'one' versus 'two' societies – may have been one that found its roots and expression within Nkore itself.

In the light of various characteristics of Nkore society it appears that this is not an invalid assumption. We have noted the historical Bairu engagement in agriculture and that of Bahima in cattle raising. In many ways this occupational separation, involving full time routines on both sides, already militated against intensive contacts between the two groups.[51]

For most purposes, socially and production-wise, Bairu interacted with Bairu and Bahima with Bahima. Moreover, not only life styles but also diets were basically different: patterns of food avoidance were in marked contrast, as many Bairu did not touch milk while many Bahima lived on nothing but milk, shunning favourite Bairu foods.[52] These basic contrasts are still largely, though decreasingly, true today. What took place was an exchange of products that appears to have been limited as regards the number of people it concerned and intermittent as to its frequency. This limited economic reciprocity mainly involved Bahima consumption of Bairu produced millet-beer, and also Bairu consumption of ghee (butter) and meat whenever they could obtain these products from Bahima. Bairu also made pipes and milkpots and some other utensils for Bahima.

These various exchanges may have taken place on unequal terms; a point to which we will return.[53] But while they obviously constituted a notable dimension of Bairu-Bahima relationships, it is evident that these exchanges were not based on a 'division of labour' which engaged the two sections in separate specialised activities in the context of one common economic process. Many Bairu were only occasionally engaged in any economic exchange with Bahima, and most Bahima appear to have been no more than intermittently involved in exchanges with Bairu. The latter, at any rate, tended only to trade when they had a disposable surplus. Generally the two groups as a whole were inclusive, self-sufficient and each basically dependent only on their own means of production; in a sense, the one could do without the other.

These diverse patterns of subsistence and the consequently largely distinctive networks of social relationships of Bairu and Bahima thus suggest several conclusions. First, one can see why salient notions of two different 'societies' should have coexisted with the image of 'one', insufficiently reconciled in the literature as they may have been. These images seem quite reconcilable in the light of intermittent Bairu and Bahima relationships on the basis of essentially different social and economic routines. At the same time, these conditions indicate basic shortcomings in viewing Nkore society as centred around a single, internally differentiated economic process with specialised inputs, let alone around a class system in the conventional sense. If one of the criteria for the designation of a society as a class system is the control of the means of production and the appropriation of surplus by a non-manual economic elite, then this hardly applied to Nkore. Even the basically exclusive Bahima ownership of cattle did not really meet this criterion, since it represented one out of two coexistent modes of production, was in practice tied to one ethnic group, and was one for which the 'owners' also provided the labour. Again, if we would instead see class positions as an index of stratificational mobility, it is also difficult to see how this fitted the case of Nkore. As we will see, there *was* a certain degree of social mobility in Nkore (as also of 'inequality'), though it appears that its frequency was all but great. But even then the extent to which this was related to any common ranking system was quite limited, so that it would stretch the meaning of 'openness' all too far to take any such instances as presumptive evidence of an open class system. Instead, reservations are called for in regard to presentations of Nkore which assume close interaction and economic interdependence between Bairu and Bahima – whether in a caste or in a class context. If anything, an open class pattern would be even more difficult to reconcile with the existence of different subsistence patterns that involved largely contrasted occupational routines, dietary practices and also ecological, hence to some extent different geographical bases, than would be the case with a caste structure. This is not to say that people did not hold differential powers, privileges or statuses in Nkore, either within the Bairu and Bahima communities or in the contact between them. In various roles and relationships they definitely did. But the range and extent of Bairu-Bahima contacts were limited and implied a basic sense of autonomy of the two groups in day to day affairs. As a result, while it would be erroneous to conceive of their relationship as one that was rigidly patterned or as one that placed every single Mwiru in a directly subordinate position to a Muhima, neither can the proposition be upheld that members of the two groups had equal chances in an open and socially mobile society; if anything, reality *approximated* the former rather than the latter type of situation.

Before trying to further identify the distinguishing features of Nkore's political system, it will be useful to first raise a question about perceptions. For if Nkore was neither a full-fledged caste system, nor an open class system, it may well be asked how – and why – some observers could have noted, and emphasised, intrinsic social inequalities whereas others perceived, and stressed, essential mobility in the system. In large measure, this must be a matter of perspectives, – applied to, or derived from, the particular context. While it is difficult to firmly establish how any of these have been formed, we can nevertheless consider some explanations.

In the first place, it would seem all too facile to simply attribute any exaggerated perceptions in either direction mainly to the channels of information which investigators employed. Even if it were true, for example, that

    'it was from [a] class of malcontents which embraced (as it still does) both Bairu and Bahima that the European researchers, in the early part of this century, recruited most of the interpreters since only they could speak some English and had no regular employment, . . . [so that it is] likely that what was collected as genuine information were the versions favoured by the particular interpreters',[54]

then it would not only seem equally likely that these researchers, if they did not themselves learn Runyankore, would check their information with other, rather more 'contented' elements (e.g. the Omugabe, his chief minister and senior chiefs, or early mission-employed teachers and catechists, most of whom were reasonably conversant with English), but it would in any event be hard to see how every piece of information could be thus re-interpreted – and so consistently, over several generations of researchers and interpreters – before it reached the researchers concerned. Such an argument, moreover, might well boomerang, for in respect to historical research that for the larger part relies on Bahima informants – presumably because they are considered the repositories of historical information,[55] it would be just as simple to suggest that the evidence thus obtained must be slanted because contemporary political divisions in Ankole make these informants apt to de-emphasise any past Bahima 'superiority'.

More serious attention deserves the possibility that *a priori* assumptions have been colouring the rapportage of some research findings.[56] For example, there can be little doubt that Victorian ideas of status and hierarchy had no small influence on, say, Sir Harry Johnston's or Roscoe's interpretations of what they heard and saw.[57] Nor should such results be particularly surprising: if one expected to find status differences in the first place, then anything that seemed observable in this regard stood a ready chance to be considered, and treated, as confirmation of such perspective.

In the case of Nkore, the possibility of such generalisations being made was even greater if one failed to grasp the elementary fact of two communities residing in the area. Bairu who were seen in the direct service of Bahima, performing low, menial tasks, were then liable to be regarded as representative of a general inferior status designation of Bairu.[58]

Thus, leaving aside the exact deductive processes which intermediated, what appears to have occurred in places is a familiar error of instances of ethnic status inequality being rapidly generalised, here to apply to 'all' Bairu and 'all' Bahima. Again, as we have seen, a similar methodology is possible in opposite terms, namely of instances of social mobility within or across ethnic boundaries being readily generalised into an 'open class system' – presumably in an effort to once and for all dismiss all categorisations of Nkore as based on a 'premise of inequality'.[59] But in respect of Nkore 'caste' is derogatory, while 'class' is a euphemism.

In the final analysis, perhaps the major hindrance to fruitful dialogue and understanding of a society such as pre-colonial Nkore are some of the concepts and models used to typify its specific socio-political structure.

Foreign-derived terms such as 'caste' or 'class' society, in more than one sense, appear inadequate to describe the particular characteristics of Nkore, especially its juxtaposition of a Bahima superstructure with two more or less separate and autonomous socio-economic poles, of which only one was directly and more intimately related to this superstructure. Though most individual ingredients constituting the Nkore structure were familiar enough (institutions of power and authority, dependency relationships, etc.), the point is that for its particular combination our vocabulary – of social science or other terminology – simply does not seem to contain a proper general term. In its absence a tendency apparently develops to mould research findings into one or another of a variety of 'familiar' models – with the result that such models begin to be selective in the first place (since some information fits it better than other), and may finally complicate distinguishing empirical evidence from the generalisations in which they are cast. Ironically, amidst a wealth of observations, we may thus find difficulty understanding reality.

The problems of interpretation and re-interpretation which we encounter in the case of Nkore have their parallels in various other African situations. Generally, the identification and analysis of patterns of stratification in pre-colonial African societies has hardly been known for its conceptual clarity and scientific rigour. By and large, patterns of social ranking and inequality have long tended to be dealt with implicitly, in the context of wider-ranging classifications and typologies of social structures. But while few investigations have been explicitly addressed to the subject, the traditional literature nonetheless has contained quite categorical notions about stratification in pre-colonial societies. Most familiar among these were blanket categorisations of certain societies as egalitarian (or stateless, acephalous, as their corollaries used to be), of others as tiered (hierarchical, centralised) structures. It is common knowledge how long these categorisations have enjoyed the status of axioms in African social studies. Increasingly, these and other propositions are now being subjected to re-appraisal. Recent historical research suggests that some societies were not quite as egalitarian as they first were believed to be. Conversely, the hierarchism and inequality attributed to others appears to have been less pronounced – or not so much structured on a single, simple principle – as originally presumed.

These changing perceptions carry implications which reach well beyond the realm of purely historical interest. Whether or not in a pre-colonial society there was a system of stratification in the first place, and in the affirmative case how it was structured, is of basic and obvious importance if we are to understand the nature of social transformations which took place during colonialism. Such base-line information is essential in order to grasp whether, and in what sense, criteria for social ranking were either altered or sustained within the colonial framework, or else by what processes and on what basis a stratified structure emerged where previously there was none. Again, a clear understanding of pre-colonial stratification configurations is no less essential for evaluating the premises and objectives, if not the rationalisations, of colonial policies impinging upon African socio-political structures. For a society might be treated as if it had a pattern of stratification and in the end find these assumptions, however erroneous, fulfilled as a result of colonial policy. As in the case of Nkore, among a variety of factors responsible for such misinterpretations and distortions, often the employment of western-derived concepts in regard to a pre-colonial African polity appears to have been of critical importance.

POWER, PRIVILEGE AND PATRONAGE IN NKORE

In the light of what appear to be not fully adequate designations of the format of pre-colonial Nkore society, we need to carry the reconstruction of the Nkore state a few steps further.

To this end, there are a few simple ground rules which we can employ. One is to accept that, if stripped from some of the broader characterisations with which they have been associated, there must be some valid hard core to statements of both status hierarchy and equality and of both social mobility and ethnic exclusiveness which have been handed down over time. Another is to situate these elements in the context of Bairu-Bahima contacts, which, as explained, was limited both in space and in purpose. If we adopt these rules, then the second at once serves as a check on the first: it is difficult to conceive of either extremely rigid ethnic barriers, or of very great elasticity in opportunities for social mobility, in a situation in which the relationships concerned were between two more or less separate communities in the first place. Put differently, maintenance of caste-like structures and relationships is unlikely in what is essentially a two-group situation. Any generalisation that transgresses this context can therefore be taken with a grain of salt.

Thus, beyond some of the broader structural aspects of the relationship between Bairu and Bahima which we have considered so far, there are two questions in particular that now need to be answered. One is empirical and concerns the nature of the major roles and status differences – and the access available to them – that existed in Nkore. Among other things, this requires identifying the major power positions in the system, the privileges these might entail and the patronage they might give rise to. The other is more speculative and asks why the Nkore system, juxtaposing a Bahima superstructure with two relatively autonomous socio-economic poles, was structured and operated the way it did – rather than, for example, on a more straightforwardly hierarchical, or egalitarian, basis. This, therefore, raises the crucial question of the relationship between state and society in Nkore. Finally, to find answers to these questions will also be necessary to better understand the role of Nkore kingship.

Thus, within the range of Bairu-Bahima contacts a few major social, economic and political spheres can first be identified in which different roles, resources, and relationships of members of the two groups were exemplified. Socially, at one extreme, a low position of Bairu was most in evidence in those relatively few instances where Bairu were directly in the service of, and dependent upon, Bahima. Even if a highly placed Muhima might also have Bahima in his service, it was his Bairu servants who would commonly be required to carry out the lowliest tasks and who might also be restricted from taking part in particular household activities. Bairu cite examples such as their duty to carry off their lord's urine, or their prohibition to touch Bahima milkpots, lest these would turn 'unclean', as evidence of this category's past inferior social position. It is probably these people, or at least some of them, whom Morris, Karugire and others had in mind when discussing Bairu living in the vicinity of Bahima kraals, cultivating some short-term crops for their own subsistence while performing services for, and moving on with, the pastoralists when the latter trekked elsewhere.[60]

It is even more likely that it was within this context that the term 'Bairu' carried its specific meaning not just of 'cultivators', but also, and perhaps in the first place, of 'servants' or 'serfs'. One might note here that from the early colonial period onwards, most of the reporting on Ankole history has occurred on the basis of contacts with leading Bahima, who, when referring to the Bairu, cannot but primarily have had in mind the Bairu who lived in their immediate surrounding.[61] Yet even in the context of Nkore with its comparatively large Bahima population only a minority of the Bairu stood in any direct master-servant position *vis-à-vis* Bahima, the majority remaining outside such an immediate hierarchical relationship or being more loosely involved, if at all, in client relationships with Bahima (or other Bairu). If this majority nonetheless shared in some of the stigmas associated with Bairu status, these were evidently exhibited in a much more remote sense and also, perhaps, counter-balanced by their own attitudes in respect of Bahima. Notwithstanding any stereotyped reciprocal attitudes, contacts between 'ordinary' Bairu and 'ordinary' Bahima in view of the distinctiveness of their life patterns could hardly have involved salient and direct inequalities.

Economically, beyond basically diverse modes of production of Bairu and Bahima, and again with the exception of the Bairu minority in direct Bahima employment, their (intermittent) contacts on the whole seem to have taken place on terms which tended to be more favourable to Bahima than to Bairu. In the absense of a fixed means of exchange this cannot be verified in anything like exact, monetary terms. But, according to older men in Ankole today, Bahima exercised what may have amounted to a certain 'market-monopoly': for purposes of barter they left it to the Bairu to carry their (heavier) products to the Bahima kraals and they also were in a stronger position to decide whether or not to trade in the first place and what value to give in exchange. If these accounts have not suffered exaggeration, they might indicate that Bahima products were more eagerly sought by Bairu than Bairu products by Bahima, or else that Bairu felt a stronger need to remain on good terms with Bahima than the latter felt in respect to them. Aside from barter, Bairu from time to time were also liable to certain requisitions by Bahima, for products or for labour. This would often be 'tribute', usually presumed to be in return for 'protection' or favours; there might also be 'gifts' with the same ends in view.[62] Bahima also were subject to tribute duties, but never to Bairu, a distinction which may have strengthened the 'imposed' character of it in the latter's case.

Underlying these economic contacts between Bairu and Bahima a few factors were of special significance. One was that of a higher premium being placed on the possession of cattle than on the control of land, at least by Bahima. As noted, in pre-colonial times the two coexistent subsistence systems in Nkore were not directly equatable and could thus hardly be 'hierarchically' ordered. Different values became only more manifest later, when in the colonial period monetisation made it *theoretically*[63] possible to buy a 2 or 3 acre plot of land, a common Bairu holding, for roughly the price that one or two cows would fetch. Considering that a small Bahima herd would consist of a dozen head of cattle and that herds of one or two hundred were not unusual at all (the exceptions rather being those of one or two thousand head), one can see that in a (colonial) economy in which different modes of production were made comparable through a system of agreed prices, cattle ownership emerged as an economically very strong and strategic proposition. But indirectly – and again whether or not there was any 'statutory' ban on the possession of productive cattle by Bairu – one can see that the value placed by Bahima on the control of cattle made it extremely difficult, if not in practice impossible, for Bairu through exchange of products or labour to submit realistic claims on cattle ownership – assuming they were interested in obtaining it. This economic basis instead suggests that exceptions might only occur if Bairu distinguished themselves, as warleaders or otherwise, in the service of the Nkore state. But such roles themselves were exceptional given the structuring of Nkore society.

Economically (and politically) as important as the Bahima's predilection for cattle was their disinterest in the control of land. Pastoral land was relatively plentiful in Nkore and it was indeed its unique ecological features in this respect that enabled the sustenance of a larger and more purely pastoral community than existed virtually anywhere else in the interlacustrine region. Since availability and access to grazing land posed few problems, the need for instituting control over (Bairu) land hardly arose and the Bahima's capacity to effect that was never tested. We will return to this point, which is of crucial importance in understanding the nature of the Nkore political framework. But it should here be noted that the economic contacts between Bahima and Bairu did not include any landlord-tenant relationships. In this respect, too, Nkore's economic system thus was not one in which one category 'owned' the means of production while another provided the labour as tenants.

Finally on the question of different economic resource-bases we should take account of the fact that while the Bahima's advantages lay in cattle ownership and their 'market'-position, the Bairu's lay in a less vulnerable agricultural subsistence base and in their 'monopoly' of the manufacturing of utensils and arms – hoes, axes, spears and arrows. Thus, while 'military power of the state was provided by Hima, ... the weapons of war were not manufactured by those who waged it'.[64] However, it is not certain – but actually quite doubtful – whether this monopoly has ever given the Bairu any 'strategic' advantage.

Lastly, whatever differential roles and benefits accrued to Bairu and Bahima in the social and economic spheres, the most visible differences were political. Asymmetrical positions of political power among Bairu and Bahima were exhibited in at least two main ways. The most crucial was the fact that the Nkore political system was largely based on the Bakungu or territorial chiefs, who wielded substantial powers and were mostly, though not exclusively, Bahima of the royal Bahinda clan. In more heavily populated Bairu areas a Mwiru might occupy a chiefly position, but as a rule all incumbents were Bahima, which listings of exceptions only seem to confirm. For purposes of recruitment to political office, therefore, the Bahima constituted an elite stratum from which the Nkore ruling class was drawn, a fact of key significance on which all sources seem agreed. We will return to the operation of this system below when discussing the institution of kingship. A second area of differential access to power was that of court litigation, which was similarly dominated by Bahima. To be sure, most cases were handled outside the royal court, through other chiefs or clan notables and commonly within a Bairu or a Bahima context.[65] The cases that did come before the Omugabe's court mostly concerned Bahima; as we will see later, the way these were dealt with was of vital importance to the existence of the Nkore state. In cases involving Bahima and Bairu, however, the latter's chances to get an equal hearing, or sanction, were less certain than the former's. Theoretically, for instance, the right of vengeance might be passed against a Mwiru for killing a Muhima, but in the opposite case that penalty was unlikely.[66]

Besides, for a variety of more minor infringements, such as the destruction of his crops by cattle, a Mwiru would find it difficult to get any legal redress at all. Indeed, as already cited, 'the legal and security system was heavily weighted in favour of ... the Bahima'.[67] Politically, therefore, more manifestly than in social and economic respects, the Nkore framework was a Bahima-oriented one.

Against these basic patterns of separateness and unequal access to power, it is necessary to note a few avenues that historically seem to have allowed some social mobility and eventually even the possibility of assimilation among Bairu and Bahima. In the first place, as mentioned above (p. 20), it appears that clans could over time achieve such a change of status that what used to be a predominantly Bairu clan would eventually, after many generations, come to be ranked as primarily a Bahima clan. The more pronounced corporateness that Nkore clans, in all likelihood, possessed may have facilitated such a process, though it is nonetheless difficult to assess how frequently it might have occurred. The example most often cited in Ankole is that of one clan, the Abasingo, which perhaps suggests that this particular status mobility was rather exceptional. (The reverse, namely what was once a predominantly Bahima clan becoming essentially a Bairu clan, is never mentioned in Ankole.)

Another process leading towards assimilation focussed on a small sub-category of individuals called Abambari, members of which had a status somehow in between that of Bairu and Bahima. It has usually been accepted that Abambari were the 'half-caste' offspring of Bairu 'concubines' taken by Bahima men, but it is possible that the category included also opposite relationships.[68] Today the term Abambari is only a historical referent, as different conditions no longer sustain this particular mid-way status designation. As a status it would now not be desired by anyone in Ankole, and besides the dichotomised and exclusive agricultural versus pastoral poles between which it was placed are no longer valid. Banyankore continue to debate whether the category included 'upwardly' mobile Bairu only or also Bahima who had lost their cattle and were relegated to a 'lower' status. The latter seems debatable in the light of Kinyankore traditions which relate that control over cattle was to some extent distributed through the kingship, so that a Muhima who had suffered losses could theoretically ask to be favoured with new cattle; also, an impoverished Muhima could still be a herdsman for other Bahima.[69] But there seems in any event consensus that any change from Bairu through Abambari to Bahima status would take several generations to be completed.

Finally we should keep in mind that not all Bahima were wealthy and powerful and not all Bairu poor and prestigeless. While many Bahima were 'commoners' in more than one sense, several Bairu achieved considerable power and influence. Again, the examples frequently given refer to some Bairu leaders who distinguished themselves in warding off external attacks, some of whom stood in control of peripheral areas of Nkore – presumably where there was also a larger Bairu population. However, precisely the fact that there were some Bairu who were renowned for their achievements and power, but who were not and did not become Bahima, suggests that transition from a Bairu designation to that of Bahima, if it was desired, was not as smooth or frequent as would be associated with anything like an 'open' class system. In many ethnically differentiated or stratified societies, such as the 18th-century Hausa states, individuals from one category have held positions of high influence and esteem within the framework of another, but such relatively exceptional instances have often served as outlets mitigating, if not sustaining, the general social distance or stratificational rigidity and must not be taken as evidence of the latter's absence.

In Nkore, as noted, a variety of conditions militated against easy transition from Bairu to Bahima status, especially the full-time and differently orientated engagement in agriculture or cattle-rearing, and the rootedness in these same routines and the habits, diets and social bases that were connected with them. As a result, 'short-term' and frequent transfers could in fact hardly take place, as seems confirmed by the stress laid by Banyankore on the fact that any such transitions would take generations to be completed, and also by the limited range of examples they cite. It is hardly necessary, therefore, to point to socially recognised physical differences between Bairu and Bahima or to a rather universally displayed disinclination on the part of socially prestigious groups to share their sources of wealth and influence, to recognise that there was a basic and continued separateness and social distance between Bairu and Bahima in Nkore which was anything but consistent with a picture of an open and mobile society.

As a focus on patronage relationships shows, individual socio-economic and political relationships in Nkore reflected, and in part sustained, this patterning of aggregate groups. Four defining criteria can be attached to 'patronage', or its corollary 'clientship': the relationship must be entered into by individuals of unequal political and/or economic influence; it must be of relative durability; it must be based on reciprocal expectations of rewards and returns; and it must involve an aspect of personal favouritism, as opposed to consideration of merit.[70] Applying these criteria to Nkore status categories we can, to an approximate extent, derive where these relationships occurred and where they did not. It appears in any case certain that Nkore society was not wholly structured on the basis of an intricate network of these relationships and thus from that angle differed again from, for example, neighbouring Rwanda.

First, the members of one particular status category, the Bahinda, were not, *as Bahinda*, engaged in patronage relationships with other individuals. Though mythology suggests unequal statuses between Bahinda on the one hand and Bahima and Bairu on the other, the fact that Bahinda in most regards were identified, and identified themselves, with other Bahima, implies that only a consideration of them as Bahima, or in their role as Bakungu, can inform us about patronage relationships in their case.

Bahima and Bairu as we have seen occupied generally different roles and statuses in Nkore society, based on different syndromes of occupation, wealth and ethnicity. But since not all Bairu were in direct and continuous contact with Bahima and since many were only intermittently engaged in exchanges of provisions and services with Bahima, it was only in certain cases that Bairu and Bahima maintained exchange relationships which had the durability that would be characteristic of patronage. The Bairu-Bahima juxtaposition, in other words, as such was not generally based on patronage but on an individual basis patronage relationships could be and were established between Bahima and Bairu. The structural basis of these relationships becomes clearer if we bear in mind that reverse linkages, i.e. in which a Mwiru was the patron and a Muhima the client, did not occur.

Durable relationships involving reciprocal benefits might, on the other hand, occur between Bahima, or between Bairu. Whether and which of these could actually be called patronage relationships depended on whether they also involved an element of unequal status.

These arrangements definitely occurred: an influential Muhima might be the patron for another Muhima, or a Mwiru for another Mwiru.

Where patronage existed between Bahima and Bairu, among Bahima, or among Bairu, this was not necessarily based on political office. Yet the most salient examples of patronage appear to have occurred where the senior partner held a chiefly position. The Bakungu, who were largely drawn from the ruling Bahinda clan, to a lesser extent from the wider Bahima sub-stratum, and in quite exceptional cases from amongst the Bairu, commonly had a following of clients, Bahima and Bairu, who supported them while expecting return benefits. These relationships were personal, relatively durable, and might involve the exchange of cattle, or in the case of Bairu-clients the gift of a bull. To maintain these relationships enhanced the security of office of Bakungu, while at the same time it provided a mechanism for the distribution – and redistribution – of rewards and benefits among a Mukungu's retinue. It was, therefore, at the level of the Bakungu that a pattern of patronage occurred most clearly and frequently, involving the key aspects of inequality, durability, and reciprocal benefits. As we shall see, its significance for the functioning of the Nkore state was considerable.

Similar to the Bakungu, the Omugabe could and did enter into patronage relationships. Some such relationships were in fact with Bakungu and then had a particularly strong political overtone. Others were with non-chiefly Bahima, or at times with Bairu as well, and then involved the more usual exchange of benefits and supports. Patronage was especially important to Bahinda aspiring to become Omugabe. As the choice of an Omugabe was largely determined by superior strength among rival candidates, it was essential that pretenders commanded a strong body of loyal supporters. Patronage was the major avenue to build this support. Once installed, an Omugabe needed to keep his support to obtain an untroubled tenure of office. He had to master sufficient strength *vis-à-vis* neighbouring states and to ward off internal fissures. Yet, while patronage helped to maintain an Omugabe in office, it did not finally define the role of that office. Patronage as a pattern of relationships converged with others in the institution of kingship. This, as we shall see, in its political sense served to uphold the integration of the political system partly through reference to values of high authority with which it was identified. For the performance of this function, however, the incumbent needed to maintain lines of support in a rather more concrete sense, thus necessitating patronage, the more so because he functioned basically as a *primus inter pares*.

Thus, patronage relationships at different levels at once reflected, and in part made possible the particular format of group and Bairu-Bahima relationships in Nkore. It 'facilitated' them in the sense that it was partly through individual patron-client relationships that contacts between Bahima and Bairu were maintained. It reflected them insofar as clientage relationships might be found in which a Muhima was the patron and a Mwiru the client, but not in the opposite order. But more illustrative of the Nkore system than the occurrence of these arrangements across the ethnic division were two other facts. One was that patron-client relationships do not appear to have formed a pyramidal network integrating all individuals – and thus the whole society – into a single system of socio-economic and political relationships, and the second, that almost certainly the frequency of patronage arrangements was greater among Bahima and among Bairu themselves than between members of the two opposite groups.

The different roles, resource-bases and relationships of Bairu and Bahima in the social, economic and political spheres allow us to draw some further conclusions about the nature of the Nkore socio-political framework. In particular, what deserves attention is the manifest preponderance of Bahima in the political sphere, as opposed to a generally less clear edge they had in social relationships and also to their economic role that – in the context of Bairu-Bahima relationships – was less based on control and domination than it derived from an exclusive involvement in a particular mode of subsistence. Evidently, therefore, a certain contrast between characteristics of political 'inequality' on the one hand and of social and economic 'autonomy' and 'coexistence' on the other suggests that in Nkore, less than in many other systems, 'social', 'political' and 'economic' aspects could be regarded as merely different dimensions of the same set of relationships. Instead, in an important sense all evidence indicates that politically, the Nkore framework was primarily a state of the Bahima, as well as for the Bahima, but that this hegemony was not necessarily, at least not fully, extended to other spheres of life. While some of the Bairu, as we have seen, were directly subservient to Bahima and while Bairu generally enjoyed some fewer rights and privileges than did Bahima in contacts between the two groups, a major part of the Bairu definitely lived a fairly autonomous existence. Even more certain is

that the political life of the kingdom mostly revolved around matters
that were virtually the exclusive concern of Bahima, such as warfare,
cattle raising (and raiding), adjudication of disputes, and other related
matters.[71] Hence, while some Bairu were expected to provide products
and services to the Omugabe and other senior Bahima, and whereas at
times the requisitions demanded from them may have been rather
arbitrary, there is little indication of a pervasive and continuous
political control exercised over all of them. An observation by Roscoe
about – note well – 'the Banyankole', in this connection acquires a new
significance: 'Evidently, their nomadic habits, combined with their
complete disregard of everything unconnected with cattle, prevented
their making much impression either on the surrounding countries as
warriors or on their own country as reformers'.[72]

In this light, also, except for the cardinal fact that there was a
Bahima-based political organisation operating in their immediate
surroundings, the Bairu's position may in fact not have been altogether
different from that of the nearby Bakiga (in the adjacent Kigezi
District),[73] where such central political institutions did not exist. Thus,
if in a general sense the Bairu have often been considered a 'subject'
category, their lack of participation in the political process seems
primarily explained by the characteristics of the 'Bahima state', which
was especially geared to the requirements of pastoralism.

To try and further assess the 'power-balance' that obtained in
Nkore, we might speculate for a moment about the implications that
any significant demographic changes might have had for the above
pattern in pre-colonial times. For example, the emergence of a mixed –
i.e. agriculture and animal husbandry based – economy and some
form of more direct and pervasive central control would have seemed
some of the possible outcomes in the event of a drastic expansion of
the agricultural sector. Both of these possible developments, a mixed
production system and a stronger centralised control, might then have
centered upon, as much as resulted from, the need to resolve
competing claims in the area of land utilisation.

In the Nkore situation, as already indicated, there was hardly a
shortage of pastoral land, nor, it seems, much in the way of pressure for
agricultural land that might have affected the requirements of
pastoralism. Nkore's population was much smaller than that of the
area today and until well into the present century people could open
up new land in various areas – an opportunity which was especially

seized by immigrant groups, mainly Bakiga. Since therefore the availability of the basic resource of land was relatively unproblematic in Nkore, there was in any event no compelling reason in this regard for the state system to strongly involve itself in matters of land control. In turn, it is therefore conceivable that what appears to have been a less than maximal political control, particularly as concerns the Bairu population, was not just consistent with but also explicable in terms of these particular conditions. By the same token, it might then be further hypothesised that a different demographic and ecological balance would have induced the Bahima to bring into play any underutilised, 'reserve' political resources at their disposal in order to safeguard their continued control over the system. In that case, the Nkore political system would 'in principle' have been stratified as a power hierarchy, with Bahima on top and Bairu near the bottom, but one in which the surplus of resources, land in particular, lessened the assertion and visibility of social and political rankings.

Such a hypothesis, however, is entirely speculative, dependent as it is not only on assessments of the relative 'strength' of political resources of Bahima and Bairu but also of other imponderabilia such as the former's capacity and preparedness to involve themselves into the social and economic aspects of agriculture. We thus have hardly a way of deciding whether to assign it a greater weight than an alternative, rather opposite hypothesis, which we can also consider. This is that in the conditions of Nkore and for the purposes it served, a Bahima-dominated state structure commanded an advantage of resources, which it might no longer have been capable of maintaining had its capacity to directly control the agricultural sector ever been put to a test. In that case, the Nkore system would not 'in principle' have had hierarchical, but largely unused powers of Bahima over Bairu, but instead its stratification would have been stretched as far as it could be the way it was. Again, however, we would run into similar difficulties of evaluation in trying to verify this proposition.

Confronted with these alternative speculations, we can do little more but note, with Thomas and Scott, that certain 'geographical factors appear worthy of consideration. ... The nature of the country enabled the Bahima in Ankole (and, farther south, in the present Kigezi District) to dominate the whole area from their grazing grounds, while following a semi-nomadic life.'[74]

In other words, a certain power advantage was maintained by

Bahima in the contact and horizontal relationships with the Bairu communities, strong enough to have given rise to various asymmetrical roles and benefits. But while the 'interest' to extend this control does in any case not appear to have arisen, it is neither certain that it could actually have been effected – at least not without the Bahima giving up their exclusive involvement in a pastoralist mode of subsistence as a major condition.

In broader terms, therefore, Nkore's political system appears to have comprised two types, or levels, of political relationships. Between Bahima and Bairu, relationships tended largely to be intermittent, though based on often unequal advantages. Within the Bahima stratum the relationships that pertained to the state organisation by comparison were much more frequent and intimate, and appear to have been roughly of the kind characteristically existing between 'freemen'.[75] But these latter kinds of relationships (as also the former) must be understood in the light of the pastoral community's mode of subsistence and social organisation, not as primarily a result of the juxtaposition of the two groups.

In a provisional typology of ethnic group contacts based on different forms of ecological interdependence, Barth distinguishes, among other types, between situations in which two or more groups 'may occupy clearly distinct niches in the natural environment and be in minimal competition for resources, [in which case] their interdependence will be limited despite co-residence in the area, and articulation will tend to be mainly through trade, and perhaps in a ceremonial-ritual sector' on the one hand, and situations in which 'they may monopolise separate territories, in which case they are in competition for resources and their articulation will involve politics along the border, and possibly other sectors' on the other.[76] The Nkore case essentially was one that by virtue of its different and minimally competitive modes of subsistence approximated the first type, although the degree of separate territorial concentration of Bairu and Bahima added an element of the second. But unlike a third type, in which '[if] they also compete and accommodate through differential monopolisation of the means of production, this entails a close political and economic articulation, with open possibilities for other forms of interdependence as well',[77] the political articulation that did occur was largely confined to an intra-Bahima context and addressed to intra-Bahima objectives. Failure to recognise this but instead to assume that Nkore politics, though dominated by Bahima, applied equally to Bairu and Bahima, has been at the root of many misunderstandings, including the creation of the colonial framework imposed on the society.

It was also within this context that juxtaposed a basically Bahima state framework with Bairu communities, that the institution of Nkore kingship functioned and in fact stood as the pivot around which the affairs of the state revolved. Against the background we have seen we are now in a better position to appreciate the role of the kingship in Nkore. It is already clear that the office of the Omugabe, while to most Bairu he undoubtedly was an ultimate symbol of power and, in principle, the supreme arbiter of conflicts among men,[78] in fact was quite far removed from day to day Bairu affairs. While the Omugabe clearly stood as the central figure in the Nkore political system and his position no doubt inspired considerable awe for many Bairu, the ties that linked them to the Omugabe were not especially conducive to strong affective identification with the political system. For the Bahima, on the other hand, the Omugabe was the centre-piece of their political relationships. They certainly enjoyed a much more intimate relationship with the Omugabe. He was closely involved in their affairs and he in fact often used to move camp with his cattle as other Bahima did. Moreover, not only was his way of life much the same as theirs, but he was also regarded as the protector of their interests. In the light of the ethnic division, therefore, the historical Nkore system differed fundamentally from, for instance, traditional Buganda with its more homogeneous population structure. Again, contrary to what its mythology would imply, traditional Nkore was not a system in which Bairu and Bahima were basically united in a mystical identification with its kingship. Instead, the institution of Nkore kingship must be understood within the context of the state system, which itself was primarily based on intra-Bahima relationships.

THE TWO FACES OF NKORE KINGSHIP

Not unlike the study of social and group relationships, the analysis of Nkore kingship[79] appears hampered by a conceptual problem which is more often encountered in the study of historical African states. When glancing through the available literature, or talking to the reputedly knowledgeable members of such societies, one of the more persistent images presented shows the traditional ruler as holding absolute powers. Further queries, however, may well yield an entirely different picture. A consideration of the distribution of authoritative functions, or of the consultation, bargaining and conflicts involved in the political process, can suggest a far greater dispersal of power than might have been anticipated.[80]

Such an ambivalence of interpretations is characteristic of much of the literature on Nkore. On the one hand, the Omugabe figures as omnipotent and despotic, as a ruler who wields unlimited powers and who has an absolute, autocratic sway over his kingdom. On the other hand, he emerges as essentially a *primus inter pares*, a mediator between conflicting interests, and an instrument in the settlement of disputes. Not surprisingly, these images are not altogether unrelated to some of the differences in perception of socio-political relationships we have discussed above. For if one perceives a society as being rigidly patterned, in terms of different power and status categories, it should be quite difficult *not* to see a powerful, autocratic ruler at the pinnacle of its political structure. Conversely, if one understands status differences to be less directly equated or more diffuse in the first place, then such views can hardly be related to a pattern which assumes the existence of autocratic or absolute kingship. Nonetheless, it remains intriguing that in the literature on Nkore both images should sometimes coexist within the same source, leaving the reader rather at a loss to reconcile one with the other.[81]

When reviewing some of these images, we can find an 'absolutist' view of Nkore kingship stated quite strongly in the work of Roscoe, who wrote in 1923: 'The government of the country of Ankole was autocratic and the power was in the hands of the Mugabe or ruler, whose rule was absolute and his decision on any matter final'.[82] Furthermore, Roscoe asserted, 'The Mugabe had the power of life and death over all his subjects, and it was believed that his people held their property solely through his clemency, for he was the owner of all the land and all the cattle'.[83] This last point was re-emphasised in an official publication of 1938, which stated that 'the Omugabe laid claim to all the cattle in the country, being as much the ruler of cattle as he was of men. This claim, furthermore, was no idle one, for the Omugabe could and did take whatever cattle he wished from whomsoever he pleased . . . .'[84] A few years later, in 1940, Oberg expressed himself in much the same vein: 'The position of the Mugabe was exalted, his authority supreme, his leadership all-embracing'. Oberg further concluded that 'Power ... both physical and spiritual, was the inherent quality of kingship'.[85]

These views have been echoed virtually till the present day. For instance, in an essay prepared some years ago by the Ntare History Society it is claimed, 'before the British brought in democracy [*sic*], the type of government which prevailed was ... despotic. The king's powers were unlimited. He could, with a word, prevent or make a man's fortune.'[86] Another illustration is provided by Vansina. Having constructed a typology of African kingdoms on the basis of a scale of decreasing centralisation, i.e. ranging from the most centralised state structures on one end to federative arrangements (in which the king is 'only *primus inter pares*') on the other, Vansina goes on to characterise Nkore as a 'clear case' of the first type, namely a 'despotic kingdom' in which 'the king appoints all other officials and wields absolute power in practice and in theory'.[87]

These examples could be multiplied, but for our purposes they suffice to indicate one persistent trend of thought according to which the traditional monarchical institutions of Nkore were synonymous with those of a 'despotic' state. At the root of this misrepresentation lies a confusion between the actual and ideal aspects of authority vested in the Omugabe, which we will discuss below. But it should be noted that, on the face of it, there was much in the traditional political culture which seemed to support the idea. In monarchical ideology, the Omugabe *was* seen as possessing extraordinary and divine faculties, unequalled in other human beings. He was known, for instance, as Rubambansi, 'He who stretches the Earth',[88] which clearly stressed his omnipotence; as Rugaba, 'The Giver', meaning that it was he who gave (or could withhold) prosperity and wealth; as Omukama, 'The Milker', again typifying him as the benefactor who supplied his people with their food; and as Nyakusinga, 'The Victorious', who overcomes all enemies. Moreover, as Omugabe, 'The one who has been given authority',[89] he posed as the direct descendant of the Creator, Ruhanga, which again exemplified his supernatural powers. In the ritual he engaged in and the ceremonial with which he was surrounded, these aspects were all symbolically expressed. On his accession, for instance, he would purify the country, and when disease came to the land he would curse it to dispel it. In the night, it was believed, he could not turn or he would turn his kingdom over.[90]

Finally, tradition relates that the Omugabe could not die a natural death, but was obliged to take a poison when his powers began to fail him.[91] When this happened, the word for death was not used, but it was said that 'heaven has fallen' or 'fire has gone out'. Again, his body was not buried, but taken to a place where his spirit would reincarnate itself into a lion.

All these notions thus seem to underscore the supreme and exalted position of the Omugabe. In practice, however, the Omugabe's powers to impose his will were severely restricted.[92] A variety of groups and individuals participated in the making of decisions and their influence could not be easily circumvented by the Omugabe. We might first note here the position of the Omugabe's ritual mother and sister, who were consulted on many issues and whose opinion, if only because of the closeness of their relationship to the Omugabe, carried no small amount of weight. But of special importance in this respect were the Bakungu or senior chiefs, who were responsible for territorial divisions and who also served as the Omugabe's counsellors. Decisions were discussed at great length in the assembly of these chiefs, usually until a consensus emerged which would then be articulated by the Omugabe. The duality of functions of the Bakungu had significant consequences, for it meant that the officials involved in formulating major decisions were also responsible for their implementation, while the Omugabe had no other administrative instrument to override their influence.[93] Although the Bakungu were expected to spend a good deal of time paying court to the Omugabe, and while this obligation might conceivably have prevented them from asserting their independence from the centre, the reverse side of the coin is that they were thus given the opportunity to gain considerable influence over the Omugabe. Various early travellers have in fact referred to them as the 'power behind the throne'.[94] Moreover, despite their involvement at the political centre, it appears that the Bakungu retained considerable freedom of action in their own areas. Willis, for instance, who was in Ankole when the British assumed their overrule, and whose refreshingly naive journal affords many useful insights into political relationships during his time, commented in 1901: 'Hitherto each chief had done what he liked . . . ' (and added: 'Now there will be a settled, responsible government').[95] But while the Bakungu were thus relatively autonomous *vis-à-vis* the Omugabe, within their own territorial jurisdictions they were themselves restricted in their powers.

Roscoe stated it quite strongly: 'The authority of a Mukungu in his own district was limited, for he had no control over the movements of the subordinate chiefs and other people who might take up their residence or pasture their cows there . . . . There was no animosity between the Mukungu and the subordinate chiefs in his own district, but the latter were quite independent and only acknowledged him as their superior when some dispute arose among them and required authoritative settlement'.[96] It suggests that political power was not only dispersed spatially ('decentralised'), but also did not reach down very deeply.

In these conditions, there was not much the Omugabe could do to enhance his influence, except through his personal leadership qualities. A large number of the senior chiefs were Bahinda, and while they had pledged their loyalty to the Omugabe, the latter was in no small respect dependent upon their continued support. His obligation to cater for their interests was perhaps even stronger since in Nkore there had not developed, as in Bunyoro and Toro, special functions of heads of the royal clan which were distinct from the office of the monarch.[97] This may indicate a lesser amount of political role differentiation in the Nkore situation and suggest that in times of crises, the office of the Omugabe might be more vulnerable to demands by the royal clan than was the case in Bunyoro or Toro. Moreover, although formally all senior chiefs were appointed by the Omugabe, these appointments in fact tended to confirm, and in a sense disguise, hereditary succession to office. Roscoe wrote that 'When one of these [Bakungu] chiefs died, the king appointed his successor who was generally, though not necessarily, his heir'.[98] Also, the Omugabe may have been able to demote one of them, [99] but then most probably not without the backing of the other Bakungu. There was always the possibility of a chief withdrawing his allegiance, which had to be countered by concession or punitive measure – depending upon the amount of countervailing strength available. Some Bahinda were in fact potential rivals to the Omugabe. Succession to the kingship was commonly determined in a contest between warring factions of princes, in which victory fell to the one who succeeded to take possession of Bagyendanwa, the royal drum. 'The choice, therefore,' commented a senior prince, 'was by spears. Spears are in fact the nation, they indicate where the will of the nation lies.'[100] It was possible, however, that even if one contender had come out victorious and had been installed as Omugabe, rival factions would continue their opposition and consider him as *Ekyebumbe*, a usurper. Full legitimacy was therefore not bestowed upon an Omugabe until all fighting had subsided.[101] The potential challenge which came from the Bahinda was also exemplified by the rule that the Omugabe's chief adviser, the Engazi, could not be a member of the royal clan, since a Muhinda might conceivably use his position to seize power. The office of Enganzi was filled either by a Muhima of a non-royal Nkore clan, by a member of a royal clan of a neighbouring kingdom, or even by a Mwiru.[102] These various arrangements are tokens of real or potential limitation to the excercise of power by the Omugabe. If, therefore, as Stenning has suggested, 'In Nkore there seems to have been little conflict between the hereditary principle and that of appointment',[103] then this was appearance rather than actual fact, achieved through a delicate balance of forces in which tension between these principles was contained. Basically, the traditional political structure of Nkore was highly fragile, and its kingship served to provide it with a sense of unity.

Some aspects of the jurisdiction attributed in theory to the Omugabe accordingly present a different picture in practice. For instance, while theoretically the Omugabe was the owner of all land, in actual fact this title had little or no bearing on the way land was allocated. Aside from inheritance, in principle people could occupy a vacant plot unless someone else had an earlier claim on it. In cases of dispute, the issue would be settled by the chiefs. Again, if people desired to move into an area which had not been their traditional habitat, the chief would commonly allocate a stretch of land to them.[104] All these tenure arrangements were naturally of importance to the Bairu cultivators. In respect of the Bairu, it is clear that a man who cultivated a piece of land had certain rights in it, his clan members or neighbours had other rights, the local chief had a further say, while the Omugabe was seen as the notional 'owner' of all land. For the Bahima, again, land was historically of little concern. Not only was it relatively plentiful, but since Bahima were constantly moving with their herds of cattle, there was also little reason for them to submit claims on any particular piece of land.[105]

The Omugabe's 'ownership' of land, therefore, rather than connoting any strictly defined property relationships in a western legal sense, was primarily a symbol of ultimate control by which legitimate authority over the society was claimed for the Nkore kingship.

Similarly, the Omugabe's theoretical ownership of cattle contrasted in significant respects with reality. In theory, it will be recalled, all cattle belonged to the Omugabe and he 'gave' it to Bahima in reward for their loyalty, particularly in times of war. In practice, however, the relationship appears rather to have been the reverse. Bahima enjoyed virtually unrestricted use of the cattle under their control and paid tribute to the Omugabe through the gift of cows, in return for which they could expect protection from the political centre.[106] The prevalence of this arrangement can be gathered, among other things, from the fact that the Omugabe had his 'own' herds, which were taken for grazing by his herdsmen in various parts of the country. For such cases the term 'clientship' would seem the proper description and here the 'giving' did indeed initiate with the Omugabe.[107] However, as this by no means applied to all cattle, and as other senior chiefs similarly entered into such clientship contracts, this contradicts the view that ownership of all cattle in any concrete sense rested with the Omugabe. The Omugabe's theoretical claim to all cattle should be seen rather as a symbolic device to assert the political unity of the Bahima of Nkore, which had little to do with actual control and usufruct arrangements.

Again, the pervasive political role attributed to the Omugabe contrasts markedly with his actual function. As noted, the theoretical claims to absolute rulership need serious qualification in the light of the role of Bakungu and other officials in decision-making. Moreover, it appears that the office of the Omugabe was in large part a judicial one. Most of the meetings of the Omugabe's court, the assembly of chiefs, were concerned with settlement of disputes between Bahima litigants, ranging from cases of theft and murder to various other infringements of rights and privileges.[108] Willis attended this council in 1902, and it seems reasonable to assume that his description is in essence applicable to the preceding pre-colonial period:

'The Native Council . . . is delightfully informal . . . . The King and Katikiro sit at one end . . . and all the chiefs are arranged in more or less order of precedence, down two sides, the poorer people thronging near the door. There is no attempt at any formal opening: no one stands up to address the rest, for all are speaking at once. In the midst of business anyone who likes strolls up, bows down, and salutes the King in a loud voice.

Most of the business consists of hearing(!) cases, for the Council is a rough and ready Court of Justice. Witnesses are of course entirely unnecessary. Two scantily clad men, unannounced, come in: each begins accusing the other violently to the King . . . .

. . . [The] claimant, finding the King otherwise engaged, looks anxiously around for someone who appears to be listening and shouts at him. By this time the discussion has become general, and everyone is talking at the top of his voice: no one hears anyone, for everyone is shouting. The marvel is that out of the hubbub, a verdict emerges, given quite decisively and without hesitation.[109]

The nature of the cases dealt with by this court was no doubt more varied than those before any ordinary modern court, covering matters of administration and politics as well as more narrowly defined 'legal' issues. Of key importance was also the fact that in all the cases brought before them '[the] function of the Mugabe and his chiefs lay more in giving judgments than in meting out punishments'.[110] Moreover, 'there was no police organisation to guard life and property'. Instead, as in the case of murder, 'the Mugabe would grant the right of blood revenge, which, however, had to be carried out by the members of the injured extended family'. The structural implications of this are of no small significance. *Prima facie*, the arrangements would appear to re-emphasise the limitations to the Omugabe's powers. However, the importance of his role should not necessarily be judged primarily by his executive powers. As with kingship in ancient times, the essence of Nkore kingship was law-giving. Law-giving was not carried out by the promulgation of sets of abstract regulations to which behaviour would henceforth need to conform. That would only have made sense if there had been a body of specialised agents, an administration and a 'police organisation', to whom the task of applying such rules could be delegated. In Nkore, where the Bakungu were involved in the law-making process, such a body was lacking. Law-giving in traditional Nkore appears rather to have been a matter of articulating the considered opinion of the leading members of the society on questions of social behaviour for which the solution was either not quite obvious or involved such drastic action to settle that a higher sanction was necessary. In either case, recourse was had to what was intuitively *known* as the law of the land and it was this to which the Omugabe finally gave expression. Kinyankore law was a living code, and its function was probably even more important than that of law in a society with more specialised organs of government. Nothing less than the cohesiveness of the political community depended largely and directly on the meaningfulness of the judgments passed on the relationships between its members.

Evidently, therefore, while in theory the Omugabe was all-powerful, in reality his powers were quite limited. In theory, he was the supreme decision-maker, but in practice the system depended heavily on reaching agreement among the political elite. Again, in theory the Omugabe could rely on coercion to have his will followed, but in practice he depended largely on voluntary compliance with the judgments he pronounced. Yet one should not *a priori* assume conflict between these images. In fact, the Nkore political system may have been able to function the way it did, and perhaps to function at all, because of the way in which the two notions of power complemented one another. Let us look at this more closely.

We have seen that the Nkore system was highly vulnerable to fragmentation due to the claims of Bahinda and other Bahima. The absence of a cadre of officials solely loyal to the political centre meant that integration of the system could only be maintained by invoking higher values to sanction decisions which had been arrived at through debate and majority opinion. At the elite level there was widespread participation in the decision-making process, which had to cope with conflicting interests and fairly autonomous political strongholds in the system.

Inevitably, therefore, two closely related problems presented themselves when decisions were being made. Firstly, if they were to be believable, it was essential that decisions should have an àura of higher sanctity than would be normally associated with the opinion of a body of individuals, even if these were leading members of society. If justice and law were to be more than a bargain, they had to be characterised by universalistic and transcendental qualities which should be able to command acceptance. If the Omugabe had been actually an absolute ruler, presumably he would have been considered as embodying these qualities. But as he was not, the attribution of omnipotence and ultimate benevolence which was bestowed upon him still served to sanction the *communis opinio* which it was his prerogative to articulate. Secondly, once a decision had been taken, the problem was to secure adherence to the judgment passed. In the absence of machinery for implementation, compliance basically rested with mechanisms of social control. Here, too, the exalted notions of the Omugabe as a political giant wielding unlimited powers came in, not to conflict with, but to complement the characteristics of the political structure. Decisions carried weight because they were ordained in the name of high authority, even if this authority was highly symbolic and only partly involved direct control over subordinates. The coherence of the political community depended critically on maintaining this myth, which was its main antidote to centrifugal tendencies. The myth's personification, the Omugabe, who transposed elite deliberation into state law, constituted the major formal institution of the Bahima state. Indeed, he had sounder grounds than Louis XIV on which to claim '*l'État, c'est moi*'. Hence, it was through the validation of this myth that a synthesis between two seemingly contradictory notions of kingship was obtained. The ideological link between the distribution of political power and notions about authority thus formed a key connecting element in the traditional Nkore system.

3. Colonial Incorporation and
Instruments of Control

Nkore's distinctive political structure was abrogated at its incorporation into the British colonial framework. The British had had their influence established in adjacent Buganda for some time when, after the 1884 Berlin Conference, they extended their interest further west and north. In the case of Toro (1900) and Ankole (1901) this expansion was ratified through 'treaties' with the royalty and chiefs of the two kingdoms. Bunyoro, which had resisted British intrusion – realised nonetheless with the close support of its rival, Buganda – only in 1933 was given the status of 'Agreement State' similar to that of Ankole and Toro. None of these three Agreements provided for delegation of similar powers and prerogatives as had been given to Buganda (1894). They were largely nominal recognitions, though nonetheless with some discernible effects on local status categorisations.

That Ankole was brought into the wider orbit of Uganda was evidently of far-reaching consequence, since from that moment the perpetuation of its political system rested no longer on any intrinsic strength but depended basically on considerations of political expediency which were extraneous to Ankole. Initially there was the familiar stratagem of employing traditional structures of authority, if only in rudimentary fashion, as a convenient way of gaining colonial control. Before long, however, this rationale lost much of its strength as the colonial administrative network itself gained in effectiveness. Ankole soon became fully immersed in this network, although a sense of distinctiveness, partly based on the retention of the kingship, was maintained throughout. Indeed, this was to be made use of as late as the post-independence period in order to counteract the dominant weight and image of Buganda.

Even if exercised with the utmost of benevolence, in the early self-confident period colonial rule was strongly authoritarian. It established a bureaucratic state in which all actions originated as a result of orders sent down by more highly placed officials to their subordinates and in which elaborate reporting at all levels placed further controls upon the execution of policies. Its prevailing tone was one of the briskness between sportsmanship and military style.[1] Its values were rational and concrete and centered upon law and order. Its lines of command comprised colonial officers as well as African chiefs, and while the distinction between these ranks was strenuously maintained, both had to observe comparable criteria of hierarchy and administrative competence. These qualities applied in Ankole as much as they did elsewhere. The dispersed power structure of the traditional Ankole system was replaced by a hierarchical framework, while concrete and pragmatic values were substituted for the metaphysical authority notions of the traditional system. The link between traditional values and the traditional authority structure became altogether lost in the process and one effect of this was to eliminate the role for kingship 'old style'. A semblance of continuity was kept up, however, for the Omugabe was retained and old values were still being referred to. But the essence of the changes was to turn the Omugabe into an instrument of bureaucratic hierarchy, and to relegate traditional values to the level of folklore.

The colonial apparatus into which the kingdom was fitted developed from rather humble beginnings. In Ankole unlike some other cases, establishing the British presence did not involve prolonged violence. Somewhat euphemistically, a former Governor of Uganda described the process in this fashion:

> 'a British officer could arrive at some remote place, as I have myself done, accompanied only by a couple of native policemen and perhaps a clerk or two, and carrying with him a union jack, uniforms and rifles for the score of local policemen to be enlisted, and the requisite stationary and books, and in a few weeks have some sort of government functioning . . . [If] there was acquiescence, as was usual, there was ready to hand a piece of machinery which might be primitive, but was in working order.'[2]

From that point, at any rate, there tended to be a steady expansion, and consolidation, of the administrative framework, and almost invariably the piece of machinery showed itself capable of coping with a rapidly increasing number of tasks. Boundaries were drawn and

redrawn between administrative divisions and sub-divisions; administrative ranks of county, sub-county and village chiefs as well as a host of
other positions were created; and in a never-ending flow of directives
the tasks of all these officials were specified in ever greater detail. The
result of it all was that the whole district was converted into a single
system of command.

At the pinnacle of this structure stood the District Commissioner (in
the very early days known as the 'Collector'), in whom executive
authority within the district was vested. To him an elaborate cadre of
civil servants, African and European, were made responsible. This
meant, in fact, that 'Not only must the District Commissioner
supervise the "Chiefs"; his responsibilities extend to the conduct of
every minor official down to the village clerk or constable.'[3] The
'Bwana D.C.' on tour of the district became a familiar sight and
reputedly was always expected to outpace the Africans accompanying
him as a way of asserting his prestige. To the District Commissioner
were added Assistant District Commissioners, police, law and public
works officers, and as time went by an increasing number of specialised
officials were put in charge of such fields as agriculture, forestry,
health, veterinary services, marketing and social welfare. The District
Commissioner himself was accountable, always through the Provincial
Commissioner, to the Governor of Uganda, and final responsibility for
the conduct of affairs in the Protectorate rested, of course, with the
British Colonial Secretary. Taken together, the establishment of this
whole complex amounted to the creation of an administrative state,
which in some sense could be said to have been superimposed upon the
traditional framework, but which should more properly be viewed as
replacing it. Only much later, in the period after the second world war,
did a policy of delegation of administrative functions introduce
important changes in this structure. An expanding number of
administrative tasks was then devolved upon African local authorities,
themselves in large part new creations. But at its establishment, at
least, colonial rule was characterised by strong centralisation rather
than decentralisation, a quality which was very much evinced through
the measures it introduced.

As a way of facilitating their entry into Ankole the British had
promised, in the Ankole Agreement of 1901, the Omugabe and other
senior chiefs the right to nominate their successors.[4] In addition they
were to enjoy some other amenities, such as a share of the revenue

collected, land grants, and various other fringe benefits. By the Agreement, the 'Chief' Kahaya was 'recognised by His Majesty's Government as the Kabaka or supreme chief' of Ankole, and it was further stipulated that 'so long as the aforesaid Kabaka and chiefs abide by the conditions of this Agreement they shall continue to be recognised by His Majesty's Government as the responsible chiefs of the Ankole district'. However, the document added the stick to the carrot, for it was made explicit that, 'should the Kabaka of Ankole – Kahaya or his successors – be responsible for the infringement of any part of the terms of this Agreement, it shall be open to His Majesty's Government to annul the said Agreement, and to substitute for it any other methods of administering the Ankole district which may seem suitable'. Clearly, the terms of the Ankole Agreement were British, just as the new order it inaugurated.

The conditions under which this treaty was concluded are not without interest, if only because the only available text of the Agreement was written in English. The missionary Willis, who had barely begun learning Runyankore, was invited to attend the ceremony only to find out, to his utter despair, that he was asked to give an off-the-cuff interpretation of the Agreement in that language.[5] Local understanding apparently was not considered a crucial element, as long as the Ankole representatives duly placed their X-marks, which they readily did. At any rate, it soon transpired that the Agreement, while repeatedly recognised as a 'valid' document, had no force of law, or at least not if Bayankore wanted to base an appeal on it.[6] Regulations governing many kinds of behaviour were put on the books and applied just the same way as elsewhere in Uganda, and notwithstanding the eloquent references made to the Ankole Agreement in subsequent documents and public speeches, its function was no other than to provide a convenient cloak for the exercise of power by the British.

Whether or not they were aware of what they had been contracted into, at first the Omugabe and chiefs of Ankole were not unwilling to comply with British directives. Of course, they had no choice. But aside from that, British backing provided a new, and perhaps an even more secure, basis for the enjoyment of prerogatives. Moreover, a semblance of traditional authority was kept up, which tended to conceal the loss of status suffered by the incumbents. To the average villager or herdsman, at any rate, the implications of the take-over were not immediately visible. There followed a period of incubation, during which the old order continued to shape popular allegiances (although for decreasing numbers of people), making it possible for the Omugabe and chiefs to draw upon residual traditional allegiances. The colonial administration was naturally interested in making use of this goodwill to facilitate their own entry and consolidation of control; hence one major consideration suggesting the retention of traditional authorities. Moreover, it was felt, in Ankole as elsewhere, that to remove traditional chiefs might cause consternation and resistance, and such reactions were definitely to be avoided. On these grounds, the Omugabe and his chiefs were enlisted in the service of His Majesty's Government. Nonetheless, we will see that many senior chiefs were to be much sooner replaced than was anticipated.

THE EXPANSION OF ANKOLE

Simultaneous to Ankole's incorporation into Uganda, the kingdom itself experienced considerable expansion, a development which constituted another crucial base-line. After the redrawing of the kingdom's boundaries, at the turn of the century, Ankole came to comprise an area which was more than twice the size of the nineteenth century kingdom of Nkore. This spectacular expansion was a result of conquest as well as of colonial policy. Spheres of influence had always been fluctuating in the interlacustrine area, but during the latter half of the nineteenth century Nkore ascended to a considerably enhanced role in the region. As we have seen, this 'imperialism' of Nkore was directly related to the decline of its northern neighbour Bunyoro and it reached its peak during the rule of Ntare V, shortly before the arrival of the British. Several smaller neighbouring kingdoms, Igara, Buhweju and Buzimba, had been made to recognize Nkore's paramountcy and pay tribute to its ruler. Then, at the turn of the century, the British assumed control over the entire region and subdued additional areas, including Bunyaruguru as well as a large section of Mpororo kingdom. Thus, in addition to the original Nkore kingdom (which it should be recalled lay in the present Isingiro, Kashari and Nyabushozi counties), Ankole's expansion was largely based on the annexations to the west of Rwampara and Shema counties (at the cost of Mpororo) and of Igara, Bunyaruguru, Buhweju and Mitoma to the north (the latter at the

expense of Bunyoro).[7] Following these operations, the parts added by
the British as well as the areas over which Nkore had begun to claim
suzerainty, were all firmly amalgamated with Nkore. Formal
expression was given to these annexations in the Ankole Agreement of
1901, although Kajara was not added until later. On this basis, the
Ankole Agreement could lay down that 'that portion of the District of
Ankole to which the present Agreement applies shall be divided into
the following administrative divisions:

(a)   Mitoma   (f)   Buzimba
(b)   Nyabushozi   (g)   Ngarama, Shema and Kashari
(c)   Nshara   (h)   Igara
(d)   Isingiro   (i)   Buhweju, and
(e)   Rwampara   (j)   Bunyaruguru.'[8]

During the next decade Ankole's territory was further modified. First,
within the next few years, southwest Shema and southwest Igara were
brought under the influence of the Protectorate administration.[9] Next,
in 1907, the chief of Bukanga placed himself under the administrative
control of Ankole. For several decades henceforth, Bukanga continued
to rank as a county. Meanwhile, Ankole 'lost' Kabula and Mawogola
counties to Buganda, of which it was regretfully reminded even in
1962.[10] Similarly Ankole's potential claims on Kitagwenda, which
went to Toro, did not materialise. Ankole's external boundaries finally
reached completion in 1914 when Kajara was added as a county.

Within Ankole, actual and proposed boundary changes continued,
which is a phenomenon of no less interest. Buzimba and Bukanga
ranked as counties until 1932. In that year Buzimba was made part of
Mitoma, except for a small section which went to Buhweju, while
Bukanga was amalgamated with Isingiro. Nyabushozi, for long one of
the least effectively administered parts of the district, continued as a
county until 1924, when it was added to Kashari. In 1940 it was
reconstituted as a separate county, with parts of Kashari and Mitoma
added to it, all in an attempt to open up the area for administrative
purposes. Nshara, which until then had been a separate unit, was also
incorporated into the newly constituted 'Bahima county', as
Nyabushozi was often referred to. Meanwhile, Kashari, Shema and
Ngarama until 1924 were jointly administered by the Enganzi, Nuwa
Mbaguta. In that year their administration was divided once again.
Shema became a separate unit, as did Kashari which came to include
Nyabushozi until this was retransferred. Ngarama was incorporated

into Isingiro and ceased to exist as a distinct entity.

This chronicle of external and internal boundary rearrangements is significant for several reasons. One is the changed demographic basis that arose after Ankole's expansion. Within its traditional confines Nkore had been essentially a Bahima state; we saw that it was so notwithstanding the fact that many Bairu lived within its territory. Though they constituted a majority, most of these Bairu did not live in the core of the kingdom, but rather to the north, west and south of it. The central parts were given over to Bahima-controlled pastoralism. Moreover, as also noted, in Nkore Bahima constituted a larger minority than they did elsewhere in the interlacustrine origin.

The enlargement of Ankole crucially modified the relative numbers of Bairu and Bahima. Virtually all annexed areas, with the exception of Kajara, had known more overwhelming Bairu majorities than existed in Nkore. Igara had had a Bahima-based monarchy but otherwise a predominantly Bairu population. More pronouncedly, still, Buhweju's royalty was of Babito derivation (though by and large identifying itself with Bahima during the present century), while the rest of its population was Bairu. In Bunyaruguru there were no Bahima, though its agriculturalist population was not known as 'Bairu' (and would neither, in effect until today, call themselves 'Banyankore', – since in their conception Ankole's boundaries begin south at Igara). Parts of Shema, Rwampara and Mitoma had also known hardly any Bahima residents until colonial rule, or only relatively recently so through encroachments from Mpororo. Only Kajara, therefore, which was amalgamated later and which included another plains area, added any substantial number of Bahima to the expanded Ankole district.

As a result of these population distributions there was a significant decrease of Bahima proportional to Bairu in Ankole, as opposed to Nkore. While earlier Bahima may have constituted as much as 40 to 60% of the population of *Nkore*, after its territorial expansion (and simultaneous epidemics and political upheavals),[11] the figure in *Ankole* was closer to 5 to 10%. If it was thus remarkable that the Bahima stratum would nonetheless provide most of the administrative and political leadership, in terms of senior chieftaincies occupied in Ankole, this fact was even more striking considering that Bahima administrative rule during the colonial period for the first time extended directly to many Bairu communities.

Closely related is a second point of interest to Ankole's boundary changes. Nominally, all the incorporated areas were placed under the rulership of the Omugabe of Ankole, which should thus be remembered when considering the role of Ankole kingship in the present century. Evidently, from that moment on the Ankole dynasty had few traditional roots, if any, in more than half its domain. This does not necessarily mean that kingship per se was an alien element in incorporated areas. Several of the areas comprising Ankole exhibited significant similarities in terms of language, ways of life, and social organisation, including the institution of kingship. In historic times the fluctuating balance of power had often caused rulership to change in the area, and as it was for long expressed in Ankole, 'it does not matter who takes over, they are all kings'. Nonetheless, for a kingship which was to be put to the test of generating new meaning and functions, the lack of direct historical roots in a large section of its domain would doubtless make this task more difficult. In terms of territorial overrule alone, therefore, the Ankole monarchy found its traditional legitimacy significantly reduced at the beginning of the century. We will return to some of its implications later.

Lastly, the scope and frequency of Ankole boundary rearrangements is no less of interest if one considers the apparent 'ease' with which they were effected. With little exaggeration what seemed to happen was that socio-political divisions during the first part of this century were created and eliminated at the stroke of a pen. There is at any rate no record of opposition or protest having been raised against these enactments. This may tell us something about the climate and nature of administrative relationships of the early colonial period. Certainly, this effectiveness at administrative penetration, repeated in various other fields, contrasted sharply with the reception of similar measures, or proposals of them, during a later period. As it happened, proposed boundary changes and amalgamation within Ankole in the 1950s and 1960s invariably met with vehement opposition from local groups, usually expressed through manifold representations and petitions and leading to prolonged discussion and correspondence.

We will see other differences between the two periods later. But we should note here the correlation of the 'easy' implementation of these administrative measures with, first, the pronounced centralisation characteristic of early colonialism (coupled, one might add, to a nearly naive sense of zeal and self-confidence among many of its officers), as opposed to an increasing decentralisation and local representation during its terminal period and the early independence years. Besides, there was a lack, by and large, of literacy and proficiency at handling the administrative channels among the population of Ankole during the early part of the century, so that any opposed views to administrative measures in any case would have had little chance of getting expressed in a way that would be heard.

But by the same token it should be evident that it was initially difficult for local groups not only to be informed, but simply to be aware of the implications of various measures initiated within the colonial administration. In the case of Ankole this may suggest another hypothesis. In effect the only people likely to have any access at all to some of the relevant information were members of the new chiefly elite; but, perhaps, the ease with which various administrative divisions seemed nonetheless created and changed may indicate that this cadre had not begun to develop strong claims on particular domains, as opposed to stakes in their positions per se. If valid, we may link this to a factor explored earlier, namely the basic separateness of the Bairu and Bahima communities in historical Nkore; that factor would indeed suggest that, with a few 'traditional' exceptions, the Bahima who came to occupy the majority of senior chieftainships in the colonial system were lacking strong prior links and identifications with the Bairu communities over which they were placed. As we will see, this lack of attachment became especially manifest after about 1908, since, following a struggle for pre-eminence within the new system, many of the initial appointees were replaced during the first few years of colonial rule.

Colonial transformation initiated various other concurrent developments which impinged upon political relationships in Ankole. Administrative impacts combined with basic economic, educational and religious effects to profoundly restructure the society, creating new socio-political categories and new sets of cleavages and alignments. We should now examine these effects particularly insofar as they changed the pattern of Bairu-Bahima relationships and defined the role and composition of the new political-administrative elite in the expanded district. Again, the early colonial period was one in which several base-line developments took place in this regard, determining the direction in which subsequent change and relationships would move.

THE SUBSTITUTION OF THE BAHINDA ELITE

One such development, which we must consider first, brought a pre-colonial rivalry to have a direct bearing on the composition of the new Ankole elite. Once the colonial framework was established, a struggle for influence was waged on a clan basis between groups which aspired to positions of reward and privilege. The result of this was that, early in the century, the Ankole monarchy was put to a test by the elimination of a large part of its traditional entourage, the Bahinda clan, as a political force. The British entry led to the culmination and final decision of a longstanding rivalry between the Bahinda and the Bashambo. The Bahinda, it will be recalled, formed the royal clan of Ankole, whose members had exclusive title to the Omugabeship and to various senior chieftainships. The Bashambo were the royal clan of the neighbouring kingdom of Mpororo, of which parts were incorporated into Ankole at the time of British intervention.[12] Both were Bahima clans and stood in a similar relationship to the Bairu population in their respective areas. In the nineteenth century, the Bashambo had been gaining ground as rulers in various other areas which came under the suzerainty of Ankole, and the Bashambo thus had to be counted as a force of no small significance in the expanded Ankole kingdom. But not only did the Bahinda-Bashambo strife become increasingly salient due to the incorporation of annexed territories into Ankole; it was also directly related to the superimposition of colonial overrule. While the British had a golden opportunity to exploit this clan conflict to consolidate their power in Ankole, it was actually the Bashambo who readily took advantage of the British presence. As it turned out, however, their interest appeared to coincide largely with that of the British, so that the result might not have been very different if the British had taken the initiative to manipulate the clan conflict.

It is not surprising, therefore, that the struggle between Bahinda and Bashambo took a decisive turn precisely during the years which immediately followed the introduction of British overrule. From shortly before the signing of the Ankole Agreement in 1901, the Enganzi or principal chief in Ankole, was a Mushambo, Nuwa Mbaguta.[13] Mbaguta would remain on the scene almost as long as the then ruling Omugabe, Kahaya, namely until the late 1930s, but after an apparently cordial relationship during the first few years of their tenure, immediately around 1900, virtually the entire four decades which followed were marked by mutual rivalry and hostility. In the eyes of the British, Mbaguta was cooperative, interested in innovations, and eager to follow their instructions. With their backing he asserted himself throughout as a shrewd and powerful potentate. From the point of view of Protectorate officials, therefore, Mbaguta was the ideal kind of native authority to work with. Through him many administrative measures were introduced and implemented in Ankole, earning him many laudatory commentaries in the records of British officers. As he was an effective and reliable instrument to make use of, the scope of his influence was in no small way promoted by the administration. Almost unnoticed, the office of Enganzi rose in accordance with the stature of the incumbent, imparting to Mbaguta a role unequalled by any of his predecessors. In fact, only one pre-1900 Enganzi seems to be vaguely remembered in Ankole, as against several generations of Abagabe.[14] And so, Mbaguta, the 'brightest star near the moon', as was the original meaning of the word 'Enganzi', came to eclipse even the Omugabe himself in actual influence.

Being an outsider to the traditional establishment of Ankole, Mbaguta was seen as a more neutral and manipulable agent of transformation than might otherwise have been the case. Being the leader of a clan which was engaged in continuous rivalry with the royal clan of Ankole, Mbaguta was keen to exploit all possible opportunities to curtail Bahinda influence and to further Bashambo interests. As a key contact man of the British, several such chances offered themselves to him. The establishment of a colonial administration, which necessitated a considerable amount of accommodation on the part of the senior chiefs, in large number Bahinda, was by far the major of these opportunities. The traditional chiefs were incorporated in an administrative command system which, notwithstanding its benefits, not only imposed specific duties but also implied considerable restrictions to their exercise of authority. The Bahinda chiefs soon felt that the objectives of bureaucratic control were encroaching much further upon their freedom than they were interested in, and their reactions to these innovations accordingly varied between reluctance and resistance.

Early in the century this culminated in a series of incidents. Government officers were engaged in strong actions against Igumera, the leader of the discontented Bahinda, and his followers. For some years after the death of Ntare V in 1895, Igumera had been the strongest chief and virtual ruler of Ankole.[15] Upon the establishment of British control he was relegated to the position of a county chief and more generally found his influence severely curtailed. When these restrictions caused him to rebel, the British exiled him to Buganda, a measure for which Mbaguta deserves special credit. Many other chiefs were also dismissed during these early years, as we shall see later. The effect of these measures was thus to leave Mbaguta's power virtually unchallenged among the Ankole elite. Many Bahinda took refuge in Buganda and elsewhere, an evacuation which was accelerated after the murder of a British officer, St. Galt, in 1905. (The background of this murder has largely remained a mystery, although many people in Ankole believe that it originated directly from the Bahinda-Bashambo conflict.)[16]

While to date Ankole historiography has been surprisingly inexplicit or inconclusive about this episode, its importance is suggested by the fact that by far the larger part of the Bahinda aristocracy fled from Ankole out of fear for punitive sanctions by Mbaguta and the British. So widespread and lasting was this evacuation that it necessitated, in the 1930s, a special recruitment effort in Buganda to find an eligible Muhinda candidate to become a successor to the incumbent Omugabe. This was Gasyonga, virtually unknown in Ankole when he was brought back there, and with only a doubtful claim to the Obugabe.[17] The more immediate consequence of these developments, meanwhile, was that of the ranks of Bahinda only the Omugabe, Kahaya, and very few others remained in Ankole. A number of the positions which fell empty were taken by Bashambo and other Bahima, and a good many chieftainships were filled by Baganda especially recruited by Mbaguta. Divorced from his Bahinda kinsmen, Kahaya thus came to stand rather isolated and, where possible, Mbaguta did not fail to by-pass him further.

Clearly, therefore, with the elimination of the Bahinda stratum an important departure from the traditional political structure was effected. Severance of the links with the Bahinda aristocracy was a source of uneasiness and frustration especially for the Omugabe, as it deprived him both of the power structure and the traditional frame of reference that once defined his position in the system. The ties of patronage had been ruptured, and for political resources the Omugabe would need to turn elsewhere. Inevitably, the legitimacy of the kingship suffered. Had the Bahinda retained their influence in Ankole, a more prolonged conflict of conceptions of authoritative institutions, focussing particularly on the kingship, might have marked the years of colonial rule. As it was, the British design for the administration of Ankole did not meet an effective opposition after the initial abortive resistance, which made it all the more easy to implant. Basically, therefore, the Bahinda-Bashambo strife could be regarded as one which accelerated processes of colonial transformation.

ETHNIC COMPOSITION OF THE ADMINISTRATIVE ESTABLISHMENT

The implications of this strife for the staffing position were considerable. This is reflected in available data on the administrative establishment in Ankole, particularly of the senior, that is, the county and sub-county chieftainships. For many years these chieftainships (which notwithstanding the connotations of the word were appointive administrative offices) have been locally considered of key importance, because of the power and status commonly attached to them. Staffing data of these ranks indicate many mutations during the early colonial years. Though the data are not systematic they can nonetheless be used to show the pattern of composition on the basis of which the system was maintained, and eventually changed.

In a sense the first staff list was the 1901 Ankole Agreement, whose signatories on the Ankole side were the Omugabe and ten senior chiefs, for each of whom a sub-division was marked out. Of these ten chiefs, nine were Bahinda and other Bahima, whereas the identity of one is debated.[18] It is clear therefore, that Ankole's chiefly hierarchy at the establishment of the colonial framework was an overwhelmingly Bahima-dominated one.

During the first years of the colonial presence, however, there were many transfers and demotions. In fact, between 1901 and 1908 all but three senior chiefs in charge of counties were replaced, thus largely reflecting the eclipse of the traditional Bahinda ruling stratum. The three who were unaffected by these replacements were Duhara, the county chief of Rwampara; Ndibarema, the traditional claimant of the chieftainship of Buhweju; and the Enganzi Mbaguta, who administered Shema, Kashari and Ngarama. Chiefs were replaced in all other counties which at that time constituted Ankole, namely, Mitoma, Bunyaruguru, Igara, Isingiro, Nyabushozi, Buzimba and Nshara. Clearly, these replacements were evidence of an early and major reconstitution of Ankole's top political-administrative elite. However, they did not alter the ethnic basis of its composition, as the Bairu's lack of involvement was perpetuated by recruiting outsiders to Ankole, mainly Baganda.

An unusually detailed list of chiefs is available for 1907 in an official report entitled the *System of Chieftainships of Ankole*.[19] In that year the ten county chiefs included six Bahima and (possibly) one Mwiru. In addition, three Baganda, Abdul Aziz, Nyemera and Abdul Effendi, had made their entry, as chiefs of Mitoma, Isingiro and Nshara respectively. Of the six Bahima, only one, Liamgwizi of Buzimba, was a Muhinda.[20] Thus, while replacements were made, the ethnic composition unfavourable to the Bairu remained.

By 1907, steps had also been taken toward a further sub-division of administrative tasks. In addition to the county or saza chiefs, therefore, the Ankole system of chieftainships then comprised sub-county chiefs or *Batongole* (later called Gombolola chiefs following Kiganda nomenclature), which were no less than 74 in number. In the 1907 report the ethnic background of these sub-county chiefs is categorized as follows:

Bahinda	12
Bahima	30
Bairu	8
Baganda	22
Batoro	2
Batongole total	74

Adding county and sub-county chiefs together, the report came to the following 'Summary of Races or Tribes':[21]

Mhinda (The Princely Mhima tribe, to which the Kabaka belongs)	13
Mhima (other than members of the Mhinda tribe)	35
Mwiro (the peasant race to which the majority of the Ankole people belong)	9
Total of persons of Ankole Extraction	57
Mganda	25
Mutoro	2
Total of persons of Alien Extraction	27

The *System of Chieftainship of Ankole* thus gives quite an illuminating picture of the staffing situation as it had come into being shortly after the establishment of British rule. The Bahima (including Bahinda) preponderance is evident. Nonetheless, only a few years after the creation of Ankole as an administrative unit, nearly one-third of the chiefly positions were filled by people from outside. Moreover, the report indicates that the reduction of the Bahinda element had taken place primarily at the level of the county chiefs, whereas among the sub-county chiefs Bahinda still retained a relatively larger representation. Finally, it shows that the Bairu, who then probably constituted as many as 90% of the population, held no more than nine out of 84 chiefly positions in Ankole.

Except for the Baganda chiefs, however, one thing the report does not quite show is the full extent to which the new administrative elite was composed of members of non-Ankole derivations. Only the two Batoro mentioned are an indication in this direction. But it needs to be pointed out that the Ankole ruling elite had come to comprise various individuals whose origins lay outside Ankole. These included Batusi from Rwanda, high-status Banyakaragwe from the Bukoba area, Babito from Toro,[22] and Bahororo from parts of Mpororo which were incorporated into Kigezi rather than Ankole.[23] Most of these entrants came at the end of the 19th and the beginning of the 20th century, the period when Ankole's Bahima elite was seriously weakened as a result of the combined effects of epidemics and the intra-elite conflicts we have noted. While these sources of strife caused deaths and migration of Bahima, Ankole's social divisions were partly perpetuated, if not accentuated, as the vacuum was filled by newcomers. The assimilation of these people into Ankole society, and specifically its Bahima elite, was rapidly realised and perhaps accounts for the absence of further differentiation in the above-mentioned report.[24]

Returning to the development of the senior establishment, a relative lack of statistical data complicates the making of breakdowns of the ranks of chiefs for the years after 1907. Nonetheless, by analysing transfers and appointments it is possible to infer the trends which occurred in the staffing position of senior chiefs over the next few decades.[25] In 1920, for instance, when Duhara was replaced, the ten county chiefs came to include nine Bahima and one Muganda. By and large, the position at this level thereafter remained the same for the next two decades. By 1942, a slight change had taken place, in that the ten county chiefs then included seven Bahima, two Bairu and one Muganda. Meanwhile, more significant modifications occurred at the sub-county level. The number of Bairu gombolola chiefs in 1942 was 39, as against 18 Bahima, five Baganda and one 'partly Hima'.[26] Thus, not only had the proportion of Bairu sub-county chiefs substantially increased, but there had also been considerable reduction in the number of Baganda chiefs employed in Ankole government service. This reduction occurred mainly in the 1930s, when repeated complaints about the demeanour of chiefs, Bahima and Baganda, induced policies of withdrawal which tended to be particularly directed at the 'alien' element. The increased number of sub-county chieftainships filled by Bairu hence appears to have been based primarily on vacancies resulting from the retirement of Baganda and only to a lesser extent by positions vacated by Bahima. They were still a long way, however, from giving Bairu a degree of influence anywhere near their numbers in the society: despite their 90% majority they now occupied 39 out of 63 sub-county chieftainships.

RECRUITMENT POLICIES AND COLONIAL CONTROL

It is thus clear that, far from initiating any significant alteration and expansion of the social basis of chiefly recruitment, colonial rule for a long time perpetuated and supported the ethnically restricted composition of the Ankole ruling stratum. But in a basic sense the British had also created this situation, either unwittingly or deliberately. Both possibilities are quite plausible and deserve some further exploration. The situation was unwittingly created if indeed the British did erroneously base their policy on an understanding of history which assumed the existence of a rigid ethnic hierarchy in Nkore, with Bahima the rulers and Bairu the ruled. Several factors might support this possibility: the fact that the British entry was effected through contact with the Bahima, the difficulty which we have noted of establishing the historical meaning, let alone the position, of 'Bairu' in Nkore society,[27] and possibly the belief that hierarchy and subordination were givens in all societies. As for the latter, the fact that four decades later the distinction between states and stateless systems should have been received as a major landmark in the scholarship and understanding of African society might confirm the long-standing prevalence of such a belief.[28]

Nonetheless, the possibility that the policy of differential ethnic recruitment in Ankole was deliberate, intended to secure the support of one strategic section of the population so as to more effectively control the whole, deserves serious attention in the light of colonial practices elsewhere in Africa. Examples abound, but in two that were quite close to the Uganda scene, Burundi and the Sudan, the Belgians and the British respectively placed members of one section (Batusi; Northerners) in a position of greater political supremacy over another (Bahutu; Southerners) than they had known before. In Uganda itself the point is illustrated by the employment of Baganda agents to help subjugate and rule annexed territories, which constituted an important ingredient of British strategies for control in Uganda. Some elements of this policy were even present in Ankole, though by and large the function of the Baganda chiefs recruited to the district turned out to be supportive of the new Bahima establishment. The nominal authority given to the Ankole monarchy over various smaller entities amalgamated with the kingdom might also be seen as an expression of this 'unite and rule' approach.

These different lines of explanation for the creation of an ethnically tiered administration do not necessarily exclude one another: the establishers of the colonial system in Ankole may have erred in their grasp of history but nonetheless also have been determined to use ethnic divisions as a means of control. What matters is that beyond the question of the exact causes and calculations that intervened, for purpose of administering Ankole the British clearly put their cards on the Bahima. Nor should it be overlooked in this connection that they were highly impressed with the Bahima: early reporters were nearly unanimous in their praise for the pastoralists' qualities, calling them 'born gentlemen', 'born rulers' or a 'superior race'. Thus, for example, Johnston, whom we have cited earlier, expressed as his view that '. . . the men of Hima blood are born gentlemen, and one is so struck with their handsome bearing and charming manners as to desire ardently that this fine race may not come to extinction',[29] thereby advancing opinions which no Muhima had asked for.

In the process, however, a more rigid and divisive ethnic cleavage was created than had existed before. Basically, the Bairu were treated as a subject category, the Bahima as an elite. For this the policy also provided its own justification; as noted already, the appointment of

Bahima to the senior chieftainships entailed a self-fulfilling hypothesis, namely that the Ankole polity (also implying pre-colonial Nkore) had 'always' been so constituted. These appointments soon obliterated any traces to the contrary, – that is *not* that Bahima had not been chiefs, but that they had been directly involved with and in control of the Bairu communities.[30] That the theory proved persuasive can be gathered from the subsequent literature: most writers, and not only those concerned with 'caste', have accepted it for fact and proceeded with their rapportage.

The reverse side of the coin was inevitably that Bairu for many years had only a chance of attaining the lower ranks of the chiefly hierarchy, a situation which neither was changed by the withdrawal of the Bahinda chiefs and the new recruitments this necessitated. Instead, the staffing of these positions with other Bahima and with Baganda not only seemed to confirm that Bairu were considered ineligible to fill them, but for a prolonged period closed these ranks to them.

The significance of these arrangements should be measured not merely by the perquisites and the status which these offices entailed, however important they were to the individuals (and their retinue) concerned. In the context of colonial Uganda they above all meant the power to control others, even if its exercise was kept within the bounds of formal jurisdictions. Through most of the colonial period this power extended over widely different areas, as wide as the notion of law and order could be stretched, and thus in effect implied broad and pervasive domination over large population groups. But in a case where power was largely exercised over one ethnic group while it lay in the hands of members of another, such an arrangement had particularly severe implications for the structure of society.

It transpires from the record that the Bahima establishment was given a fair amount of leeway in matters of recruitment, and that Mbaguta's role was especially influential.[31] Nor should one probably have expected this to be otherwise. During the early phases of British occupation colonial officers inevitably would have experienced acute problems in identifying alternative, meritable candidates. Consequently the pattern initially approximated one of cooptation, with the tacit approval of colonial officers. The Bahima elite thus could feel they were in control, as in a sense they were. But what perhaps they little realized (with the possible exception of some of the Bahinda who opted out) was that the control they exercised was itself a means of control for other objectives, the policies of British colonialism.

This approach to colonial administration through 'franchise'[32] required a minimum of overseas investments and personnel, and in that sense was effective and economical. But its low expenditure was more than offset by the social costs inflicted upon the society. The policy of 'self-rule' in the case of Ankole meant that one section of the population was set over and against the rest, thus creating a profound, and lasting, divisiveness which negatively affected socio-political relationships. Ironically, while the costs of colonial administration were thus 'internalised', it nonetheless placed the colonial power in a role of 'arbiter' of local conflicts. During a later period, as we shall see, the various sides presented grievances about the opposite group to British officials and institutions, not fully realizing that the pattern of their conflicts resulted largely from the way in which colonial policies had been inserted. Indeed, Ankole (or much of Uganda for that matter) might well have emerged as a more unified and vigorous society had the British undertaken the tasks of colonial administration in a more direct manner.

STIMULATING ELITE INTERESTS: THE MAILO CASE

Beyond the creation and ethnically selective staffing of novel positions, the colonial system also stimulated new and active interests in these offices and the fringe-benefits they entailed. The effect of this was to more deeply entrench the division between Bahima and Bairu in Ankole, not only because the senior chiefs concerned were eager to hold on to their sinecures but also because various benefits were obtained at the cost of the population under their control. These interests thus added another dimension to the colonial social framework, the significance of which is hard to overrate.

As noted, on the establishment of colonial rule the Bahima elite were granted a number of privileges, the most important of which were formally laid down in the Ankole Agreement. Chieftainships themselves constituted a key element among these benefits. Also, the British allowed the Bahima chiefs to participate in the collection of tax and the employment of labour; this not only enhanced their political powers, but significantly promoted their economic welfare. Tax and labour excises from the Bairu were often quite considerable and were in no small part used for personal enrichment. Last but not least, the distribution of mailo land – a term adopted from Buganda, where 'mailo' had developed as the local expression for the square miles also allocated there, though in even greater numbers – similarly tended to accentuate the social and economic gap between the chiefly Bahima and the Bairu.

It is illustrative to consider the mailo policy as an example of how interests were induced through the grant of colonial benefits. This policy was simple in origin, complex in its consequences. The British 'gave' away square miles to members of the elite who signed the Ankole Agreement and thus sanctioned and facilitated British entry. At the original allocation the Omugabe received 50 square miles, the Enganzi 16 miles, while the ten most senior chiefs were given ten miles each.[33] With one possible exception, all these beneficiaries were Bahima. Mailo estates were further granted to churches, while later (notably between 1921-1924) additional allocations were made partly to reward newly recruited chiefs who replaced some of the original mailo allottees who had been removed from office, partly to some World War I veterans, and partly to some incumbent chiefs who were successful in pressing for more. Each of these allocations were of private freehold land which could be alienated; in addition the Omugabe and chiefs received official mailo land, i.e. specified distributions of square miles as lifetime estates or as long as their holders remained in office.

Technically these alienations were made possible because the British had also in the Ankole Agreement declared all land in Ankole to be Crown land. Another technical provision, however, was not followed up. It was that, according to the terms of the Agreement, the mailo grants ought to be demarcated in 'waste and uncultivated' land.[34] Instead the allottees were allowed to carve out their grants in populated areas and their interests were almost immediately focussed on some of the most densely populated, central parts of the district. This enabled them to levy rent as well as to demand food and services from the Bairu peasants living on their mailo. Not until a very late stage, too late to make any alterations, were questions asked about the deviation from the principle that only waste and uncultivated land could be considered for demarcations. Meanwhile stipulations that were introduced on the books about the amount of rent and other privileges derivable from the mailo estates suggested that this shift met with definite official approval.

That new interests were stimulated by the policy of mailo grants was evinced in several ways. One was that even very early some transfers took place from less to more heavily populated areas, indicating an appreciation of the capitalised value of the new estates. Also, interpretations of the 'traditional' system of land rights were advanced which tended to provide rationalisations and claims for benefits in the new system. In fact, the pursuit of material interests was partly made possible by exploiting the area of terminological confusion with regard to land rights. What was advanced were at best narrow translations of 'rights', and then only one kind of rights, that had existed in the old framework. Thus in 1907, an Acting Collector in Ankole reported,

'It is not even easy to tell what were in fact the old-time customs, and what are the changes in these. For in most cases one finds that the stories of witnesses have a way of coinciding with their interests. The Kabakka (king) and those who follow his lead bring forward the view that the Kabakka had absolute and unqualified ownership of all Ankole and all the property in it. Certain of the chiefs lay stress on the idea of a system resembling the Feudal. The peasants are of course for the most part inarticulate, in so far at any rate as the Government Official is concerned, but from what has been said by the Revds. Father Le Tehic and W. E. Owen, from certain remarks let fall by chiefs, and from what has been told me by a few of themselves, I think that they may be credited with considering that they possess something in the nature of ownership of the lands they occupy.'[35]

Such observations illustrate how different 'rights', traditionally exercised at various levels – each of a different order and specificity – were asserted to support particular positions, all couched in the term 'ownership'. But the inducement of interests was further evidenced by an appetite for more. Instead of appeasing the Ankole elite through the special privileges bestowed upon them, the policy came to be understood as one that contained the possibility of being extended and thus created an interest group that was disgruntled because pleas for more were not readily accepted. Misunderstandings further complicated the situation and prolonged haggling evidently was the result. For instance, in 1923, according to a statement of the Enganzi, 'the chief dissatisfaction over the land settlement is over the 800 miles [*sic*] which was promised to the Ankole Chiefs . . . and which have not yet been granted.'[36]

Piecemeal adjustments were nonetheless made from time to time and possibly stimulated escalation of demands. In the same statement quoted above, the Enganzi continued to say that as for himself 'I was not grumbling as my miles were increased to 30'. District reports and minutes of Baraza meetings with the Ankole chiefs throughout the 1920s and 1930s (the period in which this reporting became more complete and elaborate than it had been in previous years) almost invariably contained a standard item on mailo issues. Some examples may be helpful to show this recurrence; they also indicate some of the complexities of administration – and some apparent inconsistencies – that arose following the introduction of the mailo system:

1922. The Land Officer who was able to attend for a few minutes informed the Baraza that their Mailos could not be marked out by Surveyors till next year. He reminded them that no land could be transferred or sold until final Certificates had been received, and that no work could be done at present on any land other than Agreement mailos.

Shamba Evictions: This always has caused ill feelings and tends to lead to emigration. Owners cannot turn people off their land unless they refuse to pay rent. The people must be made to feel that their homes are permanent. P.C. gives a public warning that such evictions must stop, as the Government is strongly opposed to them, and will if necessary take action by Legislation.

Ntende (brewing): Is illegitimate and further is cause of increasing drunkenness. On private mailos Government will not interfere. But on Official mailos it is expressly forbidden; this also applies to Lukiko Estates.

1923. January, Land: (a) All claims that have been passed must be marked out at once. Those that have not been passed may be heard in the Saza Courts, and if undisputed will be recommended forthwith by D.C. If disputed, they will be forwarded for D.C.'s decision. (b) No claims for private mailos which include cultivated land not belonging to claimant, will be entertained. (c) Chiefs should check the extent of Mission plots. In the majority of cases they have much more than they are entitled to.

Rents: P.C. cannot agree to Lukiko's proposal that hut tax should not be reduced. It must in future be Rps. 2. instead of Rps. 3. Until further notice rent will *only* be collected from private and official mailos and in every case a receipt will be given and Registers kept.

Extra land: P.C. cannot agree to the extra private mailos asked for.

Shambas for Banyiginya (Babito): Reference yesterdays petition for land for Babito, Mukwende requests Gombolola chiefs to be included. P.C. says no. If a man who had done really good work retires he may get a grant of Lukiko Butaka for life which was the reason for the Lukiko Butaka. Out of a very large salary and large number of private mailos the Omugabe has he should make provision for the great majority of his relations.

1924. Mailos: Certain lists of miles still outstanding. . . .
. . . Informed the Lukiko that the Provincial Commissioner will be coming in August to finish the Mailos and that if the men entitled to Mailos don't send their lists they will have to mark them on wasteland.

Markets on Chief's Private Mailos: Pokino asks if Mailo Owner can get some part of market dues in these cases. Told him not on any account. Rather than that the markets must be moved to Official land.

1926. There would be nobody turned out of his shamba if he cultivated outside a private mailo unless that shamba were wanted for public purposes; then compensation would be paid to the shamba owner. That had been provided for by the Land Rules given out by the District Commissioner.

Mutuba II Kashali asked what was to happen to the coffee planted on a chief's official land on that chief's transfer elsewhere. The P.C. replied that coffee need not necessarily be planted on their official land. It could be planted on their chief's land and they could leave somebody in charge of it . . . . The Muwali asked if in mailos the chiefs should include shambas of others. The P.C. replied that land was given for the use of the church and the growing of teachers' food and was not to be used for collecting rent.

1930. The Katikiro enquired about the position of Native Landowners under the new arrangements whereby Poll Tax and Busuku are paid on one ticket. The Provincial Commissioner repeated the assurance of H.E. The Governor that these Landowners would not lose financially; and reminded the Chiefs that money was available for refund when the Landowners applied for it. He trusted they would do so with greater promptness in future.

1934. Three Saza chiefs to be given a mile: Kihimba said that we recommended three saza chiefs, Rubuga and the son of Igumira to be given a mile each. But D.C. answered that I will have to answer you in future.[37]

These entries not only suggest how mailo land over the years continued to attract the attention of the Ankole chiefly elite, but also that all sorts of arrangements in regard to demarcation, registration, transfer, rent collection and other obligations and privileges became necessary following the initiation of the policy. In effect the instrument of colonial development that the chiefs were designed to be itself came to command a very central share of time, energies and resources. Not surprisingly, perhaps, in his farewell address a departing district commissioner thus told the chiefs: 'When you are in your barazas, you prefer discussing about chieftainship, about your salaries, your cattle and so on; but you discuss nothing regarding the peasants'.[38]

We shall later return to the anomalies which the mailo system produced in Ankole society. But there can be no doubt that in the give and take of mailo land it was the peasants who received the short end of the stick. Mailo land for a long time entitled their owners to rent, labour and tribute from the peasants living within the estates. Besides, the Bairu tenants often found difficulty in upholding their property rights on their crops and belongings, faced restrictions imposed by their landlords on the improvement of their houses and gardens, and for long lacked any security of tenure and could be evicted at the whim of the mailo owner. These burdens and constraints were felt even more strongly because peasants who happened to live just outside the mailo estates could develop their land without this restriction and interference.

The mailo system thus represented a policy that helped to entrench the colonial framework and which in the process drew profound divisions within the society. Parallel policies – of taxations, labour requisitions, and the chiefly recruitment itself – produced similar effects. Together they stimulated interests in newly defined, though scarce resources, and also a nascent consciousness among those that had access to them of belonging to a privileged group. These interests and orientations were not (or at least not in the first place) centered upon 'ownership' of any means of production, as class interests have been commonly defined in Western conditions and (especially Marxist) terminology. But they were quite definitely oriented towards the control of important resources, which were extracted from the society to help maintain the colonial state and which had a key bearing upon stratification divisions. In that sense these interests were early but clear expressions of a growing class awareness, – emerging among those who at a local level had come to occupy the strategic ranks in the colonial bureaucracy, and perhaps first recorded by the district commissioner cited above.

The nascent consciousness of a privileged position had also another effect, however, – one which in an ethnically divided society such as Ankole could not but be manifested in a pronounced way. Structured superiority of Bahima chiefs led to affections of arrogance and assumptions of Bairu inferiority which increasingly coloured social relationships in Ankole society. The newly gained statuses, the close exposure to colonial practices, education and religion, and also the praise and admiration bestowed upon them by early European visitors, all added to an assumption among the Bahima elite that they constituted a 'select few' and to their expression of a low regard for Bairu.[39] Pre-colonial Bahima experiences with Bairu servants tended to be extended by the Bahima chiefs to the Bairu communities as a whole, with whom there had in the past been less close and less hierarchical contacts. Among other things, these tendencies appear to have led to a changing use and emphasis of the term 'Bairu' itself, stressing its low-status, serf-like connotations in applications to the agricultural population as a whole.[40] Bahima stereotypes of Bairu as unclean, ignorant and unable to perform worthy tasks did not remain a monopoly of the chiefs but tended to be shared by other Bahima. Derogatory terms increasingly circulated in regard to the Bairu population and the infrequency of intermarriage, based previously largely on practical grounds, acquired the additional quality of a taboo when animosity between Bairu and Bahima grew. In the decades preceding the mid-sixties only a handful of intermarriages have been known to take place. As these attitudes thus gradually involved the two population sections as a whole, Ankole society gained an additional dimension of social cleavage.

A number of myths have developed about the behaviour of Bahima chiefs during the early colonial period. There is now a widely circulated assertion, for instance, that they first burnt the cotton seed before distributing it among the Bairu peasants. Although this remains unproven, it is no exaggeration that the Bahima chiefs, who traditionally had not been involved in agriculture and had little more than disdain for their subjects, have taken only a limited interest in the agrarian development of the district. As a result, Ankole remained for a long period a relatively backward corner of the country. Perhaps also in consequence of this situation, Bairu resentment over discriminatory attitudes and treatment by Bahima was articulated only much later.

EDUCATION, RELIGION AND ELITE DIFFERENTIATION

Beyond the central vertical axis on which it rests, an elite's configuration comprises several more or less specific aspects which largely derive from a society's particular experience with historical processes. Among the main factors in Ankole's elite formation, we have thus noted the replacement of the Bahinda as a key political variable by another, still basically Bahima ruling group; the continued ethnic basis of the staffing of Ankole's senior administrative ranks for half a century and its implications in terms of colonial policy; and the articulation of interests and a consiousnesss which typically accompanied this elite's formation. In addition to this, the particular orientations and socio-political position of the Ankole establishment were also significantly shaped by the impacts of western education and religion.

In Ankole as much as in other parts of Africa, the factors of education and religion were closely related. Originating from common sources (schools being founded by church agencies), education spread with religion and religion with education.[41] Also, missionary activity was closely tied up with (for some the justification of) the colonial enterprise; among other things, the colonial administration was largely dependent on mission schools for the training of its African recruits and their familiarisation with clerical skills.

But while these policies and relationships were quite general to

African situations and the colonial world, in Ankole they worked out in a way which added further complexities to the prevailing pattern of social cleavages. Religion in a sense produced another ethnicity, while formal education added one more basis for entry into the elite. The two factors had the potential of either reinforcing or reducing the existing juxtaposition of ethnic and status variables; in the end their effect was to do both, the difference being a matter of phasing.

Briefly, (Protestant) education first bolstered the position of Ankole's Bahima elite, later eroded it. It supported its continued tenure for at least half a century, until both the more massive schooling of Bairu and the minimal impact of the same on the rank and file Bahima caused the Bahima elite to lose their educational lead and find their position becoming increasingly isolated.

Religion also initially strengthened the position of the Bahima elite as they opted for wholesale conversion to Protestantism (the administration's most favoured denomination), while the Bairu became divided into Protestants and Catholics.[42] Since moreover the latter were in slightly larger numbers than the former and generally had very little chance of administrative employment, the potential challenge to the Bahima ruling class was at least temporarily minimised. But the shared Protestantism that embraced the Bahima elite and nearly half the Bairu did not prove very effective as a basis of support: in the end it was primarily the Protestant Bairu who would challenge the role of the Bahima elite.

To better appreciate the working of these factors, the qualities which appear to have been required of chiefs during the first years of colonial rule may serve as a convenient starting point. We can take it that formal educational backgrounds (in any event hardly available at the time) did not count heavily then, being at best one of several criteria employed in the selection of candidates for chiefly positions. During these years chiefs had a key role as (the major) instrument of command and communication between colonial officers and the population. *Barazas* or public gatherings were the characteristic medium of this communication, which was largely oral. Chiefs were posted to maintain order and ensure compliance with government directives in their areas. Hence they were especially assessed on the basis of their capacity to command obedience: the ideal chief was at once a strong potentate, an effective conciliator of disputes, and a skilful manipulator of local allegiances and sentiments. Such qualities, it was expected, would ensure that political tranquility be maintained, taxes levied, and the population mobilised in orderly fashion for road building and other labour duties.

As time passed, however, the administrative apparatus grew inordinately complex, far more intricate than the system which had established the colonial presence in the district. Not only were the roles of chiefs increasingly differentiated, but reliance was more and more placed on specialised officers for the fulfilment of an expanding number of tasks. Increasingly, the nature of the operations became that of a complex bureaucratic organisation, in which administrative norms and clerical proficiency necessarily were stressed. Over time, therefore, chiefs of all but the lowest ranks, far from being stereotyped lordly power holders, typically became men who were running offices and routinely worked their way through an unabating flow of correspondence, reports and other documents. This tendency, which would reach its peak during the terminal colonial period, applied to Ankole as much as to other parts of Uganda. Evidently, therefore, not only the roles but also the qualifications for these functions began to differ from those of their antecedents. Over time, the training needs increasingly demanded familiarisation with reporting procedures, filing systems and byelaw regulations rather than with the whys and hows of traditional communal behaviour. Mission schools by and large provided the kind of education that was basic to these changing roles, and the curriculum of the schools established by the (Protestant) Native Anglican Church was considered to be especially close to the administration's requirements.

Thus the intensity and average length of school experience of the chiefs increased. It would be possible to chart the rise in formal educational qualifications of the senior Ankole chiefs as running from (at most) one or two years of schooling at the beginning of the century to at least double or triple this length some decades later. But even that would still only be one way of describing the changing role and position of the chiefs. More telling perhaps is the fact that chiefs in 1907 were listed according to the amount of cattle they possessed, while later categorisations were rather made in terms of the number of years of school attendance.[43] As the former criterion stressed wealth and power and the latter clerical proficiency and bureaucratic acumen as a basis of ranking, the contrast suggests at least one important way in which the system changed.

Against this background it is significant that the Bahima elite, whose incorporation into the colonial framework had been largely based on qualities of the wealth and status variety, were able to make the transition and continue their position through acquisition of requisite aptitudes in the colonial administration. That they were thus able to hold out so long is even more remarkable considering not only the spread of colonial education and new skills among the Bairu majority, but the fact that this elite comprised only a small segment of the Bahima, who were themselves a minority. Bahima domination during the first half of the century was in fact maintained by a surprisingly small chiefly class. Beyond the basic colonial support for this stratum and their own efforts to perpetuate their tenure, the explanation of this partly appears to lie in their early lead in educational advantages.

Since early in the century the Protestant Mbarara High School was the main training ground of Ankole's elite. Opened in 1911, its educational facilities initially benefitted the Bahima most. During the crucial first few years of its existence (crucial in terms of administrative recruitment open to its students), over 75 per cent of the student body were Bahima, eight per cent Baganda, and the remainder were Abambari and Bairu.[44] Many of these early students were appointed to high positions, thus giving the Bahima a strong buttress to the perpetuation of their chiefly class. Earlier some other Bahima had already been attending Mengo High School near Kampala. Various Bahima students also went from Mbarara High School to Buddo College in Buganda for extended education.

In considering this advantage, it must be born in mind that Bahima were generally in a better position to pay the necessary school fees for their sons than were Bairu. School fees at the time constituted one of the few and, apart from taxes, probably the major item of cash expenditure for the local population. Ability to pay these fees thus also determined who would finally become eligible for administrative employment. Even with little monetisation during the early part of the century, cattle ownership commanded a better bargaining position in this respect than reliance on subsistence crops. For Bahima who already were chiefs and earned a salary the payment of school fees presented even fewer problems.

However, these economic advantages were a necessary but not sufficient condition for Bahima school enrolment. Their attendance was in fact rather difficult to achieve, as many of Ankole's pastoralists showed a pronounced indifference, at times verging on resistance, towards formal education. The routine of school attendance conflicted with Bahima views on what constituted relevant education, with the tasks of cattle husbandry, and with diets.[45] The lead which Bahima nonetheless gained in educational qualifications was therefore not least the result of enforced school attendance, – especially of chiefs' sons at the beginning of the century. Thus, one of the things for which the Enganzi, Mbaguta, is remembered in Ankole was his pressing the chiefs and other notables to send their children to school; if they failed to turn up he would send down an askari to fetch them. During his lifetime, Mbaguta himself paid school fees for quite a large number of students, including some Bairu.

The basis was thus laid for the prolongation of the Bahima establishment during colonial times: many of the Bahima students who attended Mbarara High School in the 1910s since then manned the Ankole government, and a few were influential even until the 1970s. As already noted however, the conditions were also created for an increasingly tenuous position and the eventual replacement of this elite.

Bahima were conscious of the likelihood of this development and it is often argued in Ankole that they made deliberate efforts to minimise the pace of social development of the Bairu to maintain their political supremacy. Examples cited include discouragement of Bairu from seeking an advanced education and discrimination in the allocation of school bursaries. Nonetheless, the spread of schools virtually ensured that members of the non-elite stratum, the Bairu, in time would outdistance the Bahima in educational attainments and in the long run lay claims on the majority of administrative positions. Schooling was thus again of considerable importance in this transformation. As was also to be expected, however, the alteration of the ethnic basis of elite recruitment it implied would not be realised without problems. Instead, the friction that ensued made this transition a rather critical landmark in Ankole's development, one to which we shall return in the next chapter.

At the same time the educational and occupational experiences of the Bahima elite had another significant effect, namely a measure of cultural re-orientation which led to a growing social distance between them and the pastoral Bahima. As noted above, the majority of Bahima were long disinterested in the educational facilities introduced during colonialism. Only in recent years, the last decade or two mainly, have these attitudes begun to change. This has been partly a result of the proselytising efforts of the Protestant Balokole sect, which in Ankole finds its adherents mainly among Bahima.[46] Until this development, however, the distinction between the numerically small Bahima elite – of chiefs, some clergy and others who occupied high positions on the basis of educational skills – and the majority of Bahima who remained engaged in pastoralism, was growing wider. The distinction involved basic differences not only in educational standards, but in life styles and orientations, deriving from sedentary versus semi-nomadic existences and above all from quite different occupational involvements.

Still, the distinction between the two Bahima categories did not grow into a fully fledged division between antagonistic or otherwise clearly separate groups. In that sense it differed for example from the division between the urban-based Fulani Gida and the cattle Fulani in the northern parts of Nigeria. In Ankole the two groups maintained closer relationships than was true among the Fulani, whose diverse occupational patterns were of course also of much longer standing. Members of the Bahima elite continued to demonstrate great affection for the pastoral life. Even today most are still cattle-owners and when on leave often try to spend some time around the cattle kraals. It has also not been unusual for high ranking Bahima to devote themselves to their cattle upon retirement. Recently, for example, the ex-Omugabe of Ankole retired to his cattle ranch upon the abolition of his office.[47] Other Bahima chiefs have done the same, at times practicing new methods of animal husbandry. During the early colonial years it was of course even more common for Bahima chiefs to continue an active involvement in cattle-keeping as an adjoint to their office.

Thus the Bahima elite's involvement in pastoralism, even if only sporadic or intermittent, did give them a continued sense of belongingness with the wider Bahima community. It might be noted in this connection that no Runyankore terms developed to distinguish between the two groups of Bahima, which tends to confirm the continued existence of a shared identity. Yet the endurance of these links perhaps obscured but could hardly reduce the extent of divergence of their respective ways of life. Among other things, the latter's reality can be gathered from a sense of regret often expressed by members of the Bahima elite that they lost 'control' or 'guidance' over the pastoralists. The elite were disappointed, perhaps also a little embarrassed, that the latter kept trekking through Ankole, Buganda and beyond and remained unresponsive to their suggestions for change and adaptations.[48]

The differential social development among the Bahima entailed profound implications for the position of its elite. These consequences, and the relationships on which they rested, were essentially two-pronged. On the one hand, the economic wealth which cattle-ownership represented continued to provide a source of social and political security, to the Bahima generally and in turn to its elite:[49] the elite-'mass' relationships which during colonial times developed internal to the Bahima community were somewhat unusual in that they hardly involved a juxtaposition of a rich and an impoverished section relative to one another. In that sense the pastoralists were, if anything, rather a support than a burden to the elite. Nor were they economically exploited as this is commonly understood: pronounced and antagonistic socio-economic dependency relationships tended to develop between the Bahima elite and the Bairu peasants, rather than with Bahima herdsmen. On the other hand, while the Bahima elite were already drawn from a minority section of the population, the social basis for prolonged elite recruitment was thinned further due to the non-involvement of the larger part of the Bahima in the educational and occupational channels of the colonial framework.

Thus, inasfar as numerical size and its rough proportion among the general population may count as a basis for an elite's political support and sense of political identity, one can see that there was a certain logic – or even a need – to the Bahima elite's continued affiliation with the pastoral Bahima. This affinity was facilitated by the elite's continued, if limited contacts with pastoralism, and the relative absence of economically based conflict of interest between the two Bahima groups. But it would not be sufficient to lend support to a rejuvenation and prolongation of the Bahima elite's tenure, for in the end this increasingly demanded social and administrative orientations in which the Bahima as a whole, so much in contrast to their elite, were lagging behind.

Finally, the position of Ankole's Bahima elite was also determined by the particular inroads of western religion in the society. In terms of staffing, it should be noted that from the early years of colonial rule onwards administrative positions in Ankole, especially the higher ones, tended to be filled by Protestants rather than Roman-Catholics. Protestantism became known as the 'king's religion' in Ankole; in more than one sense it was also the colonial government's religion. Without exception all Bahima chiefs appointed during colonialism were Protestant. In addition there was also a marked preference for Protestants in the recruitment of non-Bahima chiefs. Whether a condition or a consequence of this bias, there was long a closer liaison between the requirements of the administration and the curriculum of Protestant schools than was true for Catholic schools. The result has been that throughout colonial times the number of Protestants on the staff of the Ankole district administration has been way out of proportion to their membership among the population at large.[50]

This configuration is partly explained by the way in which Christianity made its entry into Ankole society. As already noted, virtually all converted Bahima became Protestants, belonging to the Native Anglican Church.[51] However, the majority of Bahima did not become Christians. On the other hand, most Bairu became Christians during colonial times, and slightly more became Roman Catholic than Protestant. The background to this was that Protestant missionaries had the advantage of arriving first, and, moreover, they enjoyed the support of the authorities. Initially, they concentrated their efforts on the Bahima ruling stratum at the center, whereas the Roman Catholics started among the Bairu in more distant locations. As a result, the Protestants gained their near monopoly of Bahima converts. Besides, following the pattern of establishment of mission stations by the two denominations, Protestants became relatively predominant in the central counties of Shema, Igara, Kashari, and Rwampara, whereas Roman Catholics tended to be concentrated in the northern peripheral areas of Bunyarugu, Buhweju, and Ibanda, as well as, though to a lesser extent, in Isingiro to the south.

Christian religion was introduced in a rather competitive fashion and for many years the limited contacts between Protestant and Roman Catholic missionaries remained cool and strained. Among the Ankole population different orientation grew following the spread of Protestantism and Catholicism, again of an often strained and competitive quality. In part these differences resulted from the nature of education offered by the two denominations. Whereas Roman Catholic missions combined broadly based, low-level education with finally a specialised, mainly seminary-type, training for a selected few, the Protestants from an earlier date offered wider opportunities for intermediate and extended instruction. Again, in the tradition of schools for chiefs' sons, the latter curriculum was more closely geared to the requirements of the administration.

But an equally crucial factor in the growth of different orientations lay in the Protestant complexion of Ankole's ruling group after 1900. Not only did this group, with the tacit consent of the British District Commissioners, generally support the interests of the Native Anglican Church and its schools, it also gave better chances of employment to Protestants than to Roman Catholics. These Protestants included Bairu adherents of that denomination, who were appointed in greater numbers than Roman Catholics as lower ranking chiefs, clerks and askaris. On the whole, therefore, the opportunities open to Protestant Bairu, though far more limited than those of the Bahima, were better than those of the Roman Catholics. As a result of these conditions, the Roman Catholic Bairu for long remained engaged in self-sufficient traditional cultivation while the Bahima elite and, to a much lesser extent, the Protestant Bairu began to actively partake in the new framework.

As we shall see later, the divergent social developments among the Bairu in time were to have important political consequences.[52] But from the early years of the century till the heyday of colonialism they produced a pecking order which placed the Bahima elite first, the Protestant Bairu second, and the Roman Catholics third in their access to differential advantages. In a sense a pyramidal structure of statuses emerged, roughly reflecting the allocation of administrative ranks among the three groups: Bahima on top occupying the senior (especially the county) chieftainships and the most important roles in the district administration, Protestant Bairu with a few sub-county chieftainships but mostly at the lower echelons as parish chiefs and in other minor posts, and Roman Catholic Bairu on the fringes of this system, enjoying the least benefits and influence.[53]

For purposes of control, then, this system gave the Bahima enormous advantages as long as the pyramid retained its basic shape. Few other arrangements, planned or unplanned, might have given such a small ruling group such a large sway over the entire system. The division of the Bairu into Protestants and Roman Catholics itself was conducive towards this control; it reduced and divided potential opposition. Also, the preferential treatment of Protestant Bairu over Roman Catholics in regard to minor benefits tended to stimulate a Protestant Bairu stake in the system, which at a crucial point in time might lead them to lend their support to the Bahima hegemony. Protestantism could serve to symbolise a 'unity of interests' and reduce the visibility of the ethnic basis of the command structure. Religion, in other words, in Ankole produced forces which tended to exacerbate the effects of other social divisions, and thus in a sense came to rank on a par with the latter. For a prolonged period its effect was hardly to mitigate ethnic inequality in the colonial framework, but to conceal, and thereby reinforce it. Precisely the fact that it did not create a one-to-one, cumulative relationship, say, between Protestantism and Bahima status and between Catholicism and Bairu status (which might have strengthened the ethnic strata, but not the stratification system), tended to lessen the exposure of the ethnic gap and consequently the latter's chances of an early conflict.

These arrangements also served the purposes of British colonial control. It was consistent with a policy of 'franchise' and 'self-rule' that local statuses should be so allocated and arranged as to result in a system which largely rested on its 'own' checks and mechanisms of control. This is not to assert that the socio-political framework which developed in Ankole was entirely a product of willful social engineering. But it does imply that the divisiveness which originated in the district's ethnic cum religious cleavages facilitated external control and, indeed, gave no reason for change or intervention.[54]

As suggested above, the effectiveness of this structuring for Bahima — and colonial — control might endure as long as its pyramidal shape did not basically change. That condition, indeed, constituted a critical linchpin for the perpetuation of the system, which was basic to its format throughout the early decades of colonial rule. In the end, however, it was no longer fulfilled. Once the colonial framework had been firmly implanted, the second quarter of the century saw the beginning of a gradual but accelerating expansion of the intermediate stratum of its ranking system, followed by growing demands for increased involvements among its members. The result of these developments, combined with the narrowing basis for Bahima elite recruitment discussed before, was to make inroads into the entrenched position of the Bahima elite which eventually inaugurated its erosion. Their significance thus lay largely in the revised socio-political relationships they generated within the Ankole colonial framework.

But these processes go well beyond the phase of early colonialism we have been concerned with here and will need to be taken up in the next chapter. Meanwhile, we must now examine the effects of colonial arrangements on another structure of Ankole political relationships, the institution of kingship and historically the polity's linchpin.

THE REDEFINITION OF KINGSHIP

Not the least important effect of colonialism in Ankole society was that which it had on its institution of kingship. Colonial rule impinged upon the institution of kingship, the Obugabe, in several crucial ways. The institution's incorporation into the colonial command structure, the reduction of the Omugabe's traditional entourage, the Bahinda, and the expansion of scale of Ankole at the establishment of British rule, all seriously affected the position of the kingship. Already the context which was so redefined weakened its potential support in the society and reduced its chances of an adaptation which might have been anywhere comparable to that shown in the case of some other monarchies. In addition, colonial government drastically transformed the role of kingship itself. The basic fact that the continued existence of the institution came to depend on colonial policy rather than on its own functionality led to major inroads into the authoritative and symbolic roles of Ankole kingship, eroding its traditional functions and causing it to loose its essential meaning.

For a proper perspective on this role transformation the ingredients of the traditional system should be kept in mind. Structurally, we saw that the system was charcterised by dispersed powers and a high degree of collective decision-making, — mostly among and for Bahima — while normatively it featured strongly hierarchical values about authority.[55] Moreover, these aspects were significantly interconnected, since the hierarchical values made sense primarily in relation to the collective style of decision making. In this context there was a central focus on the institution of kingship, whose role was of critical significance.

Colonial rule fundamentally changed these characteristics and their interconnections. It could not tolerate an institution with any measure of autonomy, but sought to make it a mouthpiece of colonial policy. The kingship was fitted into the bureaucratic structure and in time the institution was adorned with a thick overlay of new ceremonialism. As a result, new distinctions developed between the assumed and actual powers of kingship. But contrary to the historical example these lacked any complementarity and what would finally emerge was rather a caricature of the traditional institution, accelerating the erosion of supportive sentiments it had once inspired.

The key to this development was that the employment of traditional authority entailed some profound ambiguities which were to seriously threaten its effectiveness. Even if some early European administrators had a passing interest in the exotic, or took a delight in exploring the role and meaning of historic kingship, in the day-to-day execution of tasks, they commonly assessed traditional authority mainly in terms of its command over the popular will or the obedience it might be able to provide. The assumption was that 'all you could in fact do was to explain what you wanted to some "Native Authority"; and as he – or she – was generally only too anxious to please, the result was usually that it was done'.[56] Thus, in the eyes of the population, the legitimacy of traditional authority had to be maintained if it was to remain effective. But, in those early days, to treat a king or chief with all the pomp and protocol which later became more common might have stimulated a renewed consciousness and taste for actual authority on their part; this could easily have come to conflict with the conduct of regular colonial administration and could by no means be allowed. Obviously, therefore, there was a fragile balance if not tension between the requirements of continued legitimacy and external control, and it is not difficult to imagine that the subtleties of the compromise may somehow have escaped a man like the Omugabe of Ankole. He was told time and again that he was supreme chief or Kabaka. Moreover, there was the fresh memory of the traditional period in which his position, as we have seen, was indeed symbolically exalted.[57] Yet the tendency was clearly to employ him as an instrument with which to gain popular acceptance for administrative measures. An incongruous element in the new bureaucratic edifice he was, in effect, ordered around by British officers to explain colonial policies to induce compliance among the people of Ankole.

Ambiguities were especially noticeable in regard to the Omugabe's position *vis-à-vis* the administrative chiefs. For long these relationships were not explicitly laid down and, moreover, the official line in respect of these matters tended to change over time. The policy was evidently to have it both ways, that is, to keep full control over the chiefs in the hands of the district administration while yet adhering to the idea that all authority was exercised in the name and under the supervision of the Omugabe. Chiefs of counties and lower divisions were appointed by and held responsible to the district administration.[58] District officials inspected their books, kept records of their adminstrative performance, and reported on their diligence in implementing bye-laws. Yet the Omugabe was put forward as their superior, and this was done in more than a purely nominal sense. From the British point of view, it seemed practicable to make use of his influence over the subordinate chiefs. For this, however, he somehow had to be given an opportunity to display his authority. The Omugabe was therefore also asked to tour and inspect and report. Clearly, this entailed some problems, of which duplication of supervision was only the least. For one thing, the standards of good administration entertained by the Omugabe were not necessarily the same as those of British officials and as a result differences almost inevitably arose. Chiefs would either find themselves confronted with two kinds of demand and possibly be unable to decide which to give priority, or the Omugabe would follow the official line and communicate directives which he himself did not quite accept. Moreover, the relationship between the Omugabe and the chiefs was entirely different to that in the pre-colonial situation. The Omugabe came to perform in an administrative command system and it was expected that his traditional legitimacy would ease his assumption of this new role. But because this legitimacy was associated with an earlier and different authority relationship, the new role was not an instant success; instead, it left puzzles and embarrassment on the side of the Omugabe as well as of the chiefs. Moreover, as the exact scope of his authority had been left exceedingly vague, the chances of a successful learning process were all the more problematic. Finally, to function effectively in any capacity within the district organisation, a certain amount of administrative proficiency was a *sine qua non*. The whole system was designed on the basis of paperwork and bureaucratic codes, and whoever did not master their essentials was at a loss. No wonder that the Omugabe, who was wholly untrained for these purposes, should have felt a sense of inadequacy in discharging the administrative tasks devolved upon him. Rather more surprising is that the problems created by this situation were not readily appreciated by British officials; it was only as late as 1938, when the

Omugabe asked for copies of reports to be sent to him, that a District Commissioner began to wonder 'has the Omugabe facilities for starting a filing system of his own?' [59]

These ambiguities and contradictions led to increasingly strained relationships between the Omugabe and British officials. Lack of interest and resentment of the British administration came more and more to characterise the Omugabe's attitude, and a vicious circle ensued in which growing impatience and irritation on the part of colonial officers and increasing apathy and surliness on the part of the Omugabe were some of the more salient elements. Painstaking reporters of everything happening within their jurisdiction, colonial administrators have left an extensive record of these difficulties. A letter sent on March 3, 1907, by the Acting Collector in Mbarara to the Sub-Commissioner, Western Province, reporting one instance of friction with the Omugabe, deserves to be quoted at length as it typifies the attitude and tone of the earlier administrators towards the Omugabe:

Sir,

I have the honour to report that Kahaya, Kabaka of Ankole, was yesterday guilty of conduct of such an unseen nature that I feel that it should be brought to your notice.

This consisted in misbehaviour towards myself and insolence of such a sort that it should in my opinion be recorded. The immediate and apparent cause of this lapse upon his part was that I found it necessary to speak somewhat seriously to Kahaya with respect to the manner in which he treated certain requests I made to him in connection with the arrangements for the Anglo-Congolese Commission. My reproofs which were certainly not more severe than the occasion demanded were received by Kahaya in a spirit of mixed sullenness and impertinence. He informed me that he could see that I wanted to quarrel with him, that he would henceforth refuse to visit me if sent for, and that he would not attempt to carry out my requests. Thinking that he had momentarily lost control of himself I endeavoured for a space to remonstrate with him. But he either maintained an obstinate silence, or replied with sullen impertinence. Seeing that further conciliatoriness could serve no useful purpose, I told him that I would tolerate his tone no longer. I told him that he had been grossly impertinent to me, and that I would see that his behaviour was reported. I then ordered him to leave my house, and not to return until he could behave himself.

Kahaya has not of course adhered to the wild statements above-described. He received my Interpreter within two hours of the occurrence, and gave directions that what I required should be attended to. And he has today met an inquiry from me as to whether he will come to see me in a proper manner, in a becoming spirit. And did this outbreak of temper stand by itself I should not give to it much heed. For Kahaya is liable to fits of extreme and hasty temper, joined at times with an ineradicable obstinacy. I have seen him before quite inarticulate with rage against Baguta. But the whole trend of his conduct of late, and his normal demeanour when any attempt has been made to guide him or to induce him to regard seriously the responsibilities of his position compel me to think that we need to be very careful in our treatment of Kahaya. During the past few weeks in particular I have been very dissatisfied with his manner and conduct. And because two weeks ago I thought fit to censure him for repeating to me five days in succession a statement which he knew to be a deliberate falsehood, he used language which if taken seriously would seem to indicate that in his opinion the Kabaka could not be found fault with by the Collector.

This is of course an attitude which cannot be allowed for a moment. It is needless to say that it will be a bad thing for Ankole if Kahaya and the Bahima Chiefs in general are allowed to persist in the notion, which they undoubtedly entertain, and have cherished for some time, that specious promises are all that is required, and that performance is scarcely even expected; it will be worse if the idea gains ground that the Collector can always be put off by perfunctory excuses, and will not venture upon strong re-monstrances. The Bahima will need wise handling,

I have the honour to be,

Sir,

Your most obedient humble Servant,

In this instance, the Sub-Commissioner in turn communicated the incident to his superiors at Entebbe, adding that 'it would appear from it that Kahaya's character is not even now formed and he should be treated to discipline much as a school boy', and concluding that 'he will have to be properly kept in his place'.[60] Accordingly, he instructed the Acting Collector that

'[Kahaya] must learn that the Collector is the representative of the Government in his Country and any disrespect shown to him, or other Government Officers, is a slight which will not be lightly passed over. Please also inform him that I have reported the matter to His Excellency the Commissioner and make a note of the occurrence in your record book of Chiefs' characters.' [61]

A few days after the incident, the Acting Collector was proud to report that Kahaya had visited him again and that 'his behaviour on this occasion was all that could be desired'. 'But I venture to think', he went on, that 'every opportunity should be available to cause Kahaya to realise more clearly his responsibilities as Kabaka, and the attitude it is deemed to assume towards a Collector and towards Europeans in general.' [62]

The problem was not solved, however, and over the following decades a long series of reprimands reached the Omugabe. In 1921, for instance, the District Commissioner of Ankole issued a warning to him in the following terms:

'I notice that these days you never seem to go to the Lukiko or take part in the work of your country, why is this so? Your people are complaining that their Head Chief is no longer there to look after them. You must realise that it is your duty to preside at the Meetings and Courts of the Lukiko, and not allow other people to take away your power, so I hope that it will not be necessary for me to have to write again about this.' [63]

A few years later a letter from the Provincial Commissioner to the Omugabe conveyed the same concern:

'1. I am informed by the District Commissioner, Ankole that you are taking little or no interest in the Administration of your country. 2. I hope when I visit Ankole in December that I shall find you have been attending Lukiko regularly and are trying your best to help on the country of which you are the Omugabe. 3. If you consider you are so ill that you can no longer carry out your duties, would you like to retire on a pension and have your successor appointed now.' [64]

Again, in 1933, after visiting the Omugabe, a District Commissioner wrote in his report,

'I explained that I was very dissatisfied with him as Mugabe and that Europeans at Mbarara, Fort Portal and Entebbe were saying that he was useless and was no good. He had spoilt his name among

them and now he was spoiling his name among his own people . . . .
I told him that I wished to help him and wished to uphold the
Mugabeship for the good of the country, but I could do nothing if he
did not help me.' [65]

In that same year, the Omugabe was also reminded

'Always remember that a Mugabe who does not see his people and
to whom they cannot come is not worthy of the post of Mugabe or
pay.' [66]

And on December 31, 1937, the District Commissioner wrote to all
local heads of departments to express his 'regret that the disrespect
shown by the Mugabe made it impossible for me to hold Lukiko'.

It had also become apparent that the Omugabe's behaviour
conflicted in several ways with the codes for prudence and propriety
introduced by the British. In 1926, for instance, the Omugabe was told
by the Provincial Commissioner that

'The Government wish to accomplish two matters, namely, (1) to
make such suitable arrangements as will prevent your money being
taken wrongly by other people without your knowledge, as is
happening now; (2) by a proper system of supervision and
accounting to prevent your having debts beyond your income and
seeing that all such debts are paid every month thus preventing
disgrace coming both on yourself and on your country. You are at
liberty to spend all your money as you like and we do not wish to
inquire as to how you spend it provided you do not get into debt and
agree to the supervision that the Government think necessary.' [67]

And in 1927, the Provincial Commissioner instructed the Officer-in-
Charge at Mbarara:

'As regards the Omugabe, will you please convey the following
remarks to him:

(a)   It is the business of the Omugabe to understand any rules
made with regard to his country, and that if he is mentally
unable of understanding them he is not fit to be Omugabe.

(b)   That there is a legal order limiting the amount of beer to be
brewed, and that he the Omugabe is guilty of an offence and
liable to severe punishment for instructing people to break the
law.

(c)   That it is the aim and object of the Government to prevent
drunkenness and that his action is calculated to encourage it
and is therefore contrary to Government orders to chiefs and

that such action cannot be tolerated.

(d)   That he the Omugabe is not above the law of the country and that if he cannot obey the law and the instructions of the Government, I will place the matter before His Excellency the Governor with a view to considering his removal.

(e)   That this is by no means the first adverse report received on his conduct, and that unless an improvement is noted, drastic action will have to be taken.' [68]

Various other irregularities, big and small, likewise occupied the attention of colonial officers. On 16 August, 1921, the District Commissioner felt compelled to write to the Provincial Commissioner 'I report that it is my duty to bring to your notice a serious scandal complicating the Omugabe, Katikiro and the Sekibobo'.[69] The scandal involved the Queen of Ankole, and in the instructions which followed she was to be escorted by 'reliable men' to Mbarara. On 16 September, 1926, renewed disappointments caused the Acting Provincial Commissioner to communicate to the Officer-in-Charge, Ankole, that he was 'directed to convey to the Omugabe an expression of His Excellency the Governor's surprise and regret that he – the Omugabe – as head of the Native Government in Ankole, should have committed irregularities in connection with the collection of grazing fees in contravention of his own Lukiko Funds.' And in 1935, according to the Ankole District Annual Report for that year, it was decided to cancel the Omugabe's Game and Elephant licence and to withdraw all privileges for five years, owing to his 'infringement of the Game Laws'.

In response to these injunctions and reprimands, the Omugabe made occasional promises to improve his conduct and meet the standards set for it by the Protectorate administration. One such pledge is contained in a letter he wrote in 1927 to the District Commissioner:[70]

Dear Sir,

I have seen the P.C.'s letter No. 694/395, which he wrote warning me that I should do my work for my country.

Now I am writing to inform you what I am going to do in future. I expect to make a big Safari rounding the District like the Katikiro has recently done, my principal work on my Safari is to see the chiefs' work and encourage them also to encourage the Bakopi (peasants) to cultivate lot of food for famine.

After coming back from the Safari I will preside (sit) in the Lukiko regularly, so I hope in that case I may be able to abolish my present habit of sitting in my house doing nothing.

I confirm this before you that I will do my best to do the Administration work as it is required by both the Govt. Officers and my people, and in future there will be no more slackness in me.

I shall be very grateful if you will kindly write to the P.C.W.P. and inform him that his warning has been strictly carried out, and that I will not cause more trouble in future.

My safari will start from here on the 15th inst.

I hope to come and see you in your office tomorrow morning at 9 a.m. and will talk to you about my Safari, etc.

I beg to remain,

sir

Your Obedient Servant E.S. Kahaya, Omugabe.

Some such statements of intent actually inaugurated a renewed involvement of the Omugabe in public affairs. He would then do some touring and address audiences on the objectives of government policy, acting as the mouthpiece of the administration. In a speech given by the Omugabe to the Bahima in 1940, for instance, the topics covered included:

'1. I want to remind you about important words which the Honourable Provincial Commissioner, Western Province told you yesterday. He told you that in former days you were brave and clever people but when you got rich, you received other people to work for you, and little by little you became lazy and good for nothing. 2. . . . the Government will help you in keeping cattle and making good butter and hides, so that they may be of good quality and good price. She will build a School here, but you must send to it your children and pay school fees for them. 3. Don't willingly break rules given to you by the Veterinary officer. The well is made for you as a sample of good will, and you will make new ones by yourselves when this is spoilt. 4. The Government will build a Hospital for you, but please do send to it your patients and have confidence in the Government Doctor rather than in your pagan witches. 5. In my last safari to Nyabushozi, I spoke to you about Poll Tax, I want now to remind you of the use of it. Money collected from poll tax is for use in: making roads, building hospitals and other buildings of chiefs, paying chiefs and all government porters.'[71]

When asked to do so by the district officials and in his rare moments of involvement, the Omugabe might also call his subordinates to their duties. In respect to a chief's behaviour, for example, Kahaya reported to the District Commissioner:

'Sir, I have the honour to inform you that I have seen Mr. Firimoni Lwaigambwa Mugyema, and reproved him fim for his drunkenness, and I have instructed him to cease drinking native beer. He has agreed to my advice, and he has sworn in my presence that he will never drink it again.'[72]

Such an intervention, made towards the end of his rulership, was surely becoming behaviour for an Omugabe in His Majesty's service. And it was in that commendable spirit that Kahaya's successor, Gasyonga, expressed himself when taking over in 1944. Thanking the Governor for his recognition, he wrote, 'I assure Your Excellency that with the advice of the Protectorate Government and the Ankole Native Administration I shall endeavour to be one of His Majesty's Loyal Servants'.[73]

INTERPRETATIONS OF CONFLICT

The point of interest in all these reports is that they offer an insight into the highly problematic relationship between the Omugabe of Ankole and British administrative officers. Not only do the communications of these officials tell us something about the areas of friction, but a certain official viewpoint emerges from the records. This viewpoint is of particular interest to us. Basically, the notion entertained by District Commissioners, Provincial Commissioners and other colonial officers appears to have been that the Omugabe did not know his place and did not know his role. They found that he lacked understanding of and interest in the tasks assigned to him. And from the tenor of the remarks they submitted, it is apparent that British officials tended to attribute the difficulties in dealing with the Omugabe largely to the make-up of his personality. He was considered weak, physically and intellectually, sullen, lacking in will and moral acumen. During virtually the whole period that the Omugabe Kahaya was on the scene, that is until 1944, this was the most common and favoured explanation. Accordingly, in the series of Annual District Reports for Ankole, the sections concerning the Omugabe together read like a long temperature chart on his condition, as the following illustrate:

1934   'The outstanding feature of the year has been the new lease of life that the Mugabe has taken. I indicated the possibility of this revival at the end of last year.'

1935   'The interest of the Mugabe in the affairs of the District has been but sporadic.'

1936   'Much the same comment applies to the Omugabe as in previous years, namely that on the pretext of ill health he confines himself to his house and takes but little interest in the affairs of the District.'

1937   'The shortness of my time in Ankole makes it difficult to pass comment on the activities of Mugabe and his Chiefs.'

1938   'The Omugabe broke his leg during the year, but though it has not completely recovered he has during the last quarter been able to go on tour.'

1939   'The Mugabe made two tours during the year and appeared interested in all activities of his people. His health was precarious but mentally he was able to deal with all matters referred to him.'

1940   'The Omugabe made one extended tour during which he visited several Saza headquarters. He continued to take an intelligent interest in all the activities of the district.'

1941   'The Mugabe toured Nyabushozi county and addressed the Bahima in a forlorn attempt to make them help in the development of their new Saza and to stop emigration to Buganda. He has been sick during the last-three months of the year.'

1942   'The Mugabe has remained in bad health during the whole year. His only public appearance was at the time of the visit of the S.A.A.F. when he attended the display.' [74]

1943   'The Mugabe has continued in bad health and has made no public appearance during the year.'

1944   'In October the District was shocked to hear of the death of the Omugabe, E.S. Kahaya II. He has been in bad health for some considerable time and had taken little or no part in the administration of the district.' [75]

In considering this chronicle, it seems beyond dispute that Kahaya was a man of limited physical powers and of no spectacular intellectual resources. Nowhere, in British or local accounts, does he emerge as a man of great vision or foresight, or as someone who would have his own will and stand by it. Of weak health and described by his early European visitors as 'a very stout overgrown youth' about whom 'there was nothing particularly regal',[76] his involvement was by and large a passive one; generally he tended to withdraw from the complexities with which he became surrounded from all sides, and these not merely British. However, to explain problems in the relationship with the Omugabe simply by reference to personality factors is not only superficial, it too easily shifts the onus from the structural arrangements he came to operate in and the way in which these were manipulated by the British. The ambiguity of his role made misunderstandings and conflict practically unavoidable, and there is every reason to believe that the problems would have been even more serious had the Omugabe had a stronger personality.[77] As it was, however, Kahaya was a boy of about 18 when he was installed, almost immediately before the British made their entry. Hence, the conception of his office, or the lack of it, was largely British-derived; if there were difficulties, these were inherent in the very definition of his role. Long after the early days of self-confident colonialism had passed, British officers developed a more balanced understanding of the structural transitions they had enacted. As Mitchell reflected in 1939:

'Few of us realised . . . that the instrument which we were using could not retain its effectiveness if we deprived it – as we generally did – of most of its powers and responsibilities, to say nothing of its revenues. I have often wondered since those early days that the Chiefs thought it worthwhile even to try to carry out our wishes, when we had taken from them the power to punish and often looked upon the tribute and service from their people, without which they could not exist, as being corrupt extortion.'[78]

This contradiction was fully apparent in the instance of Ankole. The frequency with which the institution of kingship was used to induce compliance with administrative policies was inversely related to its actual usefulness for that purpose; accordingly, its employment tended to produce ever more marginal results. For some time it was evidently felt that if only the Omugabe could be interested in the innovations proposed by the district administration, it would not be difficult to get the rest of the population to follow suit. However, the result was very different, not least because the role designed for the Omugabe was as foreign to the Banyankore as it was to the man himself. As contrived by the British administration, the role of the Omugabe departed in major ways from pre-colonial conceptions. This was not only because the Omugabe became subordinate to Protectorate officials, but the idea of a bureaucratic line of command was also highly unfamiliar. The meaning of the institution in traditional times, which was to symbolize the political integration of a pastoralist polity through the hierarchical authority values associated with it, was irretrievably deflated by the use made of kingship to get acceptance for immediate ends. This policy had assumed the existence of sources of actual power which the Omugabe had never had. It had further assumed that, whatever the original basis of his prestige, this would be prolonged within the new context to be established. Both these assumptions proved fallacious; when the Omugabe was asked to convey colonial policies to his people, they saw him perform in a capacity which made little sense, either in the old or in the new framework. Even his relatively rare visits to various areas were felt as a burden and nuisance by the people concerned, as was evidenced in the repeated complaints over the requirements to lay on food supplies for him and his retinue. Increasingly, therefore, he was met by lack of understanding and interest, which only enhanced his own disinterest and discomfort with his role, and ultimately led to the state of apathy and withdrawal which disappointed so many of his British superiors.

Kahaya did not possess the strong personality necessary to counter these trends, and his successor Gasyonga's case was not fundamentally different. But, again, had their demeanor been more powerful, friction might well have been much greater. The erosion of kingship, which, even if unintended, was the inevitable conclusion of the process of bureaucratisation, might then have been considerably complicated and delayed (or else speeded up by open conflict).

It should be clear that this is not necessarily supportive of the view held by some anthropologists that, for an innovation to be successful, it must be hooked on to existing cultural patterns.[79] On the contrary, new situations generate new orientations and values. Even if the conditions under which some new structures are introduced may be questionable, institutional change is bound to occur wherever there is any juxtaposition of new and old elements. To assume that an institution such as kingship can be transformed but that popular orientations and allegiances toward it will remain unaffected is profoundly misleading. The attempt to make use of the traditional role of kingship in Ankole was based on this ambiguity; farreaching changes were introduced while assuming that the orientations which supported the old relationships would prevail. However, the structural transformations introduced in Ankole could ultimately lead only to obsolescence of the monarchy. Indeed, the redundancy of Ankole kingship was a built-in consequence of its use as a tool in the colonial machinery.[80] Some of the manifestations of this in a later period will be examined in the next chapter.

4. Protest and Accommodation in Ankole Politics

The previous chapters were concerned with the pattern of political relationships in pre-colonial Nkore and with the processes of transformation initiated through colonial rule in the Ankole area. In both sections the focus was on the articulation of socio-political cleavages and on the nature of institutional arrangements characteristic of the respective periods. In the present section we will maintain this dual focus and try to analyse how the patterns of group formation and institutional change inaugurated during the early part of the century have worked themselves out in terms of recent political conflict and change.

It will also be remembered that the two earlier periods were marked off from one another by a distinct historical watershed, the colonial intervention. Accordingly, in the second section we took the Ankole Agreement of 1901 as a base-line which expressed and formalised that watershed. Following this, we traced the growth of a new socio-political framework during the early colonial period and we have seen how a pecking order was created which juxtaposed Ankole's ethnic and religious categories in a manner which was as broadly hierarchical as it was congruent with the objectives of colonial rule.

Dynamic processes tend to retain their momentum unless and until there is another major intervention. This is true for processes of elite differentiation as much as for other patterns of socio-political transformation. In Ankole there clearly has been such a momentum ever since the beginning of colonial times. Beyond the few decades on which the analysis was concentrated, the formative processes we have been concerned with continued in what was perhaps a rather accelerated fashion during the 'full bloom' period of colonialism in Uganda. This period was mainly the 1930s and 1940s, a time when few new policy departures were undertaken but during which the results of earlier interventions and rearrangements provided the basic format for colonial control.

Processes of elite formation and institutional change have continued into contemporary Ankole, providing a basic link between the present and the past. Nonetheless, there is a difference – one which serves as a point of departure for the present section. The socio-political framework created during colonial rule was one which in terms of its institutional arrangements as well as the social divisions it inaugurated, facilitated 'indirect rule' of a kind. Ultimate British control provided the linchpin of this system, while the 'franchise' and leeway left to Ankole's chiefly elite served as instruments of remote control. No matter how much autonomy seemed thus to be granted, in an important sense this framework was held together – and, it might be argued, could only be held together – through the colonial linchpin. Major change and conflict were bound to follow once this was pulled out. Friction and change was also likely to emerge in an additional way. The development and maintenance of social divisions as a pecking order tends to be beset with vagaries even under conditions of the most deliberate control. In Ankole, as we have seen, differential access to educational and occupational benefits for Bahima and Bairu, Protestants and Roman Catholics, constituted a key factor shaping a pyramidal socio-political order among these categories. Ankole's chiefly elite had a definite interest in maintaining this pyramid and we have noted some of their efforts to manipulate the access to it. Still, a variety of parallel factors – the dynamics of cash-crop production, the spread of denominational schools as a relatively autonomous process, the expansion of the administrative framework and the resulting need for fresh recruitments, and perhaps above all the intent of emergent groups to try and partake in the system's benefits – in the end would make this control increasingly difficult to maintain. The small numerical proportion of the Bahima elite *vis-à-vis* the Bairu added further to this difficulty, – as also to their eventual eclipse.

These two processes – of colonial withdrawal and increasing socio-economic differentiation – set the scene for the phase of decolonisation and its aftermath with which we will here be concerned. Both became of major significance from the late 1940s onwards, and then increasingly through the 1950s and early 1960s. As of 1947 British colonial policy changed to one of decentralisation, which in Uganda as elsewhere led to the establishment and proliferation of many local, regional and protectorate-wide deliberative and consultative bodies. At the same time the school system and additional training facilities were expanded, partly in anticipation and response to the demands of new roles which came with decentralisation. Other processes of socio-economic change similarly paralleled colonial policies of decentralisation.

But apart from being related as parallel tendencies, or one being seen as preparatory to the other, there was an additional and more immediate 'fit' between the two processes. Decentralisation in Ankole and in other parts of Uganda called for a certain measure of representation – biased and controlled as it may often have been. At the same time the socio-economic divisions which had been developing in Ankole had a definite, though not immediately explicit, political dimension – which 'offered' representation as soon as the occasion arose. Clearly, therefore, council and government membership on the one hand and elite and group differentiation on the other were likely to evolve as two directly and critically related variables, the particular juxtaposition of which would largely determine which status group would at which point maintain or achieve pre-eminence in the political arena. The record of Ankole politics from the late 1940s till roughly 1973 is reflective of this play for power. There are various conceivable ways to describe the period and we shall later consider some of its aspects more closely. Among its major characteristics, however, one quality in particular stood out: that of a pronounced political involvement, commonly referred to as 'politics' in Ankole. 'Politics' was manifested through complex and varying patterns of factionalism, followed widely with keen interest and continued even after, in 1971, the Amin government had declared it 'dead'. But the involvement in 'politics' could hardly be understood in its own terms. Rather, it required understanding of the kind of society which had emerged in Ankole by the middle of the century, following roughly fifty years of colonial rule and a certain crystallisation of the socio-political formations whose genesis we have explored earlier. Quite plainly, the kind of divisions which had grown up did not remain 'static', but soon proved to be specific dynamic forces. Inbuilt friction – between Bairu and Bahima, between religious categories, and between yet differently defined groups – contributed strongly to the trends and pressures for involvement which were expressed in 'politics'. The issues concerned evolved largely around matters of access: access to positions, representation, loans, bursaries, land, ranches, and other benefits. They became all the more salient as it was widely felt that there had been many inequalities of access to start with and as there was an acute perception of the fact that in the initial stages, these inequalities coincided largely with other, visible differences between the categories concerned.

Yet such a focus on political involvement in Ankole during the last few decades, though important, is only a partial way of describing its process of political change. While it is a necessary one in order to grasp reactions against inbuilt inequalities, it does not quite explain the continuous pattern of factional involvement even after various inequalities of access between recognisably different elite groups had tended to become obliterated. Indeed, one important aspect of the process we will be concerned with is the way in which ethnically and religiously based inequalities have tended to be eclipsed, being replaced by less 'ascriptive' disparities. Continued group conflict along ethnic and religious lines nonetheless remained an important factor in this transformation, if only because it provided rationalisations for elite claims to benefits in terms of the earlier pattern of communal discrimination.

To better understand late colonial and subsequent political conflict in Ankole it is also necessary to bear in mind some of the sustaining factors. In common with many other African situations, one key fact was that 'government' – the Ankole district administration and the Uganda government – constituted by far the largest employer. Over time an increasing number of qualified Banyankore found government employment outside Ankole, in Kampala and Entebbe mainly, but even they tended to be locally regarded, and to some extent controlled, within the context of the district's pattern of political cleavages. The role of government as the main provider of employment opportunities entailed an implicit but critical division between those within and those outside the system, which was strongly enhanced by the fact that the income derived from the lowest government jobs was commonly still larger than that of the average peasant-farmer. Naturally, pressure on the part of many individuals and groups to become part of the system, or move up within it, was a constant feature of the period. It is equally plain that whoever commanded some (political) leverage in the system had a ready chance to act as 'gatekeeper' – a role which tied in directly with the pattern of group politics. If there was often an irregular quality attached to its exercise, it should be realised that this role was an almost inevitable product of a system in which a monopoly of scarce but widely desired resources lay within government. The frictions emanating from these 'gatekeeping' functions were severe and had a spillover effect into other spheres: as the promotion of job seekers was generally perceived to take place in direct rivalry between different quarters, almost any such act constituted a further move in the local politics.

While efforts to seek upward mobility – into government – were exerted throughout the period, absolute and relative chances of success varied over time. These variations, too, had a bearing on the nature and style of political involvement and should be kept in mind when trying to understand the process. Until the late 1940s and early 1950s Ankole's government establishment did not expand far beyond its original size. Attention was then focused on a handful of key posts, mainly the senior chieftainships and the central administrative posts at the district's headquarters.[1] Dissatisfaction about their distribution was profound, however, as there were glaring discrepancies in terms of ethnic and religious 'representation' – a product and reflection of the socio-political pecking order we have discussed earlier. Through the 1950s, the effects of protest and a concurrent expansion of the political-administrative framework tended to mitigate some of these disparities, though by no means for all the groups concerned. For a while, there nonetheless seemed to be more room than there used to be, and in specific instances even a lack of suitable candidates. During this time the school system, greatly expanded, produced full steam in anticipation of a continued widening of demands. As employment chances tended throughout to be of considerable relevance to the fortunes of politics, and *vice versa,* it is no wonder that in the late 1950s and early 1960s a climate of expanding opportunities should have coincided with a sense of euphoria about the political game in Ankole. While there was a rush for rewards, it was not altogether understood to be a zero-sum game.

As the room was being filled up, however, pressure became more intense and bitter. The system, reaching its outer limits as an administrative framework, began to show signs of top-heaviness and its expansion was slowing to a halt. With many more prospective entrants seeking government employment, fresh frustrations tended to pervade the ranks. The styles of political conflict appeared to change accordingly. Initially, during 'nationalism' and early independence, competition between rival factions had had a certain sportive quality: it might be acted out in devastating speechmaking against an opponent, the interception and display of compromising information, or the employment of one of many techniques at election fraud, – all of which were followed with humour and interest by many people. As the 1960s progressed, however, the forms of contestation became more covert, more capricious, and more dangerous. The central government of Uganda became increasingly involved in district politics and local actions were often perceived as a threat to the center. During the late 1960s outpacing opponents at elections and recruitment made place for the hazards of prison terms – whenever X intimated that Y was a threat to the government. In more recent years even this route has tended to be cut short; with another center, hints of threats have been instantly acted upon by soldiers.

Thus, if we try to come to grips with the essence of change in Ankole politics over the past few decades, we can emphasise various dimensions which seem by and large convergent. One has been a sense of unfolding grievance and protest, with the salient cleavages of one period tending to become eclipsed, superseded and partly incorporated by those of the next. Closely related was another, namely the tendency for the pattern of socio-political stratification to change from one that stressed ethnic and religious affiliations to one that increasingly included other bases of political and economic power. In terms of the framework as such, the pattern was one that moved from a full-fledged colonial administration, centralised and hierarchical, to a more decentralised set-up with substantial local discretions, and back to a new pattern of centralisation and authoritarianism. A significant aspect of the move to decentralisation was the fact that the administrative framework was left by and large unchanged while a political hierarchy was placed on top of it. If these new political-administrative relationships did not work out, one thing they did was help inaugurate the breakdown of the socio-political formations created during colonial times. Again, once the linchpin was pulled out, there was hardly a way of recreating the original order – a point which seems to be often overlooked by contemporary centralists.

Thus, with a slight paraphrase of some recent literature, an account of the play for power in Ankole politics over the last few decades tends to be concerned with the breakdown of the colonial order. If the episode is unended in Ankole, it is bound to remain incomplete due to other than the process' own determinants. Not only did the Ankole district cease existence as an administrative unit and a political arena as a result of the Amin government's administrative restructuring in the country as a whole, but all key positions and virtually all office-holders, chiefs and others, have been replaced through army-supervised 'elections'. Moreover, the play for power in Ankole remained 'unended' in yet another sense. During one of Uganda's subsequent moments of drama – the Obote invasion from Tanzania for which Ankole provided the scene – many of the major protagonists in the Ankole political arena of the 1950s and 1960s were killed at the hands of army personnel.

In the next few sections we will be concerned with some of the major processes and transformations which have occurred in Ankole during this period. We shall first consider the development of protest against the ethnically restricted elite stratum which had been characteristic of Ankole during colonial times. Following this, we will discuss the articulation of land interests as a specific determinant of changing patterns of social stratification and then reconsider the dynamics of recent factionalism in terms of the pattern of social cleavages. Finally, we shall again be concerned with the institution of kingship and analyse how continued patterns of socio-political transformation have contributed to its decline and eventual eclipse.

THE KUMANYANA MOVEMENT

The determinants of ethnic protest in Ankole were largely embedded in the socio-political order which had been built up during the first half of the century. Just as inequality had been defined mainly in ethnic terms, so protest was expressed along correspondingly salient, ethnic lines. From roughly the end of the second world war onwards, increasing numbers of Bairu began to challenge the premises of hierarchy and subordination that underlined the Ankole structure. During the 1950s in particular Bairu protest against Bahima overrule culminated in a movement which became known as *Kumanyana* ('to get to know each other').

In a general sense, protest in Ankole should be considered a step towards, or an aspect of, the breakdown of the colonial order.[2] More particularly, this protest was an attempt to redress the inequalities which Bairu experienced in their society. As we have seen, these inequalities lay in the distribution of power; in access to the political center for the allocation of benefits; in wealth and welfare; and in dignity and social status. Hence, protest was in principle concerned with redefining the political framework and changing the distribution of power, with enlarging social and economic opportunities, and with a search for and assertion of new dignity and social identity. In the actual course of affairs, however, these objectives were to a large extent fused, just as the command of power, wealth and status had tended to be merged. Economic and social transitions provided a strong impetus to the formulation of protest against inequality. By the middle of the century, incomes rose among wider categories of Bairu than heretofore. As a result some began to share in social advantages previously concentrated among the Bahima elite. Rising material welfare, increased access to education, and the transmission of liberal-egalitarian values thus militated increasingly against continued acceptance of social and political inequality. Although the actual incidence of discriminatory practices did decline in Ankole, this did not necessarily mean a decline in indignation over remaining, as well as remembered, inequalities. To the contrary, development in the economic and social fields stimulated a heightened self-awareness and a desire for general, and especially political, equality among militant Bairu. The Kumanyana movement was an expression of these sentiments and, from the outset, its protest accordingly had strong emancipatory characteristics.

One plain but key factor which gave direction to the course of protest in Ankole was that Bairu and Bahima laid claims to the same territory. Of equal importance was that the Bahima elite constituted only a small proportion of the Ankole population, as contrasted to much stronger elite positions in other situations, e.g. pre-revolution Rwanda or Burundi. Together, these conditions induced the Kumanyana movement to press consistently for the inclusion of Bairu into the Ankole political elite – to them the most strategic and most obvious way of attending equality. In addition, there were other significant characteristics. Throughout, the Kumanyana movement sought its objectives by continuous and steady pressure for integration, rather than through a revolutionary bid for power. Moreover, the involvement in Kumanyana, far from approaching a mass movement, remained by and large restricted to the level of notables – a quality which in time would provide continuity with the pattern of factional politics. Finally, as opposed to situations in which there is a more exclusive preoccupation with political concerns, Kumanyana was stimulated to promote Bairu interests along a much wider range of fronts.

Thus among the conditioning factors which induced Bairu demands for absorption into Ankole's political elite were the particular structure of the ethnic cleavage and the proportions of the dominating and subordinate strata. In a sense, Ankole's ethnic structure directed Bairu towards some form of participation within the established framework because Bairu and Bahima had come to constitute two horizontal social layers within the district. Hence there was no territory but Ankole – and none but the whole of Ankole – which the Bairu would consider their own. As a result, opting out of the system was no real alternative. Meanwhile, the fact that the Bairu formed the vast majority of the population also fostered a certain confidence among them that political equality could be achieved in the process of constitutional transitions. Moreover, notwithstanding the differences in their customs, there were important cultural links between the Bairu and Bahima: they basically shared the same language and many traditions and had for many years coexisted within the area. Together, these factors strengthened Bairu allegiances to Ankole as a political unit, though these allegiances did not necessarily reflect an affection for the regime, nor for the political community.

There were also other aspects of the composition and position of the Bairu population which appear to have induced gradual but sustained pressure as a strategy, namely the religious division among the Bairu and the physical proximity of at least part of them to the Bahima ruling elite. The cleavage between Protestants and Catholics weakened the numbers and influence of the Bairu and introduced an element of competition among them which tended to prolong the influence of the Bahima elite. Moreover, possibilities for the development of radical programs among any one of the Bairu groups were diminished by the fact that the two religious groups lived side by side, though in varying proportions, over most of Ankole. This reduced their homogeneity and diminished the ease with which the two sections could be mobilised. Of even greater importance was the fact that Bahima and Bairu lived together in some of the areas where grievances were most articulate and where protest eventually originated – notably in Shema county. The physical proximity of the Bahima as well as their political and economic influence imposed a considerable constraint on Bairu activities. The vulnerability of those Bairu who challenged the regime thus induced cautious and secret strategems which were not to be given up until the Bairu had achieved a substantial amount of influence in the government of Ankole.

Some other related factors were of more direct influence in causing Bairu protest to take the form of continuous pressure for participation. One was that the Ankole ruling class tended to be generally accommodating to pressure for Bairu integration. This was in large measure due to the numerical weakness of the Bahima, as well as to the fact, as has been mentioned, that they were gradually losing their educational and economic advantages over the Bairu. Bairu demands for governmental positions and other benefits thus were accommodated in a piecemeal fashion since the late 1940s.[3] Although these accommodations did not prevent Kumanyana's emergence, they did cause the movement to be less revolutionary, and become less of a mass movement, than it might have been in the absence of any concessions.

Finally, the specific application of constitutional changes in Ankole should again be considered. New constitutional frameworks had gradually widened Bairu political representation in the 1950s and perhaps indirectly caused Bairu protest to remain relatively limited in scope. In part because of its relative weakness, the Bahima elite was unable to resist the introduction of the 1955 *District Administration Ordinance*, which constituted the most important constitutional change during the 1950s and provided for a widening of Bairu representation on the Eishengyero.[4] Hence, Bairu leadership gradually began to participate in the affairs of government in Ankole and the legitimacy of the regime did not become challenged in any particularly drastic way.

In 1949, a small incident touched off protest. A Mwiru, Z. C. K. Mungonya, had, under British sponsorship, been appointed Enganzi.[5] Four Bahima students at Mbarara High School, believed to have been instigated by influential elders, wrote a letter to the Omugabe, protesting against this encroachment upon positions to which, as Bahima, they considered themselves entitled. Even though its various provisions had long since been disregarded, they based their position on the Ankole Agreement of 1901, which had given the principal chiefs the right to nominate their own successors. The letter was intercepted and circulated by Bairu. Its effect was to crystallise latent antagonisms into concrete alignments, both among the Bairu and the Bahima. It was at that moment that the Bairu protest movement which was eventually to be known as Kumanyana emerged.

The situation following the 1949 incident differed from earlier protests because the expression of Bairu discontent was far more explicit in 1949 than it had been in the past and because the sense of grievance and indignation was shared by more Bairu than ever before. This is of course not to say that there had been no antecedents in the Bairu movement. In fact, the earliest organised expression of Bairu aspirations goes back to the Church Missionary Society Association Club of the 1930s. Under this name, selected to minimise vulnerability, a handful of educated Bairu had met to discuss matters of common concern. One of the most important matters so discussed was to remain a continuing, indeed major, theme of protest: that appointment to public service should be on merit.

Although the Club's direct influence was minimal, it was nevertheless significant as an early discussion ground for an incipient Bairu elite and because it stimulated reflection on discrepancies in Ankole's political structure. One should also mention the fact that in 1940 the Bairu students at Mbarara High School had organised themselves into an association named *Obutsya Ni Birwa* (after a Kinyankore proverb meaning 'The daughter will equal her mother'). They had done so in answer to an organization founded by the Bahima students, called *Kamwe Kamwe* ('One by One', an abbreviation of a proverb meaning 'One by one together makes a bundle'). After this, regular meetings among small numbers of Bairu leaders, of Bairu 'old boys' of Mbarara High School, as well as of student organisations at the school itself, had continued discussions of the position of Bairu in Ankole society.

By 1949, however, circumstances were quite different. In that year, a new *African Local Government Ordinance* had been issued which was designed to expand local administrative functions and to allow greater local involvement in local affairs. Although it remained basically an advisory body, the Ankole Eishengyero was enlarged to include more official and unofficial members, and expectations were fostered that the Bairu would be allowed steadily widening participation in local government. That the Bairu believed that the Protectorate had come to support their political advancement was clear from their pleas during the next years addressed to the District Commissioner, the Governor, and British Members of Parliament and designed to promote their participation in the local government. They also had reason to believe, however, that the Bahima ruling class did not favour such changes. And indeed the Bahima retained a substantial influence on the recruitment of personnel for local government.

Against this background, education became increasingly important. While since early in the century the Mbarara High School had been the main training ground of Ankole's elite, by the 1940s the high school had become more and more mixed in make-up. As its graduates normally took the positions of leadership, the question whether educational qualifications would be allowed to supersede ethnic criteria as the principal consideration for admission into government service became very critical. The dilemma was especially acute because the administrative positions constituting the Ankole establishment were limited in number and, at the time at least, did not seem likely to be expanded to a significant extent.[6] If Bairu were really to have equal opportunities, a major change would have to take place. And this did not seem likely. Increasingly the Bairu became convinced that the Bahima were determined to change the direction of Bairu advancement. Suspicion grew.

Thus, in the climate of expectations which had come to exist in Ankole in 1949, a minor incident such as the students' letter had consequences which would have been inconceivable in an earlier period: protest and the start of a Bairu organisation. Significantly, the chain reaction that this event produced was closely linked with past events. Thus, when protest was articulated, it was often in terms of a reinterpretation of the historical relationship between the Bairu and the Bahima in the light of what the Bairu increasingly saw as unjust Bahima domination. Indeed, discontent about a wide variety of matters became more consciously linked than before and social grievances, whether based in reality or history, fact or fiction, were more fully explained in terms of Bahima supremacy. In the course of protest each and every advantage given to the Bahima when British authority began became an object of Bairu discontent. The disproportionate allocation of chiefly positions became a focus of Bairu grievances as soon as qualified Bairu were available to occupy such ranks. Indeed, the creation as well as the activities of the Kumanyana movement in the 1950s was to a large extent stimulated precisely by discrimination in this sphere. In addition, the tax and labour contributions which were demanded from Bairu were often felt to be excessively burdensome and frequent transgressions of authority by Bahima chiefs in these matters increased the feelings of discrimination among the Bairu.[7] A sense of injustice was also prompted by the fact that the non-chiefly, pastoral Bahima, who were generally wealthier than the Bairu, were usually not only excluded from labour duties but were able to avoid taxation over a long period. As late as 1967, these facts were mentioned by Bairu as grievances against Bahima chiefs. The distribution of mailo land holdings also became an irritant to the Bairu. As we shall see later, this was because of the preference given to Bahima, as well as for other reasons.

When protest finally emerged, however, it originated mainly among the Protestant Bairu, Kumanyana therefore being principally a Protestant movement. Basically, the Protestant Bairu appeared more alert to the differences which separated them from the Bahima elite than were the Roman Catholics. Paradoxically, this seems to have resulted largely from the social advantages which the Protestant Bairu had over the Roman Catholics, as well as from their closer contacts with the Bahima. We have noted the importance of the Protestant complexion of Ankole's ruling elite since 1900 and the relatively better chances of employment it gave to Protestant Bairu than to Roman Catholics. Indeed, throughout the present century not only the senior chieftainships but also most key posts at Kamukuzi were held by Protestants. Perhaps the most notable exception to this has been the county chieftainship of Bunyaruguru, which was held by Roman Catholics for various prolonged periods.

About 1955, at the time of the survey on which *East African Chiefs* was based, the religious distribution among chiefs of all ranks was as shown on the following page.[8] This table comprises Protestant Bahima as well as Bairu. Nonetheless, it clearly demonstrates that the percentage of Protestant chiefs was highest at the most senior level and declined along descending scales of the hierarchy of chiefs. Roman Catholics, on the other hand, had a proportionally higher representation in the lower ranks than they had at the top level. However, even at the lower level they did not have a majority, nor, for that matter, a percentage commensurate with their numbers among the population at large. One thing these figures indicate, therefore, is the strikingly peripheral position which Roman Catholics occupied in the Ankole

	County chiefs	Sub-county chiefs	Parish chiefs	Paid head-men	Unpaid head-men	Total of chiefs
Protestants	87.5%	86%	77.4%	55.5%	29.6%	63.5%
Roman Catholics	12.5%	14%	22.6%	36.7%	38.8%	20.5%
Muslim	–	–	–	4.4%	–	1.1%
Pagan	–	–	–	5.9%	31.6%	7.5%
Actual totals	8	50	75	68	54	255

political-administrative system.

The factors which differentiated the Protestant Bairu from the Roman Catholics had been most pronounced in the centrally located counties of Ankole, where a majority of the Protestants lived. Physical proximity to the center enabled them to keep more easily in touch with developments in public matters and facilitated the marketing of the cash crops that they had begun to cultivate. Indeed, the introduction of coffee in the 1930s stimulated a rise of incomes, especially in the counties of Shema and Igara, as well as in parts of Rwampara. In turn, this rise provided a financial basis for increasing school attendance which helped to develop new skills and formal qualifications. Shema and Igara especially have competed, for many years, in claiming the largest numbers of graduates at various levels. Eventually, a majority of the leaders of the Kumanyana movement who entered the scene in the 1940s and thereafter were also from Shema and Igara; most of them in fact attended the same primary school – that of the Native Anglican Church at Kabwohe in Shema.

Thus, it was the Protestant Bairu, and not the Roman Catholics, who reacted against Bahima domination, precisely because their relatively greater opportunities, their economic welfare, and their educational attainments gave them stronger incentives and better means to strive for further social advancement. Moreover, their closer contacts with the Bahima made them more sensitive to the advantages given to their Bahima schoolmates, fellow church members, and government colleagues than were the Roman Catholics, who had least in common with the Bahima. In addition, since the majority of

Protestant Bairu were concentrated in the central areas, they experienced more directly some of the negative aspects of Bahima supremacy, such as the relationships between mailo landlords and tenants. As greater numbers of them reached higher levels of economic and educational achievement, such instances of Bahima privilege became increasingly exasperating. For these reasons, it became more and more evident that the fringe benefits granted to Protestant Bairu had laid only a fragile bridge, not a firm basis for concurrence between the two Protestant groups. Although the Protestant Bairu had become the most favoured of the underprivileged stratum in Ankole, their pressure for greater participation ultimately led to an attack on the principle of Bahima rule.

Notwithstanding the depth of animosity which increasingly came to characterize Bairu-Bahima relationships, ethnic conflict in Ankole did not lead to open confrontation. Indeed, in striking contrast to the developments in nearby Rwanda, or to the violent clashes resulting from ethnic antagonism elsewhere in Africa, the tension between Bairu and Bahima has throughout remained singularly devoid of spectacular events.[9] This absence of landmarks was not unrelated to the basically accommodationist quality of protest in Ankole. In fact, there appears to have been a fairly general conviction that incidents were to be avoided because they would serve no strategic purpose. This point is perhaps borne out most clearly by the role which the Kumanyana movement chose to play.

Generally, the Kumanyana movement opted for indirect strategies rather than for any open onslaughts on what it considered to be the wrongs of Ankole society. Throughout the 1950s when Kumanyana was actively engaged in the assertion of Bairu interests, it certainly sought to remain as inconspicuous as possible. Its members did not stage demonstrations or become engaged in fights; nor were reputations established or enhanced by prison terms. Perhaps most significant, the Kumanyana movement never initiated a large-scale mobilisation of the peasant masses. Through preliminary meetings, the movement tried to influence votes in the Eishengyero, the Ankole Public Service Commission, or other official bodies; it definitely did not put itself up as a bargaining group. On occasion, it would call upon its members to submit protests and petitions to Ugandan and British authorities if the situation demanded; again, however, these people were expected to do so as individuals and not in the name of the Bairu or of the Kumanyana movement. One reason for this circuitous approach was, no doubt, that Kumanyana was for a long time of necessity an underground movement. Challenging Bahima supremacy amounted to questioning the officially sanctioned ethnic hierarchy and could easily have invoked retaliation. In this regard, it was of no small significance that many who were in Kumanyana's vanguard occupied, and depended economically on, government positions. This made them particularly vulnerable to sanctions and caused them to refrain from bringing their actions into the open.

Other factors, however, tended to lead in the same direction. One of them lay in the paradoxical fact that, notwithstanding the pervasive nature of Bahima domination in the Ankole political and social framework, there was no legal or other concrete basis of recognition for this hegemony. Despite the long prevalence of ethnic co-optation in the Ankole government service, the formal structure of government designed by the British was supposedly neutral, and recruitment theoretically took place on consideration of merit alone; even the signatories to the Ankole Agreement of 1901 had been recognised in their individual capacity rather than as Bahima. Thus, the Kumanyana movement, whose very existence was rooted in the problem of Bahima domination, might well have found itself at a loss if it had been required to point to any explicit code or procedure as evidence of a willfully maintained Bahima supremacy. Given this lack of 'proof,' discontent could not easily be displayed as openly as it might have been with a more clear cut cause. (Hence, too, the rather disproportionate importance attached to a minor but a least tangible piece of evidence, such as the 1949 letter.) In addition, however, no Bairu movement could afford openly to propagate the doctrine of Bairu ascendancy if it did not want to lay itself open to accusations of ethnic partiality similar to that of which it was accusing the Bahima. If they did not want to weaken their argument, the Bairu could, at least publicly, only justifiably stress broad egalitarian principles and the need for merit and qualifications as criteria of recruitment. Underground, far more particularistic, and at times petty interests were nonetheless expressed.

Kumanyana's organization was in keeping with its strategies. Basically, it was a loose assemblage of Bairu leaders, without formally designated officeholders or any other explicit framework. There was clear consensus, however, as to which individuals exercised overall leadership in the movement. Kumanyana's underground quality was perhaps best revealed by the fact that for a long time contact was maintained by secret gatherings, usually irregularly called by person-to-person communication to confront immediate issues. In a very real sense, Kumanyana *was* these meetings, and vice versa. Indeed, the term 'Kumanyana' itself has connotations of fellowship, to 'get to know one another'. Never were more than about seventy people present at any of the meetings, but large sections of the Bairu population were nonetheless effectively kept in touch with what evolved. The most important convocations were usually held in or near Mbarara. The participants in these meetings served as links with various areas of Ankole and subgroups of Bairu as they communicated the results of the discussions to meetings which might subsequently be held in the counties. To reach wider groups, at the latter meetings individuals were often assigned to contact Bairu in various corners of the counties. This was frequently done after Protestant church services, which was one reason why a strong parallel emerged between Kumanyana's network and that of the Native Anglican Church. Once relationships had been established with parish congregations, such groups were asked to send delegates to future meetings at the next higher level.

Kumanyana's leadership consisted mostly of relatively educated Bairu. In addition, its leaders were men who had already achieved a certain prominence. Most of the key figures held positions of some significance in Ankole, and these were generally the highest that had been attained by Bairu. Conversely, virtually all Bairu who later held high-ranking offices were at one time engaged in the Kumanyana movement. The central personality in the movement was Kesi Nganwa, supervisor of the Native Anglican schools in Ankole. Nganwa was sometimes called Ruterengwa ('Nothing compares with him in stature'), a name which was objected to by royalist circles because it implied superiority over the king. Another prominent figure was C.B. Katiti, one of the first members of the Uganda Legislative Council and later a Uganda cabinet minister. Katiti was one of the people who would establish a relationship between party politics and the movement. Many of the leading participants were teachers, the one profession in which Bairu had been able to fill the great majority of positions. In addition, there were clerks, traders, medical assistants, farmers, some chiefs who disregarded the ban on political activities, and several Protestant clergymen. The latter had a particularly strong incentive to become involved since the hierarchy of the Anglican church in Ankole, like that of the government, was dominated by Bahima. With dramatic sermons and references to Christian doctrine, they contributed greatly to the spiritual basis of the movement. Although Kumanyana was basically a Protestant group, a few Roman Catholics remained regular members over the years. Most participants, at any rate those in the central and county level gatherings, were notables in their areas and had considerable influence over local opinion. A number sat in the Eishengyero and were thus in a position directly to represent Bairu interests as formulated at the Kumanyana meetings, as well as to influence fellow councillors. After 1955, when Bairu influence in the Ankole government was substantially increased, Kumanyana's political role became largely that of a shadow parliament, in which alternative policies were sounded out before they were officially launched and from which an important source of support emanated for the Bairu leadership, whose position in the government remained precarious.

Not the least compelling of the movement's objectives was to instill a greater sense of self-confidence among Bairu generally. One of the most important driving forces of the Kumanyana movement was undoubtedly the resentment, especially among educated Bairu, of continuing attitudes of superiority and arrogance of the Bahima. This prompted the movement's assertion of equality of status and dignity in many areas of life, and greatly strengthened the impetus of the movement's activities in the political and economic spheres. A perception of the relationship between social welfare and political influence was evidenced in Kumanyana's preoccupation with the educational progress of the Bairu. Because it was realised that the future position of the Bairu depended largely on the attainments of the student generation, Kumanyana exerted much pressure on the allocation of bursaries and itself maintained a small relief fund which was largely used to pay the school fees of needy children. It also encouraged parents to build schools in remote areas which did not have educational facilities. Similarly, its supporters campaigned for the erection of more hygienic and permanent houses, for the adoption of more productive methods of cultivation, and generally tried to awaken the people to the idea of higher standards of living. Kumanyana was of no less importance in articulating the grievances of mailo tenants and it played an active part in stimulating, without official sanction, resettlement from the densely populated counties of Shema and Igara to Kashari. It also was a strong promoter of the establishment and growth of many co-operative societies. Lastly, it was in several counties instrumental in the creation of local welfare societies which addressed themselves to the needs of the Bairu. Basic to all this activity was an urge to demonstrate that the Bairu were capable of attaining increasing economic and social prosperity. As they had felt subordinated and regarded as inferior, there was a compulsion to assert their equality with the Bahima and to imprint this same notion upon much larger numbers of Bairu. Kumanyana was at once exponent, symbol, and radiator of these sentiments.

Notwithstanding its wide range of involvements, the most critical goals of Kumanyana remained in the political realm. The movement was particularly concerned with trying to increase and strengthen Bairu representation in the Ankole Eishengyero and in the corridors of the Ankole government. In a closely related way, the movement also sought to influence the appointment as well as the transfer of chiefs and other public servants. After the initial stimulus of 1949 and subsequent skirmishes in 1952-53, peak times in its fluctuating role as a political pressure group were reached whenever major choices were imminent – such as in 1955, at the nomination of the second Mwiru Enganzi, and again around 1958 when a growing entente between Protestant Bahima and Roman Catholic Bairu created an entirely new political situation. The 1955 crisis was decisive for much more than the selection of an Enganzi alone. The Bahima group, including the Omugabe, were determined to have a Muhima county chief who had a rather unfavourable reputation among Bairu. Under the then existing constitutional procedure, laid down in the 1949 *African Local Government Ordinance,* the Enganzi would be appointed in agreement between the Omugabe, the incumbent Enganzi, and the District Commissioner. Kumanyana mobilised fierce opposition to the proposed nomination, and a deadlock ensued which was solved only by altering the constitutional framework of the Ankole administration. Protectorate officials speeded up the process by which Ankole, as the first district, could come under the regulations of the *District Administration (District Councils) Ordinance* which was being prepared in 1955. This ordinance considerably broadened the area of jurisdiction of the local government; expanded the Eishengyero by enlarging the number of directly elected members; and provided for an Enganzi elected by the Eishengyero. As a result, the Bairu henceforth obtained a substantially increased influence in the Eishengyero, and Kesi Nganwa, the man who had emerged as the leader of Kumanyana, was elected Engazi.

Once this was achieved, however, Kumanyana's political role began to change markedly. One result was an increase, rather than a decrease, in the number of its meetings and the size of its following. Another was that, during the following years, the focus for the movement's political action became increasingly narrowed to securing positions for its more active supporters who, as it was locally expressed, 'had killed the animal and wanted to eat it'. Their desire to be rewarded with sinecures was, however, thwarted by two conditions. One of these was that the tenure of most posts held by Bahima was protected by civil service regulations; the other was that Roman Catholic Bairu expressed an increasing interest in having a share in the benefits. Roman Catholic Bairu had begun to constitute a third political force in Ankole and by the mid-1950s they had been attracted to Catholic Action and other lay organisations. Through the working of electoral mechanisms they obtained a substantial representation in the Eishengyero. In 1955, they considered it in their best interests to support the Protestant Bairu in the Nganwa election, thus bringing about a complete Bairu alignment against the Bahima. They became disenchanted, however, when they felt that the Protestant Bairu were gaining most of the advantages for the achievement of which they had given their support. Protestants, on the other hand, considered that they had borne the brunt of the struggle for Bairu advancement, that they had more qualified people available to take positions, and that there was thus a stronger justification for distributing chieftainships and other posts among themselves than among the Roman Catholics.[10]

As a result, the initial alignment between Protestant and Roman Catholic Bairu was followed by a widening estrangement between the two groups. Kumanyana, which had originated as an expression of protest against conditions affecting all Bairu, played an increasingly partisan role in matters of appointment, and since the spoils were limited by the protection of tenure, its pressure to gain appointments for its own group became more intense. Whereas in a different context the Kumanyana movement might have unified all Bairu, it now grew into one of the factions dividing them.

Clearly, therefore, the nature of the Kumanyana movement changed considerably over time. As an emancipatory movement, building solidarity and self-esteem, it played a significant role in the transformation of Ankole society. Though originated and carried forward mainly by Protestants, in its earlier stages it could with some justice purport to speak for all Bairu. At one time it did indeed represent most Bairu, Catholics as well as Protestants, but when disagreements developed over the distribution of rewards, it shrank back to its basis consisting of the most militant Protestant Bairu. After its earlier concern over the need for improvement in standards of living, the successors of Kumanyana increasingly engaged on basically 'equal' terms in Ankole factional politics.

LAND INTERESTS AND POLITICAL CONFLICT

As we have seen at various points, protest in Ankole was by no means solely concerned with representational matters. While questions as to which individuals held which positions for a long time commanded considerable attention, grievances were also articulated about the way in which other privileges and benefits were distributed in Ankole society. One major area in which discrepancies were increasingly experienced as unjust was that of land allocation. We have seen how the policy of allocation of mailo lands during the early colonial period bolstered the position of the chiefly Bahima elite and had the effect of reducing the Bairu peasants who cultivated on these lands to a directly subordinate position. Inevitably, a sense of grievance about these arrangements contributed to Bairu protest and tended to be shared by far wider categories than those immediately affected.

If a discussion of land issues will thus help to understand some of the underlying dynamics of protest, there are also additional grounds for a focus on these matters. One is that questions of development in most African societies – certainly also in Ankole – will continue to be primarily concerned with agricultural development, and that therefore the particular modes of land distribution and ownership which have been adopted are of basic significance in appreciating the nature of socio-economic divisions which are presently evolving. Specifically, in the case of Ankole, we may derive a better understanding of changing patterns of stratification from a focus on land tenure arrangements. Whereas the fortunes of political factionalism have tended to change at relatively short intervals in Ankole, patterns of land acquisition over the past few decades have been more continuous and provide a significant background to these conflicts. Land issues, indeed, constitute an important link in understanding socio-political transitions in Ankole society.

Today, a rather serious land problem appears to be developing in Ankole. Land is increasingly being acquired for commercial and speculative purposes; access to land for the majority of Banyankore becomes problematic. Recently, an unexpected witness called attention to the issue in the following terms:

'On the land problem in Ankole, [President Amin] urged those land owners who bought a lot of land in the past not to evict tenants at very short notice. To ask, he said, someone who has been living on your land for 20 or 60 years to leave at short notice is not human. How would you feel, he asked, if you were the one asked to leave?'[11]

To appreciate both the protests and the interests that have been aroused by land policies during the colonial regime, we will be concerned in this section with the effects of two examples of land acquisitions in Ankole, the mailo grants and the individual freehold titles which were introduced in the late 1950s. These policies have not been the only ones governing land tenure in Ankole. Nonetheless both have clearly contributed to nascent problems, if only through their general inducement of interests in land as a commodity.

By way of background, some preliminary notes on patterns of land use and acquisition in Ankole will be useful. Generally, access to land over the past half century or more might either be called simple or complex, depending on how one looks at it and what one looks for. Avenues of land acquisition have tended to be relatively unproblematic for most of the people during most of the time. Pre-1900 there were mainly two ways in which a man could get access to a piece of land, i.e. by inheritance or by opening up a new plot.[12] The latter involved the need for consent of the local people and chief, which does not seem to have been particularly difficult to obtain. Today, in the 1970s, there are three main ways of access to land. Again inheritance and opening up new land (though the latter possibility is rapidly coming to a close) and in addition, purchase, either of land held under customary tenure or freehold (mailo or 'individual'). Land is nowadays purchased either for cultivation or for purposes of investment, speculation and prestige. The latter rationale has become increasingly popular in recent years. One of the things 'to do' for members of the Ankole elite or aspirants to it is to buy a piece of land in the vicinity of Mbarara. In other areas land is also acquired and often involves quite sizeable portions, with examples of up to several square miles.[13] Among other things this trend suggests a shift from investment in cattle as the traditional embodiment of wealth to one in land.

If both for pre-1900 and post-1970 Ankole the picture of access to land is relatively straightforward, it is more difficult to ascertain the basis and mechanisms of ownership (as opposed to acquisition). Puzzles about 'ownership' have appeared to be due partly to complexity of arrangements, to confusion in terminology, and to interests aroused in ownership. These three sources have reinforced each other in no small degree. Complexity of 'ownership' is suggested by the fact that at least at four different intervals, in 1906, 1926, 1961 and 1965, official enquiries were conducted to clarify the system of land tenure in Ankole. Without going into details, one may further note that in either period a variety of different kinds of rights were exercised in land in Ankole, thus suggesting a degree of 'real' complexity.[14] Today, ownership questions would definitely also yield diversified answers, including notions of customary tenure, individual freehold, mailo freehold (until recently official and private), leasehold and simply government land. Without detailing these forms here, it should be noted that the exact status of any particular piece of land has not always been immediately clear by reference to any of these descriptive terms; cryptically 'ownership' may well at times clash with 'ownership'.[15]

More pertinent is the fact that complexity and confusion have spiralled following new interests. This is not a novel phenomenon, but it has been basic to the kind of land issues which developed in Ankole. As we have seen earlier, the pursuit of interests has in part been made possible by taking advantage of terminological confusions about land rights.[16] This strategy did not easily subside; even at the time of issuing the first new freehold titles, in the late 1950s opposition to the scheme was in part based on the contention that all land belonged to the Omugabe and thus could not be 'alienated'.

More generally, one significant difference immediately suggested by a pre-1900 and post-1970 comparison is the commercialisation of land as a factor of production. No matter what mechanisms were used or what was the legal basis of acquired plots (mailo, freehold, customary tenure or even lease-hold), increasing frequency of sales and rents indicate a basic fact that land has acquired a new economic value, expressed in money terms. That fact would require its own explanation, for the general process of which one will need to turn to an examination of how capitalism has pervaded this rural part of Africa. But while certain policies (mailo, individual freehold) have added to this trend or provided an alternative route towards commercialisation, much of Ankole nonetheless continued to provide an example of how relatively capital-intensive cash-crop production (coffee and tea especially) could be undertaken without there being any prior 'security' of tenure of the kind provided by a freehold land title.[17] That contrast in turn suggests that if new economically-based interests can be seen to be aroused in land following certain policy innovations, such interests may not primarily be for cultivating purposes but rather in land as a commodity, hence arising from 'extra-agricultural' objectives.

Turning now first to the mailo arrangements, their effects have been almost exclusively in other than agricultural domains. We have already seen some of the immediate social, political and administrative repercussions of this system, which basically aimed at the creation of a landed class in Ankole.[18] Again, this policy was meant to provide support to the exercise of colonial rule through the stake in the system which its beneficiaries were expected to develop. A citation from another context suggests that the strategy as applied in Uganda was no novelty of British colonial policy: 'If security was wanting against extensive popular tumult or revolution, I should say that the Permanent Settlement . . . . has this great advantage at least, of having created a vast body of rich, landed proprietors deeply interested in the continuance of the British Dominion and having complete command over the mass of the people.'[19] Repeated a hundred years later on a much smaller scale in Ankole, there was at least this difference from the intended effect that the policy aroused, rather than assuaged, popular unrest.

Over time the list of tenant grievances with the mailo system became a long one and included such varied items as the demand to vote for the landlord's party, the destruction of their crops due to the landlord's cattle running through their fields (at times, it was claimed, on purpose), the extra rent demanded from shopkeepers operating on the mailo, and the landlords' practise of settling disputes in their own 'courts', in addition to the basic issues of rent, tribute, labour, property restrictions, evictions and compensations discussed earlier. Over and above individual inconveniences and hardships the mailo system had adverse economic and political consequences for the district as a whole. Economically the system's negative effects have been beyond question. Restrictions of many kinds prevented tenants from making lasting improvements to their plots and from reinvesting towards increased production. Involving some 20,000 tenants at the end of the 1960s, this category would have been able to contribute more fully to the district's development if they had not been incorporated into the mailo system.

From time to time new regulations were introduced that were intended to strengthen the position of the tenant, mainly by restricting his obligations to his landlord to rent only and by putting checks on the landlord's right of eviction. A variety of these new rules were codified in the *Ankole Landlord and Tenant Law* of 1937. While this constituted an improvement on the books, it did not alter the basic dependency relationship nor the contrast to non-mailo peasants. It should be realised that it first required a good deal of evidence of the exercise of powers by the landlords before ameliorative legislation was undertaken and that it further required a fair amount of time before the implications of the new rules would be appreciated by both landlords and tenants. As it happened the *Ankole Landlord and Tenant Law* was not published until 1957, which did not seem conducive to creating this clarity.[20] That it was not can be gathered from the fact that the recommendations of a commission appointed in 1965 by the Ankole Goverment to enquire into the question of mailo lands included the need for abolition of tenants' tribute and labour, the prohibition of arbitrary evictions and the requirements of proper compensation for the tenants' property.

Politically the system gave rise to a sense of insecurity and grievance which tended to be shared by people who themselves were not immediately affected. Coupled with the ethnic subordination of which it was both a result and a condition, the mailo system operated as a major factor in sustaining the basic divisions and moving forces of Ankole politics. Protests were picked up and reiterated over the years in the protestant Bairu camp as additional grounds for their grievances against the Bahima. The 1965 enquiry was essentially a product of this sentiment. However, one reason why it did not lead to major changes was the make-up of political divisions within the district's leadership at the time. This leadership did not wish to openly identify itself with the causes of any ethnic or religious section of the population and it consequently adopted a willy-nilly attitude both to the enquiry and to the recommendations.[21]

The Ankole mailo system has thus turned out to be one of those issues whose negative aspects have been outstanding but which are nonetheless extremely hard to undo. Its anomalies were many and stood out even more sharply due to general advancements in the areas within which mailo estates were located, particularly in Shema county. It was nonetheless continued, partly because of the fact that mailo land had been irrevocably issued as private freehold property (and part of which has been alienated by the original owners or their inheritors and has continued to change hands since then) and because general applicability of statutes forbade repealing those which happened to govern the Ankole mailo system. Moreover, political and social conditions militated against change in addition to these legal constraints. As we shall see further, the balance of powers in Ankole district politics, first between Bahima and Catholic Bairu on the one hand and Protestant Bairu on the other, then shifting to a more subtle but no less profound cleavage that also involved a division among the Protestant Bairu, prevented consensus from emerging on issues in which historically one ethnic group, or a section of it, had been the losing party. Socially this position was reinforced by a variety of conditions which might have worked out differently in another constellation. One of those pertains to the question why mailo tenants did not move out to new land where they would not face interference by landlords. Some no doubt have done so. The many others who did not, however, clearly belonged to the category whose limited resources would make such a move extremely difficult to undertake. Not only did they generally have a weaker economic base than other people in the area, but the prospect of receiving none or at best a very minimal compensation for their property was not particularly conducive to their migration.

Another factor that for long perpetuated the dependency relations inherent in the mailo system was the fact that, contrary to what happened to the much larger mailo grants issued in Buganda, mailo land was for a long time sold little in Ankole. Part of the mailo land is still now with the original owners or their successors. Of particular significance was the fact that by and large the Bahima elite who acquired the mailo estates for a long time did not sell it and neither felt induced to turn them into agriculturally productive propositions. In part they lacked these inducements because their major concern was commonly with cattle. Cattle itself required a certain freedom of movement, which was to an extent guaranteed by the rights in mailo land. In addition, and perhaps more basically, the mailo arrangement was a convenient and strategic way of ensuring a domain within which ethnic inequality, and the prestige derivable from it, could be maintained.

The mailo system tends to lose this function with the spread of new economic roles which are no longer based on a syndrome of relationships that involves cattle-ownership on the one hand and landlord-tenant roles on the other. Perhaps this factor already accounts for the fact that exchange of mailo land has become more frequent during the last two decades or so. However, such transfers did little to change the tenants' position in the estates. Despite various waves of protest, this position was maintained by a combination of legal and political obstacles. In recent years, one more such obstacle was added, a major one indeed. As the 1960s progressed and sales of mailo land became more frequent, various leading members of each of Ankole's ethnic and religious political groups began to acquire pieces of mailo land. Leading Bairu of both denominations thus joined the ranks of the estate owners, even if the holdings concerned tended to become increasingly fragmented. In a sense, the trend was one that made for greater equality in the 'ethnic' distribution of the mailo lands. At the same time, however, chances of any effective action being undertaken to reassess the anomalies in the system – which remained – became reduced to virtually nil. This lack of enthusiasm to initiate and implement such corrective measures was an important factor in turning the 1965 inquiry into a non-starter. As a result, grievances endured, but could less and less command an 'ethnic' outlet. Ankole's structure of ethnic inequality was being replaced by other inequalities.

The land title scheme was a second externally initiated policy applied to Ankole. Following increased attention for matters of land tenure during the terminal colonial period and more specifically on the basis of the *East African Royal Commission Report*, the Uganda government undertook the encouragement of individual freehold ownership with the declared objective of promoting economic development.[22] The policy was discussed with all district councils but met with little enthusiasm or understanding.[23] There was some interest only in Kigezi, Ankole and Bugisu and consequently pilot schemes were launched in these three districts. In Ankole the scheme was first sited in the densely populated Kagango and Shuku sub-counties of Shema county.

The scheme was rationalized in terms familiar for policies of individualisation. A freehold title would help establish clear property rights, boundaries and fences, provide the security of tenure that would permit the making of improvements on land conducive towards further commercialisation, facilitate sales and loans, and prevent transmission of infectious cattle disease. To this end a system of adjudication and certification was established which involved a procedure that seemed more characterised by concern for constraints and precautions than for complexity.[24]

A beginning was made with implementation of the scheme in 1958, but it soon became the subject of political controversy. Action was suspended between the end of 1958 to 1959, pending an appeal to the High Court that the scheme's legality was unfounded (the Ankole district council had had no quorum when giving it its approval; but that, the court ruled, was immaterial since its approval was not called for), then resumed, suspended, and resumed again paralleling changes of power in the Ankole government between 1960 and 1963.[25] Thereafter it became increasingly clear that the mechanics of the scheme required more administration and manpower than was available, so that an estimated backlog of many man-years in surveying piled up; as a result implementation on the basis of available resources was given low priority while a search for new procedures and even new tenure arrangements was undertaken.

Whether any agricultural improvement has followed in those cases where land titles were obtained is doubtful. Brock suggests that the Uganda pilot schemes, including that of Ankole, led to no discernible increase in economic activity and that as far as sales are concerned plots held in customary tenure continued to be bought and sold without the benefit of surveys, registers or titles.[26] Perhaps one may wish to reserve final judgement on this, if a period of roughly five years' practice is too short to allow such evaluation. When doing that, one should be particularly interested to see whether in fact any of the new titles have been used as securities against loans, the one purpose for which it might be claimed with some strength that they provide a new element. But such evaluations are in any case difficult to make because the farmers that applied for titles generally appear to have been those who already were in a more favourable economic position than others.

Yet, while technical complexities and constraints and the economic results of a project like the Ankole land title scheme are of interest and importance, they must not be seen in isolation from the potential social and political ramifications of the project. The latter have been of particular importance in determining attitudes towards the scheme and even in retrospect it is useful to consider these implications and see what social effects the project tended to entail. The simplest way of doing this is to relate the project's objectives to the broad interests of the various socio-political groups in Ankole and to try and see whether there was any logic to the antagonism that followed its introduction. One possible distinction to be kept in mind here is between arguments advanced and the reasons for advancing them; they may be, but are not necessarily the same.

Opinions in favour of the scheme given at the 1961 Inquiry into the Operation of the Land Tenure Scheme in Ankole included:

1. The concept of freehold land is not a new thing, many notables having held freehold since the 1901 Agreement.
2. The scheme has been voluntary and no one who does not wish to have a title need apply for one. Conversely, if anyone wishes to have a title, he should not be prevented.
3. A freehold title gives the owner a sense of real ownership, and he will take care of what is his.
4. With proper boundaries and a registered title a man will no longer be plagued by petty boundary disputes, and the courts will be spared much work.
5. With a title, a man can obtain a loan from a bank to help him improve his land.
6. Improved land will benefit the cultivator, the rancher, the mixed farmers, the trader and Ankole as a whole.
7. With a title a man will be able to fence his land (according to his needs), and thus stop the spread of cattle disease which is the result of 'free for all' grazing.

8.   With a title a man will be able to rest his land without fear of its being spoilt by the indiscriminate grazing of neighbours.[27]

Opinions against the scheme listed in the report were:

a.   All the land in Ankole belongs to the Omugabe, and it should be distributed by him through his Eishengyero. The land titles policy should not interfere with existing rights to land under native custom, and should not interfere with places of common benefit such as pastures, wells, places for the gathering of firewood, thatching material or clay. It should be administered by a body in which people have confidence.

b.   The existing policy was introduced by underhand means, the Protectorate Government siding 'in a mysterious alliance' with a few well-to-do people in order to force it on the poor. It was introduced through a court of law 'whose decision is still understood only by lawyers'.

c.   The introduction of the policy was accompanied by insults to the Omugabe, and by the arbitrary violation of human rights and the arbitrary taking away of human liberty, never recommended by the World Bank Mission, the Royal Commission on Land in East Africa or the Munster Report, 'under which the Protectorate Government is taking refuge'.

d.   .... Appeals to the District African Court included cases of people who had tried to defend their property rights against the chiefs. Because of the expense and delays in the appeal procedure, many cases went unheard.

e.   It was understood when the Shema scheme was introduced that only a man's property would be dealt with. In fact other people's land was taken and added to that of an applicant for title.

f.   Areas of pasture, sources of firewood and building materials were taken into adjudicated areas.

g.   As a result of such detestable consequences, the scheme is very unpopular, as is instanced by the small number of applicants for titles. Since 1959 about 26 people have obtained final certificates: only about 30 have paid survey fees, and applications for land titles number 800 in the pilot scheme and 1,200 outside it.

h.   The question of land titles should be decided by the London Conference, and the Protectorate Government must be undermining that Conference to implement a policy before the results are known.

i.   The chiefs take advantage of the scheme to snatch land for themselves and their friends.

j.   Communal grazing areas are taken by chiefs and given to cultivators. Cattle owners are therefore squeezed out.

k.   Chiefs compelled many people to apply for titles.

l.   People were not given sufficient time to study the scheme before it was put into operation.

m.   The survey fees were too high: only the rich could afford them.

n.   That the titles scheme is a device to enable Europeans to take the land.

o.   That the muluka chief should not be chairman of the adjudication committee.[28]

Most of these views need little further comment. Some are concrete and represent straightforward pros and cons. Others are evidently rationalisations (e.g. the Omugabe argument), attempts to refer the issue into a dead alley (the London Conference point) or justifications on other than the scheme's own merits (the 1901 analogy). However, none of these reduce the sense of controversy which surrounded the issue, some of the basic motivations for which may not have been expressed, or expressable. Also, the commissioner looked into actual grievances submitted, and felt able to dismiss most or all of them, but that did not necessarily mean that fears or suspicions of future implications were allayed.

Of the three main socio-political groups in Ankole the Protestant Bairu stood clearly in favour of the scheme, whereas the Bahima and the Catholic Bairu opposed it. One simple reason for their opposition may have been that the former group was in favour, following a pattern that was not infrequently manifested in Ankole local politics; nonetheless, that factor was by no means a sole and sufficient condition. Reasons why precisely the Protestant Bairu could be expected to be pro involved the fact that they comprised most of the advanced commercial farmers in the area, those who were more likely to be interested in the improvement, sales, loans and boundaries arguments for the scheme – whether or not in the end these possibilities would make much difference. If these were rationalistic grounds, they were strengthened by others which derived from the historic relationships in Ankole, particularly the Bairu-Bahima contacts. For one thing the land title scheme was perceived as one that would remove any final area of insecurity about tenure and in fact make any title holder as secure about his land as the mailo owners. Besides, to become in a sense like a mailo-owner promised no small amount of satisfaction, if only as a way of asserting equality of status to those who had long been regarded as an overpriviliged group. This motivation, though hardly ever explicit, was of considerable significance in Protestant Bairu quarters. Finally, population density in the Shema area probably made the project seem more desirable there than in other places as long as the right to enclose land was associated with freehold tenure. More concretely, it would help to keep off cattle from land under cultivation, which was a nuisance to the farmers. Added to this, perhaps, was also a chance to be of some nuisance to the cattle people. It was speculated with keen interest that if most of the land would come under freehold and be fenced it would almost certainly mean the migration of Bahima away from the area.

To the Bahima the scheme was objectionable for precisely opposite reasons. Cattle required freedom to move and it was felt that if increasingly the land was to be enclosed this movement might become seriously impaired. This would especially be the case if enclosures, as was likely, were to include the sections of land to which a farmer could lay a customarily recognised claim but which he would not normally, or continuously, have under active cultivation. Rights to trespass such sections with cattle have also been conventionally accorded, but would be jeopardised by the development of freehold enclosures. Bahima themselves would find difficulty claiming freehold titles for stretches of land large enough to engage in cattle production. Ultimately the possibility of forced migration from the area thus loomed as a prospect. Specifically for the pilot areas these possibilities were not always of immediate concern; but if the scheme was successful here it would be extended and pose a much greater challenge elsewhere. Hence there was considerable Bahima concern about the principle being adopted. In addition to restriction of movement itself two more limitations suggested themselves. One was that Bahima were likely to be excluded from defining the rules of the game governing access to land with the adoption of freehold arrangements, thus terminating a role which they had been able to play, implicitly at least, on the basis of the (convenient) fiction that all land belonged to the Omugabe. Loss of control was matched by a prospect of loss of prestige. To lose control was itself to lose prestige, while also the prestige of mailo ownership would be likely to suffer through the introduction of freehold of 'equal' status. Finally, the latter would point up the anomalies of the mailo system in even sharper form since it would show mailo tenants, again, as the losing party. For Bahima with or without mailo there was no conceivable advantage in the scheme but instead potential drawbacks at various levels.

Catholic Bairu opposed the scheme partly because of their alliance with the Bahima. Also, if they were against it because the Protestants were for it that was based on more than considerations of party rivalry *per se*. In Ankole as elsewhere politics was frequently, and never entirely unjustifiably, seen as a winner-takes-all game; in other words, as a competition entitling the incumbent party at least to first access to available benefits. As they had for long been out of the official establishment there was a fear among Catholic Bairu that they might lose out at boundary demarcations and that they would not be sufficiently well placed to carry through cases which were more than normally complicated. Besides, since there were fewer advanced or better-off farmers among them than among the Protestants there was a correspondingly more limited interest on the part of Catholics in land titles as a means to secure loans, to make claims for final boundary demarcations and arrange enclosures, etc. Neither for practical reasons nor prestige did these benefits have much appeal to them. Nor were they as much motivated as the Protestant Bairu to challenge the mailo system, or the Bahima, by opting for land titles. Finally, in the light of these reservations, the expenditure in fees may often not have seemed worthwhile. For up to 2 acres the total fees were Shs 50, up to 10 acres Shs 90, etc., which hardly constituted negligible expenditure for peasants who did not belong to the economically most successful category.

Evidently, then, the scheme aroused considerable discussions and controversy. The fact that it was voluntary and thus only for farmers who wished to apply for a land title did not reduce objections because in the long run the programme could lead to the emergence of a group of property owners versus a group of 'non-property' owners. Again, for Bahima it was not a matter of their own interest in the new land titles but rather of the scheme affecting them by implication. Clearly, therefore, one can see that a project which provokes such conflicting interests does not provide a particularly stable basis for the development of a society. These reactions might have been anticipated because there were clearly divergent interests involved. Instead, a project was created which, like the mailo scheme, revealed an inadequate fit with local social and political conditions (not to speak of customary arrangements). While it is difficult to show its economic utility, it was far from an irrelevant factor in Ankole society because it created a taste in land as a commodity, had potentially harmful implications for social relationships and finally, once started, was hard to undo.

Similar to the mailo scheme, albeit in a different manner, the individual freehold policy provided a link between the politics of protest and the politics of factionalism and constituted one more avenue of re-stratification in Ankole society. In a sense, the controversy surrounding the new freehold titles was a factional dispute in the first place. The conflict partly ensued as rival groups tried to ensure that their opponents – in this case primarily the Protestant Bairu – would not be able to seize a political prize; in that way the issue may be seen as an expression of 'negative' factionalism. Nonetheless, as noted, there was initially also a dimension of protest in the interest expressed in the land titles: the security of tenure and the prospect of becoming 'like' a mailo owner which the policy appeared to offer.

These questions tended to be particularly acute in Shema county where the individual freehold project was first concentrated. Shema is one of the most densely populated areas of Ankole, in which new land is virtually non-available and where pressure on or about land accordingly becomes more intense. Earlier, it had been the density of population in Shema which had first brought some of the major mailo estates there (because of the 'availability' of tenants, inevitably Bairu). Again, this density became one of the reasons for the land title scheme, since it was believed that this kind of program would be the next logical step in a situation where land was becoming scarce and expensive.

It may also be reiterated that Shema's relatively central geographic position had made it 'first' in a variety of respects: first in major school expansion, first in the impetus to cash-crop cultivation, thus first too in the spread and creation of new interests, new skills and to an extent new wealth. In part, this also accounts for why the land scheme became an issue in Shema. The land titles which were coveted by those farmers who were very much products of these transformations were resented by those that had a less active, or less profitable part in that process. Thus, a Protestant Bairu challenge to Bahima preponderance in Ankole had special relevance, and roots, in the Shema situation, while Catholic Bairu misgivings about Protestant Bairu ascendancy had an immediate origin in, and bearing upon, socio-political relationships within Shema.

If the land titles dispute did therefore partly originate in the politics of protest, it in turn helped to lay the conditions for new grievances – less articulated as they may have been. The fencing of freehold land was one of several avenues resulting in enclosures, and in a differentiation between those who 'have' land and those who 'have not'. This development, though slowed down at intervals due mainly to technical constraints, has continued and over the past ten years has been having quite visible effects in Ankole. Fences and boundary demarcations vividly demonstrate the growth of a new social category in Ankole: of commercial farmers and others who share a speculative or prestige interest in land holdings. From the outset, this category has included many Protestant Bairu, particularly from the central parts of the district. However, similar as happened in regard to the mailo landholdings and more dramatically even in the case of the allocation of ranches, discussed elsewhere,[29] once the land title issue had been 'settled' an increasing number of leading members of each of Ankole's ethnic and religious divisions began to acquire their freehold titles. Increasingly, these various elite groups have had in common a capacity to command access to resources, and also a desire to be ranked high. But there have also been other implications. As new socio-economic differentiations inaugurated changing patterns of social stratification, the play for power in Ankole tended to become more restricted in scope. Besides, the protest element in Ankole politics, too, shifted ground: as broad denominators became less available for the articulation and redress of grievances, the tendency has been to seek relief and support through more individual, particularistic and discrete channels.

SOCIAL DIVISIONS AND THE DYNAMICS OF FACTIONAL CONFLICT*

While basic socio-economic relationships were subject to change in Ankole, over the years a lively pattern of political conflict continued – though with a changing significance. Elements of ethnic inequality persisted as a determinant, if only because earlier 'first come, first served' opportunities had tended to result in enduring discrepancies. Until quite recently, various political issues indeed continued to be defined in terms of the Bahima-Bairu division – whether or not some of them reflected genuine or contrived differences. Nonetheless, as the 'room on the top' gradually began to accommodate other elite strata in addition to that of the Bahima, it became increasingly difficult to consider *ethnic* inequality as the dominant feature of Ankole society and its politics. In a strictly political sense, moreover, the Bahima's role tended to become more rapidly eclipsed than was true for their involvement in the administrative and economic domains – though even here we shall have to note some major exceptions.

No neat boundary lines can be drawn for these transitions. Nonetheless, from roughly the late 1950s onwards, ethnic and religious affiliations in Ankole appeared to increasingly acquire an essentially similar significance as they had elsewhere in Uganda politics, namely that of vehicles to maximise the political influence of factions which operated as each other's 'equal' competitors. Followings tended to be built up, and to be sustained through the promises of patronage, largely on the basis of ethnicity, religion, region, clan, or a combination of these references – or in a more negative way by calling attention to the supposedly disruptive designs of groups of another ethnic and/or religious description. Various such trends in the late 1950s and early 1960s tended to reaffirm a newly based triangular pattern in Ankole politics. One important development was that of a convergence of interests between the Protestant Bahima and the Catholic Bairu, which gradually led to their coalition in the political arena – one which thus joined the strongest and the weakest group of the colonial set-up. Beginning with the changes

*This section is based largely on unpublished documentation and on interviews with many members of Ankole society, particularly political leaders. Though most of this information has been freely accessible, much of it might officially be regarded as classified or be seen to compromise the sources concerned. For these reasons, few specific references will be stated.

which were effected in the district political-administrative framework in 1955, the Bahima had experienced a gradual decline of their political position in Ankole. As a numerical minority, they needed to look for allies when party politics made its entry in the years immediately before independence, which they found in the Catholic Bairu.[30] Their alliance was first articulated in 1958 at the nomination of representatives to the Uganda Legislative Council (Legco) by the Ankole Eishengyero. Thereafter the Bahima-Catholic alignment found its organisational basis in the Democratic Party (DP) when it branched out into Ankole.[31] Constituting a significant variant on the otherwise quite solidly Catholic membership of the DP in Uganda, they won the first general elections which were held in 1961 for the Eishengyero and formed the Ankole government from that year till 1963, when they were replaced by the Uganda People's Congress (UPC). Again, in 1961 the DP had a victory in the pre-independence national elections held in Ankole, and in 1962 they returned four of the six Ankole seats in the first (and last) general elections during independence.

As of 1960, the Protestant Bairu gave the majority of their support to the UPC, which basically stepped into Kumanyana's organizational framework. The UPC had come about as a merger between a wing of the Uganda National Congress and the Uganda People's Union, which had its basis mainly in the Western Region. Since Ugandan political parties originated largely at the center (though on the basis of local notables, mostly Legco representatives) it took some sorting out before local complexities found their expression in party rivalries. The UPU and the UNC had to some extent cut across ethnic divisions, but their membership was too small and their leadership too impermanent to be able to attach any particular significance to this fact. In the late 1950s and early 1960s, however, potential election returns became a major consideration in Ankole politics. In keeping with other parts of Uganda, the religious cleavage assumed major dimensions in the immediate pre-independence period. Since the vast majority of Ankole voters – i.e., the Bairu – were mobilised along religious lines into the DP and UPC, it became imperative for the leaders of both parties to try and tip the balance – particularly as, it will be recalled, the religious division had split the Bairu on a nearly 50-50% basis. The largely Catholic Bairu DP had Bahima support, but the Protestant Bairu increasingly felt they needed Bahima votes for the UPC. Hence ethnic rivalries were markedly played down during the 1960-62 period, while religious conflict assumed major proportions; ironically, the two Bairu groups competed actively for Bahima support in the 1962 Uganda elections. At the popular level, meanwhile, a striking identification developed of the DP with Catholicism and the UPC with Protestantism. Since members of the two denominations were assumed to vote for the corresponding parties as a matter of course, strenuous efforts, called 'political baptising', were also made to convert the remaining 'pagans' and thus conquer the floating vote they represented.

The UPC was not able, however, to attract any substantial amount of Bahima votes, even though some influential Bahima (most notably Grace Ibingira) had entered into its leadership. Nonetheless, this strategy also had a paradoxical result. After many efforts to mobilise the Bairu in opposition to the Bahima during the preceding decade, it was quite remarkable that a substantial part of the leadership of both the Ankole DP and UPC in the early 1960s came in the hands of Bahima. In 1962 Bahima obtained half of the Ankole seats in the National Assembly, gaining three of the six elective positions (UPC: 1; DP: 2), and in addition enjoyed considerable influence in each party's executive. An overwhelming majority of the Bahima remained nonetheless loyal to the alignment between Bahima and Catholic Bairu and voted DP.

This particular situation obtained until roughly 1964-66, when the strength of the DP was progressively eroded by crossings of its representatives in the Eishengyero to the Uganda People's Congress. At the national level, the DP then lost all but one of its seats as a result of crossings to the UPC. Thereafter, quite a different political constellation emerged in Ankole – and indeed in Uganda as a whole. Until that point, however, and in view of the longstanding lack of empathy between Ankole's ethnic-religious groups, it was hardly surprising that suspicions and frictions should have developed in both parties, though most pronounced and openly within the UPC. As a matter of fact, there was among Bairu a widely held belief that Bahima deliberately stirred up Catholic-Protestant and DP-UPC rivalries so as to keep the Bairu divided, and then, distributing themselves over the two parties, subsequently managed to gain control over both, all as a grand design to perpetuate their political influence. This belief was linked again to criticisms about the allocation of land and other resources, which part of the Bairu felt were handled so as to give disproportionate privileges to 'those who have fallen into things', among whom there were not a few Bahima. Also, continued overrepresentation of Bahima in high political, administrative and clerical positions caused an element of frustration among a number of Bairu, who had expected the results of their protest to be more visible, tangible, and complete.

As already noted, these arguments were not without an element of rationalisation. Leaving aside the merits of these charges, however, they unmistakably added fuel to further articulation of Bairu aggrievances. As a result, a continuation of the Kumanyana movement could be found in one of the factions which until 1971 came to divide the UPC in Ankole. For the leaders of this group, the remaining hard core of the movement acted as a ready-made source of political support. The rival UPC group maintained, on the contrary, that times had changed and that the issue of the day was no longer one of all-pervasive Bahima domination. They argued that cooperation and understanding were necessary and possible between Protestants and Catholics, Bairu and Bahima, and that accentuating their mutual differences in the long run would work to nobody's advantage, but to the detriment of the whole. The latter faction, called the Kahigiriza group after its leader, constituted the Ankole government from 1963 till 1967. They were replaced by the Bananuka group, which formed the UPC administration in Ankole until the 1971 coup. This last, 'intra-Protestant Bairu' split, commanded most attention in Ankole during the period; hence, it will be useful to consider its basis and background.

The origins of these divisions within the Ankole UPC dated back to 1963. Until that year Bananuka had been party leader in Ankole. However, once the UPC had won the 1963 Eishengyero elections, a move was made to prevent him from being nominated as Enganzi – presumably because of his more radical leanings. A confused situation arose within the UPC caucus, where at one point Bananuka reportedly had received majority support; the nullification of his nomination was largely attributed to an intervention by Ibingira, then Minister of Justice in the Uganda Government. After alternative suggestions had failed, a compromise was sought with the appointment of James Kahigiriza, who at the time was county chief of Kashari and had earlier been an Assistant Enganzi; the arrangement further provided for Bananuka, Kihuguru, and Muntuyera to become Ministers in the Ankole Kingdom Government.

Before long, however, relationships within the Ankole government deteriorated, with Bananuka and Muntuyera increasingly on one side and Kahigiriza and Kihuguru on the other. In 1964, problems were indicated when Kahigiriza, as Enganzi, reshuffled his team of ministers, shifting Bananuka from Health and Works to Finance. Though efficiency was given as a reason for the transfer, it was generally believed that the change was motivated because the post of Finance would provide its incumbent with fewer opportunities for travelling and campaigning than had Health and Works. Still, the result was that from that moment on, strained relationships were particularly characteristic of intragovernment contacts in Ankole, with frequent separate meetings being held and separate followings being built up by each of the two groups. Finally, in 1965, there was a direct confrontation when Kahigiriza dismissed Bananuka, allegedly for 'undermining' his government; Muntuyera resigned in solidarity with Bananuka.

Fortunes turned in 1967; the republican constitution which was adopted in Uganda during that year stipulated that only directly elected members of district councils would qualify for leadership in the district administrations. This caused the termination of office of Kahigiriza as Enganzi, who had been a specially elected member from the time of his appointment. Bananuka then replaced him, not as Enganzi, but in the newly styled function of Secretary-General of Ankole district. Curiously, however, this particular implication of the new constitution had not been immediately evident. For many months in 1966 and 1967, the two UPC factions were engaged in a close competition to gain a majority of votes in the District Council, expecting that these would determine the choice of incumbents in the administration. Their competition involved not only efforts to win over councillors from the opposite faction, but was also directed to the remaining DP members, whom they tried to persuade to cross to one or the other of the two UPC groups. For a long time the race appeared undecided. The strength of the divisions had become roughly equal, with about 21 elected members on each side, when a change of administration was finally effected on the basis of the new constitution.

Before and after the take-over, the styles and strategies of the two groups were largely identical. Characteristic measures included the wholesale transfer to out of the way schools of teachers suspected of siding with the opposite faction. Similarly, chiefs believed to be supportive of the opposite faction stood a chance of being posted to remote stations, where they would have minimal opportunities for political and social contacts. New appointments (even though since 1967 these were handled by a sub-committee of the Uganda Public Service Commission) almost invariably continued to be the subject of considerable lobbying and pressure. Generally, the candidate's relationship to the political factions was an overriding factor in appointments.

Each move, actual or contemplated, was usually widely discussed among the politically engaged in Ankole. During the most recent years, at least until 1971, this also involved close attention for the intentions of the 'center'. In view of the increasing involvement of the Uganda government in local affairs, and with an acute awareness that the center might make modifications to the format of district government which could turn out favourably to one party or another, strenuous efforts were made by all sides to anticipate and where possible influence any such interventions. Indeed, at times of local deadlocks, it was not uncommon for two or more groups to rush in their cars to Kampala, trying to reach there before their opponents could talk to the same cabinet ministers or other officials concerned.

Ankole 'politics' evolved towards a new moment of crisis in the fall of 1969 and early 1970. During this episode, attention was largely focussed on the Committee of Inquiry into Ankole District Council and District Administration Affairs.[32] This Committee had been appointed by the Minister of Regional Administrations in September, 1969, to enquire into the background and causes of factional divisiveness in Ankole politics. Specifically, the Committee, composed of three non-Banyankore UPC members of Parliament, was charged with examining allegations to the effect that 'tribal and religious considerations' played a role in matters of recruitment, rewards and the execution of official tasks in the Ankole District Administration. Locally, the outcome of the Committee's investigations was anticipated with much interest, for its recommendations might be an important factor determining the Uganda Government's position and possibly bring about a new change of leadership in Ankole. As it turned out, however, the Committee's conclusions were most favourable for the incumbent politicians in the Ankole district administration, most notably for Bananuka.

Clearly, this inquiry was launched in a situation where the various factions, including the incumbent group, had been competing particularly intensively for control over the Ankole district administration. As before, the major groups involved in this conflict were the two factions of Protestant Bairu and the Catholic Bairu and the Bahima; attention, however, was primarily focussed on the first two groups and the Catholics. Only shortly before the Committee began its work a resolution by the Ankole UPC Executive Committee had recommended the dismissal from the party of the Minister of Internal Affairs in the Uganda Government, Basil Bataringaya (the former Opposition Leader in the Uganda National Assembly who in 1964 had made one of the first crosses from the DP to the UPC). This resolution, which was not implemented pending the Committee's inquiry – nor afterwards – was motivated by the conviction that the Minister 'undermined' regular UPC party activities in Ankole by strengthening his own and his supporters' political influence in the district. What these allegations were largely concerned with was that Bataringaya sought to promote the interests of Ankole Catholics, particularly those in his own constituency, in Bunyaruguru and Buhweju counties, who had crossed with him, or subsequently, to the UPC. In the late 1960s this strategy had led the Bataringaya group to align itself with the Kahigiriza faction – even although at an earlier point, in 1967, Bataringaya had been known to support the replacement of Kahigiriza by Bananuka. Among the 'original' Protestant core of the UPC (the Bananuka camp mainly), however, any special efforts to promote Catholic interests within the party and the government were viewed with misgivings. Those involved in these efforts were believed to be 'still DP at heart' or 'at least 25% DP'. Thus, increasing numbers of Catholic crossings to the UPC, first hailed as a major victory in that party, began to be seen as a Trojan threat by the Bananuka-UPC which was in command. Moreover, they also blamed the other groups, i.e. the Kahigiriza faction and the Bahima, for instigating and supporting the moves of the Bataringaya group.

Expectedly, the 1969-70 inquiry into Ankole factionalism was seen as an initial answer by the central government to the proposed dismissal of Bataringaya from the party. Although having a weak political base in Ankole, Bataringaya was a powerful figure in the Obote cabinet and there was every reason to believe that he would try to hit back hard in reaction to his proposed dismissal from the party. Before long, however, it appeared that the investigation was unlikely to bring about any significant change in the stalemate between the political factions in Ankole – let alone in the factionalism itself. Not a few people in Ankole attributed this to the inquiry being itself compromised by the factionalism in the district, and to one side being more successful in influencing the results than the other. And indeed, there was no significant change, or at least not until January, 1971, when the Amin coup took place. For present purposes, meanwhile, the specific measures which were contemplated following the inquiry appear less important. More significant seemed the fact that even in 1970, several years after the Obote government had begun to centralise its control and discourage local political involvement, group conflict along ethnic and religious lines in Ankole was important enough, or at least so considered, to be made the subject of a special parliamentary inquiry. For this and other reasons, it will be useful to look at its dynamics more closely.

When considering factional conflict in Ankole, several points might be borne in mind. One is that Ankole was often credited as a district with 'stable administration' in Uganda. Particularly its tax yield and its general financial management for years were considered among the best in the country. If factionalism nonetheless seemed pervasive in Ankole, this did not therefore reduce the district's comparative standing in terms of administrative performance. Nor was the district a particularly unique or serious case in terms of divisiveness; other situations, for example that in next-door Toro, continued to be far more ominous.[33] If anything, the Ankole case would rather seem to represent more general patterns in the country at large.

Secondly, just as significant as these parallels in other districts was the enduring quality of factional conflict in a district like Ankole. The 1969 commission of inquiry had not been the first that was appointed by the central authorities to look into Ankole district affairs. Apart from various inquiries with more specific purposes – although with an immediate bearing on the general political scene, such as the land tenure inquiry – in 1962 an earlier UPC commission had been charged with largely the same tasks as the 1969-70 commission. Though at a different stage of the political game, this inquiry had come up against basically the same conditions of group rivalry. Nonetheless, especially during the late 1960s the Obote government had been taking various steps to alter the format of the political system. As noted, the general trend was one towards increased centralisation of political and administrative functions; more and more tasks were being transferred from the local governments to field officers of the central government in the districts. For the casual observer these steps may well have reduced the visibility, or even the immediate implications, of local political conflict for 'regular' administration. Yet such an observation would too readily assume a one-to-one relationship between political centralisation and the mitigation of factionalism. Political centralisation in Uganda during the Obote years by no means caused a subsiding of all factional struggle at the local level, nor a decrease in the intensity with which issues were fought. What happened was that the strategies and styles of political rivalry tended to change, becoming less open, public and visible. But the fact that factionalism was enduring despite basic changes in the form of the system is at any rate noteworthy; we will return to this point later.

Thirdly, despite the profound antagonism often displayed in factional conflicts in Ankole, it is doubtful whether the differences between the various factions were as great as they often appeared. There did not seem to be very much difference in the nature of the policies pursued and, quite naturally, each group exhibited similar kinds of interest in gaining control over the affairs of the district, particularly in order to be able to place followers in administrative positions. If these were pragmatic matters, the composition of their respective followings in a sense may have been similarly pragmatic, irrespective of what historical developments lay at their roots. Thus, whereas the Bananuka-group was able to rely on a solid core of Protestant Bairu for support and consequently needed to cater largely to their interests, the Kahigiriza-group was more strongly compelled to look for coalitions, and thus perhaps also to advocate the principle of tolerance and compromise. The leaders of the groups did not themselves distinguish essential differences in the policies of their administrations. In 1969, the differences indicated during interviews included the fact that during one administration more dispensaries had been completed than during the term of the opposite group; that one leader had used prison labour for his private garden which his successor declined to do; and, at another level, the statement of one leader that he liked to think of himself as more "socialistic" than the others.

A fourth and final point is related to a further behavioural characteristic that was manifested at the leadership level. For many years it used to be a common tendency for new incumbents in the Ankole district administration to use the personal emoluments connected with their office towards a change of life styles. The key personalities involved have in particular been noted, one after the other, to build new and larger houses (in recent times often two-storeyed) and invest in land, cattle, cars and various business ventures. To be sure, some of the salaries allowed a fair amount of scope; in addition, there were fringe benefits. More important, however, appeared not merely the fact that the quest for social advancement was common to the political elites of the various factions, irrespective of ethnic and religious backgrounds, but that to a certain extent this trend appeared to be socially 'expected' behaviour. Successful politicians were apt to show the signs of their personal growth with pride to their friends and visitors; they were tokens of success. Success for the individual tended to be seen as success for the group – though with one reservation. If a leader appeared to display a too ready inclination to spend on strictly personal objects, questions might be raised among his followers whether there would be enough left as spoils. Some such concerns were expressed in Ankole during the late 1960s; however, they tended to reaffirm the principle rather than challenge it. Explicit critique of *enrichissez-vous* tendencies came from rather limited circles, but was not necessarily enduring.

However, not only in Ankole but also more largely in Uganda there was a wider significance to these trends. What mattered were not just the interests connected with leadership positions. More basically, any administrative or other post in the government administration was (and is) regarded as highly desirable among large categories of the people, simply because even the lowest paid job would earn an income that was larger than that of the average, non-salaried farmer. Add to this that till today, and in the foreseeable future, government is by far the largest employer in the country, and that people with less than secondary education needed to look particularly to the district administrations for possible employment opportunities. It is clear, then, that to be or not to be accommodated within the government ranks became probably the most critical differentiating factor among social categories, which to a large extent helps to explain the keen interest shown in appointments at all levels. Government not only had been for years the most promising road to social mobility, but it continued to be believed that there were additional opportunities. This belief increasingly rested on erroneous perceptions, as there were definite limits to the scope for government expansion; yet as long as it was assumed that the ranks had not been closed, pressure for absorption was likely to continue – rather than withdrawal or dissent.

Patronage closed the circle: to stand any chance in a situation of scarce resources it was necessary to be in the good books of someone with influence. Support to a political figure who either now or at a future date might be in a position to bestow rewards on his followers was a common way of cultivating such goodwill. In a way, there was nothing particularly unique about these tendencies (however much patronage may tend to be discussed as a 'non-western' phenomenon in the social science literature). Nonetheless, if we relate them to the historical background and kinds of social cleavages in a district such as Ankole, patterns of factionalism become clearer. In Ankole as elsewhere in Uganda one might distinguish between mainly two bases of social differentiation. One was that which derived from the occupancy of a salaried position, while the other distinguished people by ethnicity, religion, or some other so-called 'primordial' criterion. In a sense the latter distinctions were arbitrary, at least inasfar as it would be a matter of particular historical factors whether an area might have an ethnic, religious, linguistic, or other cleavage. However, as long as additional rewards were seen as lying with the administration (and so long as, therefore, a *political* division would not develop between those within and those without the administrative ranks) there was hardly any other such ready-made basis for the mobilisation of pressure to obtain government spoils and benefits than that of the groups of some ethnic or religious description. In Ankole, without adopting the view that its politics evolved solely around the competitive claims on administrative positions and other sinecures, doubtless these potential rewards were a major focal point for political alignments and divisions in the district. With Bahima, Protestant Bairu and Catholic Bairu occupying different positions in the district arena, yet forced to compete for the same, limited amount of spoils, it seemed quite logical that these ethnic and religious divisions should have provided the main foundation blocks for the formation of political groups.

Factions so constituted along ethnic or religious lines were vehicles for upward mobility, kept together by reciprocal obligations and expectations of patronage. Ethnic-religious divisions were thus functionally related to emergent class divisions, two structural principles which have often been regarded as mutually exclusive or contradictory: in the type of political structure which was characteristic of the district level in Uganda until at least 1971, ethnic channels tended to be a major route towards enhanced socio-political power. In this situation, therefore, the tendency was for administrative growth, class differentiation and ethnic-religious factionalism to be strongly correlated.

Still, if factional strife has appeared as 'inevitable' as it was enduring, perhaps the question that remains is whether its implications should also have been as profound as they were. This question is in part one about the institutional framework; we will return to it in the final section. Meanwhile, it will be necessary for us to turn to another institution, that of Ankole kingship, and try to understand its decline and eclipse during the transformations we have discussed. A convenient starting point for this will be the moment of its termination.

THE REDUNDANCY OF ANKOLE KINGSHIP

Kingship in Ankole was formally abolished on 8 September, 1967, following the ratification by the Parliament of Uganda of a new constitution which proclaimed a unitary and republican form of government for the whole of Uganda. Together with the kingdoms of Buganda, Bunyoro and Toro, Ankole lost its semi-federal and monarchical status and henceforth was relegated to the rank of a district of Uganda.[34] Administrative offices and other institutions reminiscent of Ankole's monarchical heritage were disbanded or restyled in accordance with the pattern followed elsewhere in the country. Letterheads and placards bearing the name 'Ankole Kingdom Government' were altered with remarkable speed and instructions were issued concerning the proper way of addressing the new district officials. The Omugabe, Rubambansi Sir Charles Godfrey Gasyonga II, was given a month's notice to vacate his palace. And when, at the end of September 1967, Ankole's royal drum, Bagyendanawa, was unceremoniously loaded onto a lorry to be taken to storage in a government warehouse, the last major visible attribute of Ankole kingship was officially consigned to oblivion.

Given the historical claims of monarchism generally, it might have been quite reasonable to expect its termination to signify a profoundly emotional clash of values. After all, few things are more powerfully symbolic of corporate existence than kingship itself. Kingship has been often the object of deeply affective values and in many instances has played a crucial role in shaping common political identities. Removing this capstone from a political structure might well leave an emotional vacuum not easily filled by alternative secular symbols. On the surface, the abolition of Ankole kingship might have seemed just another illustration of these conditions.

In fact, however, the operation did not carry such momentous implications. Naturally, most Banyankore engaged in lively discussion over the issue. But more significant than the display of interest as such was the nature of attitudes in Ankole. While these varied from group to group, there was clearly no general expression of regret. In June 1967, the first announcement of the proposed termination of kingship was made. Among the opinions then expressed, some clearly suggested that the changes would upset Ankole. And, as a matter of fact, some people were upset. Others, however, did not hesitate to express their satisfaction over the fall of the monarchy, and one especially vocal group immediately staged celebrations in Mbarara.

Nonetheless, both rejoicing and regret were, on the whole, atypical reactions, as a much larger part of the population appeared basically indifferent to the whole matter. For this wider segment it made little difference whether there was an Omugabe or not, as life would presumably go on much as before. Theirs was often a reasoning based on quite pragmatic grounds, largely devoid of emotive responses. Many people, for instance, argued that since the Omugabe was no more than a figurehead, neither his presence nor the office itself were of much consequence. Pros and cons were also formulated on the basis of utilitarian grounds, or on considerations of prestige. Preference for abolition, for instance, was not seldom argued in financial terms, since many Banyankore considered the money used for the upkeep of the monarchy to be unnecessary if not wasteful expenditure. Again, if a nostalgia for kingship was expressed at all, this was often not so much founded on any intrinsic merits, but rather on the idea that it had given Ankole more status and dignity than, for instance, the districts of northern Uganda.[35]

Few of these views fit the stereotyped notion of a traditional people intensely devoted to their overlord. Even the circles closest to the monarchy took the changes with remarkable detachment and restraint. The Ministers of the Ankole Kingdom Government were obviously concerned about the loss of their titles and the perquisites they had enjoyed, but that seemed roughly the extent of their concern. As one commented privately, they cared little for either the person or the office of the Omugabe, but had found the ministerial positions associated with Ankole's kingdom status quite gratifying. Another senior official, who was more intimately associated with the Omugabe, said that however much he personally deplored the termination of kingship, he had expected this to happen for the past twenty years and thus found reason to be thankful in the fact that it had lasted so long. The comment of the Omugabe himself was that if the Government and the people found it fit that he should go, then he would do so. 'All that I am anxiously waiting for is an instruction from the Government on what to do next.'[36] Meanwhile, administrative officers who had been in the service of the Omugabe's government were dutifully engaged in obliterating the remaining vestiges of monarchism from the facade of the political system. The operation was smooth and unspectacular, as if it were merely a matter of disposing of an already superfluous appendage.

If one takes the view that affective loyalties are a necessary ingredient of kingship, then the behaviour of the Banyankore in 1967 may well have seemed inexplicable. Certainly, the argument that the people of Ankole refused to express their innermost feelings out of fear of penalisation cannot withstand critical examination. Remarkably candid discussions had appeared in the press prior to the enactment of the new constitution, followed up in the course of public debate, and whoever wished to publicly state his support of the monarchy had been quite free to do so.[37] Hence, the question remains as to why the Banyankore reacted so indifferently. Our assumption is that there is no reason to dispute the genuineness of the opinions expressed in Ankole, and indeed that there was a certain logic to these views. Thus it would suggest itself that in 1967 kingship had little meaning for the average Munyankore, either as a symbol or an institution. While there is no gainsaying that Ankole kingship served as a major focal point of political cohesiveness prior to the introduction of British rule, it is the effects of the transformations brought in the wake of colonisation which made the institution increasingly redundant.

Earlier in this study we have examined some of the major structural changes to which the Ankole kingship was subject during colonial times, and have seen how the institution, uncomfortably placed within the colonial edifice, gradually lost the functions and significance it had had. In the present section and the next one, we shall be particularly concerned with the 'effects' of these changing conditions on the monarchy, and see how a once meaningful institution had become a largely superfluous appendage of the Ankole political framework. Our main concern will thus be with the way the institution was treated during late colonial and subsequent times. Still, our first task must be to look at some implications of the ethnic and religious divisions on the fortunes of kingship.

In the light of colonial policies and their social effects we have seen, it is not surprising that a crucial element bearing on the destiny of the Ankole kingship should for many years have centered on the Bairu-Bahima division. While in the pre-colonial era Bairu and Bahima had had different orientations to the monarchy, in order to preserve its legitimacy the monarchy would have needed to 'equalise' the symbolic identification of its ethnic 'constituents' and give Bairu and Bahima a sense of shared involvement in the kingship. This requirement, however, first ran counter to early colonial policy and its implied 'premise of inequality'. Later, Ankole's ethnic stratification imposed an additional limitation on rejuvenation of kingship.

As the monarchy was restyled, Bairu and Bahima simultaneously developed divergent attitudes toward the office, which, in a sense, led to a replication of earlier divergencies. Although the Bahima maintained a close identification with the monarchy, the source of this identification changed considerably. The Bairu, on the other hand, had never been very closely related to the monarchy, and when the institution lapsed into obsolescence, their reaction was one of growing indifference. There was also another strand of opinion among Bairu, however. As the monarchy was identified with Bahima overrule, its legitimacy was questioned at the same time that Bahima supremacy was challenged by Bairu. So far from promoting the unification of ethnic segments through their joint identification with kingship, the Obugabe became a symbol of increasing tension between Bairu and Bahima.

Yet, if the monarchy became a focal point of conflict, this was not so much the result of its own doing as a reflection of the intensified ethnic antagonisms, particularly at the time of the Kumanyana movement. The influence of the Obugabe was then already at a very low ebb. In contrast with the situation in adjacent Rwanda, the monarchy in Ankole was too weak to be a significant factor in the ethnic strife; yet ethnic conflict was bound to deepen, and if for no other reason than to strengthen their respective claims, the contesting groups were likely to politicise the issue of monarchical legitimacy.

To the Bairu, kingship was a constant reminder of Bahima claims to hegemony. Whatever pronouncements the Omugabe made to the effect that all Banyankore were equally his subjects,[38] these were inevitably received with a sense of strong disbelief by educated Bairu elements. As Bairu protest became increasingly vociferous during Gasyonga's reign, the latter's attitude became the target of growing criticisms on their part. Even though they knew that the kingship no longer had a significant influence in politics, any semblance of involvement of the Omugabe with Bahima tactics was invariably denounced by the Bairu as 'proof' of ethnic favouritism.

To the Bahima, the monarchy also became a symbol in a new political sense. Traditionally, the kingship had symbolised, and in a way ensured, their political unity. Although the practical utility of the institution was now very much in doubt, the Omugabe's continued presence in office during a time of ethnic confrontation nonetheless strengthened Bahima feelings of identity and security. As they sensed the threats posed to their political supremacy most Bahima sought to reverse the trend as best they could given the political resources available to them. In the long run the numerically weaker Bahima were bound to suffer a decline of their privileged political status. Though forced to relinquish their position of pre-eminence, the Bahima derived a sense of unity and continued recognition from the conviction that the kingship was still 'theirs'. That this conviction was largely illusory is beside the point. Precisely because they were victims of this illusion, they perhaps failed to realize the full extent of their eclipse as a political elite, a fact which may also help to explain their relative quiescence during the transition. Retention of the monarchy through the period of ethnic restratification has thus probably smoothed the reversal of ethnic status in Ankole.

Somewhat anti-climatically, the contrasting attitudes of Bairu and Bahima almost never led to explicit demands for either the abolishment or the retention of the Ankole monarchy. Nor did the survival of kingship become an all-pervasive issue, as in Rwanda. Part of the explanation may lie in the Bahima-Catholic Bairu alliance. Many Catholic Bairu insist on pointing out that their coalition with the Bahima in the DP was less out of predilection for traditional authority than for reasons of political expediency. The Catholic-Bahima alignment involved an implicit understanding, however, that the position of the monarchy would remain unquestioned. Meanwhile, it will be recalled that in the early 1960s the Protestant Bairu who had moved into the UPC faced a need to attract votes from either Catholic Bairu or Bahima to stand a chance of winning elections. As a result, while the UPC membership would have been the most likely group openly to challenge the kingship, electoral considerations caused them to refrain from doing so. Ironically, the political parties were indeed so concerned not to be identified publicly with anti-monarchical opinion that at times each of them purported to represent the interests of the most loyal defenders of the Omugabe. Little of this stemmed from genuine sympathy for the kingship; but it did help to prolong the relatively undisturbed existence of the monarchy.

Ethnic tension, as we have seen, was at its height in Ankole in the middle and late 1950s. By the time of independence, in 1962, remnants of inequality were certainly still present in Ankole, but the principle of Bahima supremacy was no longer operative and Bairu protest declined. As noted, in the factional struggles which followed a core of the Protestant Bairu militants continued to press for 'full' equality. Among other things, they did not envisage the possibility of full political emancipation short of a formal abolition of kingship. Its elimination, as it turned out, came at a time when 'ethnic' equality had by and large been achieved. This was not unlike what happened to another symbol of 'ethnic' domination in Uganda, namely the statue of King George V in Kampala, from which the identifying plaque was not removed until several years after the country attained independence.

THE ECLIPSE OF THE MONARCHY

In its terminal years the kingship increasingly came to be a lonely station. So far from being the axis from which radiated an innovating tradition, the monarchy did little more than reflect the orientations of its environment. And the shine it produced was just as faint as the popular identifications which it inspired.

A lonely monarch, the Omugabe's loneliness was made even more apparent by the pedestal on which he was placed during the last phase of his reign. Whereas in earlier colonial times his status had been deliberately downgraded in the interest of administrative efficiency, throughout the fifties and the early sixties the tendency was just the opposite. Not only was he knighted, but in these later years formal recognition was given to some of the Omugabe's traditional titles. In 1951, the Provincial Commissioner gave his approval to the use of the title of 'Rubambansi the Omugabe' 'on all formal occasions as a matter of courtesy'.[39] Similarly, when discussing the proposals for local government reform outlined in the 1953 Wallis Report, members of the Eishengyero suggested that the Omugabe be treated as the political Head of the Kingdom 'as he had always been'.[40] It was further decided in that same year that from now on all bye-laws would be ratified by the Omugabe before being published in the Gazette, and should read 'The Omugabe has given his consent to . . .'.[41] Moreover, as if to reaffirm his newly-gained preeminence, the Omugabe was allowed to officiate over the annual opening ceremonies of the Eishengyero, and to award Certificates of Honour to those Ankole Government employees deemed worthy of such distinction.[42] Lastly, it was submitted in this new climate that the Omugabe should be accompanied on his official tours by 'one or two senior officials in their cars', since 'going alone would be risky to his life and would belittle his dignity'.[43]

Up until the mid-fifties the Eishengyero had remained largely a Bahima establishment. As we have seen, however, its composition underwent a major change after 1955; from then on until about 1961, the position of the Bahima elite suffered decline. This transformation was reflected in the Eishengyero's increasingly cavalier treatment of certain proposals aiming at buttressing the symbolic aspects of the Omugabeship, such as the defeat of a motion introduced in 1957 seeking the confirmation of all appointed chiefs by the Omugabe.[44] Only in a new political constellation, in 1964, could this idea be reintroduced. From then on, in fact, new chiefs were expected to thank the Omugabe for their appointment and pledge loyalty to him on Accession Day; but as it transpired, some of the chiefs never turned up on these occasions.

Thus, the loss of effective powers incurred by the Omugabe continued to be paralleled by attempts to enhance the formal appurtenances of his office. As an Eishengyero motion of 1961 stated it, the 'Omugabe was to be the Head of all people in Ankole except for Her Majesty the Queen and her representative, the Governor of Uganda'.[45] But this declaration itself only appeared to increase the imbalance between the lofty and low standings accorded from different perspectives to Ankole kingship.

The inflation of the Omugabeship reached its peak shortly after Uganda attained independence. The stature and dignity of the office of Omugabe then gained unprecedented recognition – a phenomenon which is best understood in the light of two fundamental realities of post-independence Uganda politics. One was the adoption of a special kind of federal structure for the new state; another had to do with the somewhat capricious course of party competition in the years immediately following independence.

'Federalism' explicitly put Ankole on the political map of Uganda as a Kingdom. As noted earlier, there was a variety of reasons for adopting a pluralistic constitutional framework for Uganda, the most decisive being the position of Buganda. Until this pattern was laid down, the term 'kingdom' had been used in an informal sense in respect to Ankole and the other semi-traditional units, the common official reference being 'District'. Only shortly before independence, the "Kingdom of Ankole" and the other Western kingdoms gained constitutional recognition *qua* Kingdoms. Ankole's monarchical status was formalised in a new Ankole Agreement, concluded on 30 August, 1962, and was reaffirmed in the 1962 Independence Constitution of Uganda as well as in subsequent legislation. The wording used for defining the position of the Omugabe was the same in the Ankole Agreement and the Uganda Constitution:[46]

(1)   The Omugabe (King), who is the Ruler of Ankole, shall enjoy all the titles, dignities, and preeminence that attach to the office of Omugabe under the law and custom of Ankole.

(2)   The Omugabe, the Omwigarire (Queen) and members of the Royal Family, that is to say, descendants of Omugabe Rwebishengye (Abanyiginya n'Abanyinginyakaze), shall enjoy their customary titles and precedence.'

The signing of the 1962 Ankole Agreement was hailed as the 'Biggest ceremony in Ankole history',[47] and for several dignitaries it was indeed an opportune moment to look back into the past. The Bishop of Mbarara outlined three stages in the development of Ankole – 'the period when the Kings of Ankole were supreme, their period under British protection, and the time after the agreement had been signed by the Governor and the Omugabe'.[48] The Enganzi, for his part, pointed to the changes which had occurred since 1901 and asked 'those present to join with him in asking the Governor to convey to the Queen (of England) and her Government the deep gratitude of the people of Ankole' for the work they had done.[49] The Omugabe, the Enganzi, and the Governor all expressed satisfaction with the constitutional arrangements which had just been agreed upon.[50]

While the new Ankole Agreement thus substantially enhanced the formal status of the Omugabe, this trend was curiously accentuated by the local implications of partly rivalries at the national level. It is well to remember in this connection that at the time of independence, in 1962, the central government of Uganda was under control of a coalition between the UPC and Kabaka Yekka (KY), while the Ankole government was under control of the DP until 1963. Before 1964 drew to a close, however, a growing tension emerged between the UPC and KY, in time causing the collapse of their alliance at the center. Exclusive control over the central government passed into the hands of the UPC leadership; meanwhile the tension between the UPC and KY reached unprecedented proportions.

In 1962, Kabaka Yekka ('The Kabaka Only') began to solicit the support of Baganda and non-Baganda elements residing in Ankole. In response to what was officially regarded in Ankole as an unwarranted intrusion into the political life of the kingdom, the DP government of Ankole initiated measures to counteract the KY tactics. Thus when groups of individuals in Ankole began to wear badges bearing the words 'Kabaka Yekka', the Ankole government reacted by prohibiting the display of such badges on the ground that it amounted to 'praising a King in another Kingdom' and this was contrary to customary law as it 'belittled the honour and authority of the Omugabe'.[51] One Muhamudu Kasumba was arrested and convicted for not heeding the Ankole government's instructions, and a case grew out of the incident in which the action of the Ankole government was finally upheld as valid by the Uganda High Court.[52] The matter became rather more complicated because some members of the Uganda cabinet did not, at that time, share the view that wearing a

KY badge constituted an affront to the Omugabe. At a political rally in Mbarara in July, 1962, some central government ministers went so far as to publicly denounce the order which sought to prevent the wearing of KY badges. The Minister of Justice, himself a Munyankore and UPC member (Ibingira), 'shouted praises of Kabaka Yekka and told a big gathering that anyone was free to wear a Kabaka Yekka badge in Ankole'.[53] These controversies led to a growing estrangement between the Ankole and Uganda governments, and similarly between the Minister of Justice and the High Court. The issue took a new turn when those who sought to spread KY influence in Ankole adopted an alternative strategy. With characteristic shrewdness, they substituted another label for the previous one and soon new badges were circulating bearing the inscription 'Omugabe Wenka' ('The Omugabe Only'). The display of these badges was immediately prohibited, however, and 'Omugabe Wenka' turned out to be an exceedingly short-lived affair. But it seems a fair presumption that even without the government's prohibition its impact would have remained minimal. Neither the persons wearing these badges nor the slogan itself carried much of an appeal in Ankole. The comments of the Omugabe sought to defuse the issue:[54]

'I am above politics and the use of my name by any one political partly as a slogan would only divide my people and endanger their happiness and the progress of my Kingdom . . . I do not discriminate against any of my people and I regard all of them in Ankole, irrespective of their political or religious beliefs, as my beloved subjects and for that reason I do not permit a section of my people to use my name for political ends.'

And in regard to Kabaka Yekka, the Omugabe's view was:

'My Enganzi and Eishengyero have publicly condemned Kabaka Yekka activities in Ankole and I strongly endorse their condemnations as I would not personally permit any other ruler to exercise his rule in my own Kingdom.'

The KY threat against the Omugabe's Kingdom was repeated a few years later, but now in an entirely different political context. Ironically, the renewed Kabaka Yekka infiltration caused the UPC government then in office in Ankole to use much of the same argument as its DP predecessor had done. On 14 September, 1965, the Enganzi stated 'I have today been informed that a movement called 'Kabaka Yekka' has started infiltrating into this Kingdom to try and hinder the progress of this Kingdom.' He further pointed out that 'saying Kabaka Yekka here in Ankole and wearing Kabaka Yekka shirts in Ankole means that the Kabaka is the only King . . . . even in this Kingdom of Ankole', and warned that 'I, as the guardian of the constitution under the Ankole schedule, and the Omugabe's Government as a whole cannot approve of this'.[55] To the Omugabe, the Enganzi gave his reassurance that 'this Government and your local subjects shall never allow any external movement seeking to lower your dignity. The exodus of KY to this Kingdom is truly calculated at lowering your dignity and seeks to cause division among your loyal subjects. Banyankore are well-known to be peace-loving and tolerant, but they might be forced to reach a point beyond which they will tolerate no more if KY tries to force its way through to this Kingdom.'[56]

That point was never reached, however, partly because of the restrictions placed upon KY activities, and partly because far more critical developments were in the offing. Through the spring of 1966 everyone's attention was focussed on the impending trial of strength between the Kingdom of Buganda and the central government of Uganda. The outcome of the crisis was to bring about a major change in the national balance of power and in time produced a considerable overhaul of the entire governmental structure.

It was also this crisis which provided the immediate motive for abolishing monarchical structures throughout Uganda. Significantly, just like earlier policies which had so much contributed to the exaltation of the Western Kingdoms, the measure again stemmed basically from a strategy pursued in regard to Buganda. When the Buganda crisis came to a head, the Uganda Government seized upon this opportunity to dismantle once and for all the Kabaka's stronghold. Following an open clash with the armed forces of Uganda, the Buganda monarchy was destroyed and its Kabaka fled the country. With the Buganda kingship eliminated, the smaller kingdoms instantly lost their *raison d'être* from the standpoint of the Uganda government; moreover, their abolition was positively valued because it 'soothed the pill', as it were, for Buganda.

The Ankole monarchy's last year of existence provided final confirmation of its status as a dependent variable. Following the 1966 clash, the preparation of new constitutional arrangements took some time, and while new proposals were being formulated many pre-existing arrangements and institutions were temporarily left untouched. Among these were the kingships of Ankole, Toro and Bunyoro. In 1966, an interim constitution was introduced which for all intents and purposes abolished federalism, but nonetheless reconfirmed the legitimacy of these three remaining monarchies. As the Enganzi then said to the Omugabe, in his opening address of the Eishengyero, 'nothing in this constitution has prejudiced your position as the Omugabe of Ankole Kingdom, as you will soon hear . . . Part one paragraph one to ten of the Ankole New Schedule, which honours you Nyakusinga, has not been altered either by letter or punctuation'.[57] But the provisional 1966 Constitution was in effect for a little over a year, that is, until the constitutional arrangements for a unitary republic in Uganda were ready. The Ankole kingship lasted until just that time.

5. Ethnicity and Kingship as Political Factors

ETHNIC IDENTITY AND ETHNIC INEQUALITY

Discussions of ethnicity in Africa politics have often focused on two sets of questions. One is about 'vertical' relationships and is concerned with potential conflict between ethnic identities and national loyalties. The other focuses on 'horizontal' relationships and is concerned with conflict between ethnic groups as such. Underlying both is a similar question, sometimes (in the affirmative) a premise, namely does ethnicity as such matter?[1] Usually implicit, at times explicit, answers to this question have varied, but the debate seems hardly to have been closed.

With the hindsight that we now have of roughly an eighty-year period of changing relationships between different ethnic groups in the Ankole area, it appears possible to make certain observations as regards the weight and relevance of factors of ethnicity in this particular African political context. Notwithstanding certain phases of pronounced ethnic strife in Ankole, the analysis of the Ankole experience seems supportive of the argument that ethnicity does not itself constitute a key variable but that instead it derives its significance from the context within which it is placed. Before presenting this argument, however, it will be useful to consider the two sets of questions about the role of ethnicity more closely.[2]

If we turn first to the focus on 'vertical' relationships, it appears that a tendency to view ethnicity, more specifically ethnic heterogeneity and ethnic identities, as problematic has here often been a point of departure. When discussing problems of ethnic ('primordial') diversity in the context of an 'unfolding civil order', Geertz, for example, argued that 'congruities of blood, speech, custom and so on, are seen to have an ineffable, and at times overpowering, coerciveness in and of themselves'.[3] In rather similar fashion, Pye wrote that 'the identity crisis . . . focuses on the most explosive and emotion-laden issues in political development',[4] while Gulliver speaks of the issues of unity and identity as two crucial problems pressing East African states.[5] These concerns have been reiterated over and over again.

In brief, the implication is that in many of the new states people's basic political identifications are generally not with the state but with sub-national units, such as linguistic, ethnic, religious, racial or regional collectivities. A lack of national identity may have serious consequences for the viability of the state, it is implied. Where there is not some minimum degree of 'belongingness' to the projected national framework, it is argued that such a state may lack sufficient cohesion, especially if it must face crises, but perhaps even for the smooth functioning of normal government operations.

In Africa as elsewhere, sub-national identities have indeed often appeared to be of considerable tenacity. Based on ethnicity or some other interest, in many instances they involve profound sentimental attachments. In a broader historical perspective, chances may thus well seem that sub-national units of identification will outlive some of the institutional structures superimposed upon them, finding new expressions of interests and identity in each new political framework. Europe has known quite a few examples where such attachments have continued to be of pervasive impact, for example, in Belgium, Britain, Czechoslovakia and Yugoslavia. Without holding to the view that Africa will necessarily repeat Europe's experience, there are neither any *a priori* grounds to suggest that the process will be much different. To the contrary, overarching government structures commonly being relatively new and often weak in Africa and virtually every country being divided along a variety of axes, there seems hardly a reason to expect any dramatic shifts in African ethnic identifications.

The question remains, then, whether the existence of such different ethnic attachments, in and of themselves, constitutes a problem, or even 'the' problem in African states. According to one trend of thought this would indeed appear to be the case. Leaders of many new states have often encouraged their people to think of themselves as citizens of these states rather than as members of sectional groups, or have even constitutionally forbidden any reference to ethnic membership, as in various francophone African countries. In Ankole, too, visits by 'national' officials and dignitaries usually included stern and lengthy admonitions that the local people ought to stop thinking of themselves as Banyankore (let alone as Bairu and Bahima) but should instead consider themselves as Ugandans.[6] Again, scholars have frequently echoed these desiderata, implying that such re-identifications – in and of themselves – are necessary and possible. In the extreme case the assumption appears to be that reconciliation and adjustment of ethnic attachments will eventually entail integration in the sense of full assimilation into new membership units.[7]

Still, it is doubtful that this particular concern with 'vertical' integration is valid and should be a first order of business. To assume that it would be possible and necessary for, say, Yoruba or Hausa, to become assimilated to the extent that they would no longer be Yoruba and Hausa but only Nigerians, or for Banyankore to become Ugandans 'only', might not only be a conceptual mistake but potentially could have adverse consequences. First, as regards the possibility of large-scale assimilation, the only major example to date appears to have been the United States. Here, due to quite unique historical circumstances, a process of dissolution of ethnic attachments and their replacement by a sense of American-ness was brought about to a considerable, though never to a full extent.[8] But it would require similar opportunities for massive immigration from heterogeneous origins and the attendant mixed settlement within one territory for this process to be possible elsewhere. Needless to say, African and Asian countries do not have these possibilities.[9] The Israeli case is already too different on a number of counts to enter as an example.[10] Instead, in Europe and elsewhere various forms of sub-national (and cross-national) 'belongingness' persist and seem to show no clear correlation with levels or patterns of development, whether measured by economic or other indices. Thus, even though the multitude of different ethnic identities in countries of Africa may well seem perplexing, there appears to be no basic difference between the prospect that Slovaks, Walloons or Scots will continue to be identified (and identify themselves) by those names, and the same happening in regard to Ashanti, Amhara, Baganda or any other of the innumerable ethnic communities throughout Africa. To try and radically alter such situations not only seems futile but may disrupt rather than serve to integrate.

Second, however, it not only appears impracticable to obliterate sub-national ethnic identities, but generally it seems unnecessary too.

Notwithstanding the concern frequenty expressed with issues of ethnicity, it still needs to be demonstrated that the creation of uniform and exclusively national identities would in and of itself be requisite to national development and integration. Would the fact of someone calling himself a Kenyan rather than a Kikuyu make him perform 'better' in his country's development? Put this way, the answer must be in the negative and the retort a simple 'What's in a name?' It is a different matter that Kenyan, Ugandan, Ghanaian and other new national identifications may increase as a result of processes of change; also that the latter kind of identifications may, relatively speaking, be strengthened within a multiple set of loyalties. But to call for a general sublimation of non-national into national identifications as a precondition to national development would be putting the cart before the horse and disregard the essential quality of these orientations.

Ethnic attachments themselves do not need, nor appear to be, problematic. Almost anywhere in the world, people can be categorised in more than one reference group, with which they may identify simultaneously. In most cases, no acute problems are implied; just as people may be Frisian as well as Dutch, so a relative harmony may exist between Kikuyu identity and Kenyan nationality.[11] However, a low degree of identification with the 'nation', contributing to lack of legitimacy, may arise as a result of other conditions. This is especially true for situations where a group feels that government is in the hands of 'the others', in which case 'the others' refers to people of a different ethnic identity (e.g. Cyprus, Sudan or even Canada). If one does not form part of the other group it may follow that one also does not wish to belong to that group; its extreme implication may be a refusal to coexist within a more inclusive framework which also incorporates the opposite group. Thus, in Rwanda the Bahutu had misgivings about joint membership with Batusi in the political framework, Greeks about Turks in Cyprus, and Muslims about Hindu in pre-independence India. One description of these situations would contend that particular groups do not wish to identify with the larger unit that incorporates and legitimises an opposed group, and instead either try to opt out or to claim the entire unit for themselves. But it also suggests that ethnic identity largely derives its saliency and meaning from the social context in which individuals and groups find themselves placed. Contextual analysis, not a focus on ethnic attachments *per se,* thus appears necessary to come to grips with the problem of ethnicity.

If we now turn to the other, 'horizontal' dimension within which issues of ethnicity are frequently discussed, then not only do a host of subsidiary questions at once suggest themselves, but it is clear that they are also more commonly addressed to contextual issues. A few examples of such questions may indicate this, e.g.: why do lines of cleavage in the socio-political structure of society A run a different way, based on different criteria, from those in society B? Why, for instance, is in one society religious affiliation more overriding in the formation of political groups than ethnic ties, clan loyalties, regionalism or personality factors, whereas an entirely different situation prevails in a neighbouring society? Can one determine what causes dissension of a particular type to emerge, and if so, how does it happen? Further, if dissension widens between members of different ethnic groups, does this occur *because* they are of different ethnic groups or because there are other, less obvious factors underlying these differences? Again, if a particular pattern of conflict has dominated, is it possible for a shift to occur towards another type of confrontation? How, in fact, should one account for a succession of different alignments, especially when a seemingly highly entrenched division makes place for conflict between differently based political groups? Are some structures of conflict perhaps inherently permanent, others more flexible? Also, can two or more such patterns coexist or are they mutually exclusive?

Questions such as these are preliminary to others of a directly political concern: what consequences do different political cleavages have for consensus and cooperation, both at the district and the national level? How do they affect the operation of governmental functions? Are some splits more functional (= preferable) than others from a point of view of national integration? Do some of them allow for, or perhaps even promote, the achievement of goals in the unit as a whole? Finally, of at least equal importance seems the opposite relationship, i.e. can government efforts modify, narrow or bridge these cleavages? Are some structural arrangements of government more conducive to reducing ethnic factionalism than others?

Clearly, questions of this kind require research along a variety of fronts to account for the particular juxtaposition of socio-political groups in a society and the social attachments that go with it. A broad historical account of the way relationships between ethnic, religious or other categories have developed into the present particularly is essential. Attention may need to be given to culturally determined factors which might have induced one group to develop economically more rapidly than others. At the same time, the role of education and the differential access and response to it by various categories may be crucial in explaining relative advantages attained by particular groups within political systems. Again, religion may to some degree have modified outlooks and aspirations as well as the extent of participation and the share of benefits available to its adherents. Closely linked to this are possible differences resulting from unequal economic opportunities available to various groups, or sheer demographic factors which may have given one group a lead over others. Other possible determinants, such as the type of leadership exercised, organisational structures and skills, elite composition and motivation, the pattern and effectiveness of communication, would similarly require examination for their possible effects on integrative or disintegrative potential.

Fact-finding along various of these lines will help to illuminate the nature of contact between different elements of a political system. In turn, this should increase our understanding of, among other things, whether and why conflicts are restricted to specific issues (such as competition for jobs or other immediate benefits) or generalised, affecting any contact and in any context between rival groups. Some ethnic groups, for instance, have coexisted within a single region or district in a basically non-competitive relationship, whereas in other situations there has been a long tradition of conflict on many fronts. Particularly in cases where an element of subordination formed part of the relationship, one might expect to find a relatively diffuse and lasting sense of antagonism, based on indignation over alleged inferiority on the one hand, and feelings of pride and superiority on the other. Immediate issues may no longer divide such groups, and conceivably continuing dissension may largely be attributable to a psychological lag. Nonetheless, such backgrounds would have important effects on popular identities, and in turn for people's preparedness to participate in wider frameworks. Closer examination of the nature of social cleavages should help determine whether the conflict concerned seems lasting or transitory, susceptible to intervention or rigid and inelastic, and whether, if untouched, it might gradually diminish, increase, or be supplanted by new types of confrontation.

Still, once allowance had been made for these contextual conditions, the central question that continues to concern us is whether ethnicity as such makes a difference – more plainly, whether ethnic conflict may occur because of ethnic differences. If we try to come to grips with this question, a partial answer would reiterate that in conflict between groups of different ethnicity the dispute usually involves more than these attachments alone. Often, people of different ethnic background within a single political framework have different occupations, different educational opportunities, different measures of influence in the unit, and so on. The origins of these ethnic divisions of labour, income, prestige and influence are not seldom of the chicken and egg variety, i.e. ethnicity first or occupation first? What matters is that either genuinely or contrived, much of the fuel for continuing inter-ethnic dispute is provided by inequalities in the distribution of benefits. Disputes are often fought under the banner of ethnicity, giving more meaning to the 'cause'. The question then is whether the sentiments involved would be equally strong in the absence of ongoing divisive issues or, in other words, whether ethnicity operates as an independent factor, irrespective of social and economic discrepancies (or perceived discrepancies) or comes and disappears with the latter? Obviously, these questions have an important bearing on the role of ethnicity; practically, however, it is difficult to separate the sustaining factors. Therefore, indeed, it is still only a partial answer.

Turning now to Ankole, the case is instructive because it provides us with an example of a historical development of issues of ethnicity which suggests that it is not ethnicity as such but other conditioning factors which tend to cause stresses and conflict among different population groups. The example is even more enlightening in this regard as it concerns a situation in which ethnic divisiveness and conflict first grew, later subsided. We are thus in a better position to relate this growth and decline to changing situational variables within the district context.

There are several dimensions of Ankole ethnicity in regard to which significant changes have occurred over the past half century or more and which are of analytic interest.[12] Nonetheless, other than noting that ethnic attachments and identities in Ankole have been compound and complex and than restating that the juxtaposition of identifications as Banyankore and Ugandans has not appeared to be particularly problematic, we will restrict ourselves here to the one dimension within which ethnicity in Ankole did become a major issue, i.e. the Bairu-Bahima division.

In the approximately eighty-year period with which we have been concerned, three phases can roughly be distinguished through which the relationships between Bairu and Bahima have evolved. First, in the pre-colonial era, we have seen that Bairu and Bahima had various kinds of social, economic and political contacts, and that Bahima enjoyed a certain 'power' advantage in these contacts. Notwithstanding various classifications of Nkore as a 'caste' or a 'class' society, it appeared that the nature of historical Bairu-Bahima relationships could best be understood as one between two largely distinct communities. Colonial rule, as we saw further, drastically changed this pattern and substituted it by one in which a chiefly and administrative Bahima elite came to function as a local ruling stratum in the (simultaneously) expanded Ankole district. Thus, during a second phase ethnic inequality between Bairu and Bahima grew and became even more pronounced as a result of attendant social and economic discrepancies introduced with and through the colonial framework. Eventually, ethnic protest and conflict erupted. Finally, we saw how during a third phase 'ethnic' inequality tended to subside, to be gradually eclipsed by a pattern of socio-economic inequalities in which various Bairu elites joined the ranks which earlier had been more exclusively occupied by Bahima. Ethnic conflict declined, though slowly, and new social and political alignments grew between Bahima and Bairu elites.

The analytic import of these transitions seems quite clear and straightforward. The Ankole example suggests that ethnic differences and coexistence do not appear to be problematic unless and until changes are brought about in the pattern of relationships. If one ethnic group ascends to a position of privilege and power, becoming visibly differentiated in additional respects than that of its ethnicity alone, rise of ethnic cleavages and friction is a strong probability. Thus, in Ankole, socio-economic inequalities superimposed upon ethnic differences created a sense of ethnic superiority and arrogance on the one hand, and of grievance and protest on the other. Similarly, when in the end status and ethnicity had lost their marked correlation in Ankole, these attitudes and feelings tended to change. Both the rise and the decline of ethnic hostility thus appear explicable by changing situational variables in the Ankole case, specifically of differential access to political and economic benefits for the two population groups. The conclusion that follows is that ethnicity as such does not constitute a source of conflict, but instead that ethnicity is made an issue through other factors.

Still, central though these implications appear to be, certain qualifications are suggested by the Ankole experience which appear of no less interest. One of these concerns the 'sequencing' of situational change and ethnic protest. While the evidence points to a basic connection between the growth of socio-political discrepancies and the rise of ethnic hostility, it is also clear that the two developments did not perfectly correlate in time. Inequalities in the political and economic spheres grew first – and for a considerable number of years even – before ethnic conflict broke out into the open. Later, again, the ethnic 'distribution' of inequalities had become more 'even' when ethnic hostility still tended to continue. To be sure, this qualification can itself be qualified. For example, it is quite certain that in the earlier stages grievances and ethnic resentment had developed long before protest · became open. At the other end, ethnic resentment continued to be promoted through Ankole's factional disputes as new transformations caused discrepancies in the distribution of benefits no longer to be based on an ethnically tiered pattern. Such additional qualifications are important, but do not basically reduce the apparent 'time-lag' that was evidenced between the growth of socio-economic cleavages and the articulation of ethnic hostility, and again between the decline of ethnically based inequalities and the retarded subsiding of ethnic protest. This time-lag does not appear difficult to explain, however: rather than being expressed in any mechanistic fashion, human reactions tend to develop slowly – and to linger on after the facts. But when considering the 'role' of ethnicity, and particularly when debating whether its status is that of a cause or a consequence, it ought to be noted that during such time-lags ethnicity may be neither of the two, but instead be manipulated as a tool for other purposes.

We have discussed the development of ethnic protest and a variety of conditions, demographic and other, which determined the particular course of this protest in Ankole. Without referring back to these various factors, it is worth recalling in this connection that when ethnic protest was 'on', its particular form and expression were again largely given shape by contextual conditions. A further point, however, goes beyond these contextual constraints, namely that at virtually no point did ethnic conflict in Ankole involve either one or the other entire ethnic group. Plain as this may be, it nevertheless throws up a contradiction: in Ankole as elsewhere, while ethnicity and ethnic divisions implicitly refer to general, maximum categories, the truth of the matter is that only some groups and individuals take part in conflicts understood to be 'ethnic'. In fact, though ethnic conflict supposedly concerns everyone, practically it may well prove hard to assert a common ethnic position – as among others the leaders of Kumanyana seem to have experienced.

Now, this paradox may be partly a question of nomenclature, more specifically a matter of inflation of terms. In Ankole, too, some limited disputes may well have been given a wider reference this way. Nonetheless, there is also another side to this contradiction, which appears more significant – and at least as applicable to the Ankole situation. Even in conflicts in which only few are actually active, there tends to be much wider potential support if the issues concerned are perceived to be 'ethnic' – again, if unequal rewards are more widely believed to correlate with ethnic distinctions. In such situations there is commonly a sense of self-evidence about the 'cause', one which has certainly also been manifest in the Ankole case. Thus, ethnic causes, specifically protest, may actually not need much active, massive support to be so recognised; rather, a certain blank check of solidarity appears to fill in the contradiction.

Finally, however, if this paradox seems thus to be resolved, it is precisely at this point that we should restate an earlier question: does ethnicity matter? Reviewing the Ankole experience, we have seen that the assertion of ethnic conflict, and of ethnicity, *followed* and did not precede other factors, notably socio-economic and political discrepancies. Accordingly, we have come to conclude that ethnicity did not 'cause' discrepancies and conflict, but rather that the structuring of these discrepancies 'caused' ethnic conflict. The general implication has thus been that other differences come first, and are decisive.

Now, there is no reason to change this logic, which as noted appeared to be confirmed by developments in Ankole. Here, as in many other contexts, ethnic protest was aroused by socio-economic differences – and somehow, this protest helped to change them. But what if there had been no ethnic differences to begin with? Though an entirely hypothetical question, it is useful to speculate about it in conclusion. Chances are first that in, say, a wholly Bairu society of

Ankole, colonialism might have created similar kinds of socio-economic discrepancies. Chances are further that few people in Ankole (or outside) would have paid as much attention to them as they have done to the present conflicts – for the strikingly simple reason that inequalities are 'normal'. These 'same' inequalities, however, as we have seen, provoked a major sense of injustice in an ethnically differentiated society – and with considerable effects (though including some unintended ones). Therefore, a qualified conclusion must be that ethnicity does after all make a difference. Moreover, without trying to answer what is more 'important' – ethnicity, or inequality – it also suggests itself that the Ankole peasants who get the short end of the stick now have an even smaller chance of a hearing than they might have had during 'ethnic' domination.

THE ARENA FOR CONFLICT

If we try to understand more of the dynamics, persistence and intensity of factional conflict in the Ankole district arena until 1971, it will be useful to consider some aspects of the structural setting in which it took place. In doing so, it will be necessary to present some additional data on the organisation of Uganda district government and administration up till that time, which applied to Ankole in similar fashion as to all other districts.[13] The main focus, however, must be on the channels and processes for interest-expression in that structure – or lack of these – without which a key dimension of the policy process would not be grasped. In particular, attention for the relationship between the *locus* and pattern of resource allocation and the strategies of political groups is necessary.[14]

In Uganda, the districts for many years clearly stood out as the principal units of regional government, without significant overlap with other local levels or ambiguity as to the point of gravity in local administration.[15] This is not to say that there was no overlap or ambiguity in other ways. Over time there were numerous rearrangements of the tasks and functions between the district administrations with locally recruited staff and the central government with its field officers in the districts. As noted, at some points the movement was towards greater decentralisation, at others towards centralisation; in each case these shifts tended to be translated locally into new kinds of relationships between local government personnel and central field officers. In 1971, with greater centralisation than in the late 1950s and 1960s, the district commissioner heading the central government administration in the district commanded increased powers (such as he enjoyed in a much earlier period), including that of control over local government expenditure; nonetheless, at least until that year, a degree of duality endured as there were two public works departments, two offices concerned with health, two with education and for various other functions in each district – one of the central government and one of the local government, though with some functional division of labour between them.

Such duplications were largely products of historical growth, unplanned in their entirety but difficult to undo. In and of themselves, however, they were not necessarily the main source of ambiguity. Until the district councils were dissolved and secretaries-general removed from office by the 1971 military government, ambiguity in Uganda district administration stemmed more directly from un-certainty about which authority had final say over what function: the district commissioner at the head of the central government's machinery or the secretary-general at the head of the local government administration. While the tendency was for the weight to be shifted onto the D.C.'s office, there were few, if any, guidelines to help sort out their respective tasks, and there tended to be considerable friction and dispute concerning their order of precedence.

Yet even the controversies between these two officials were epiphenomena of differences which reached more deeply. The D.C.'s and the secretaries-general symbolised two distinct administrative setups within each district, one central, one local.[16] Each headed an organisation, usually located close to one another, featuring an elaborate set-up which comprised scores of personnel at different levels. The declared purpose of both organisations was to promote the welfare of the district they served; yet surprisingly there was but little contact between the two in the fulfilment of their common objectives. The D.C. had a contact with the local government because he was charged with the supervision of their administration. Other central government officers had more incidental and specific contacts, made in their efforts to get things done within the competence of their departments; not the least important, for instance, were their contacts with the chiefs who arranged meetings with groups and individuals. With these exceptions, each of the two organisations basically went its own way. Central field officers for specialised areas such as agriculture, co-operatives, veterinary services or community development, received instructions from their respective headquarters and translated these for immediate action within their districts. Though usually a dozen or more of these specialist officers had adjacent offices at the *boma*[17], they only met from time to time to inform each other of their programmes, not usually to integrate their activities. Neither was there any institutionalised dialogue with the local government over their plans and priorities. The air at the boma was essentially technical and professional, characteristic of a style of planning from above which eschews interference from local groups and local politics. The majority of field officers appeared to prefer it that way; when asked, not a few indicated apprehension at the idea of having to subject their programmes to prolonged discussions and amendments by local groups. In any case, one consequence of this pattern of plan-making was that local individuals and groups only came into it at the final implementation stage, by which time they might try to influence the officer concerned to exercise whatever flexibility of manoeuvre was left to him in order to maximise the benefits they could derive through his office. Aside from this lobbying on a near-individual basis, more general consequences of this pattern appear to have been the potential lack of local interest in programmes and schemes and the lack of relevant information for plan-making.

If one had wanted to fill these gaps, the obvious body to bring into the planning process would have been the local government. For all its elaborate organisation and personnel, the local government structure in Uganda was not directly involved in plan-making. Its structure was that of an administrative hierarchy, for narrowly administrative tasks, headed by a local political leadership. The responsibilities of its largest component, the administrative structure of chiefs, had changed a great deal since the system was first established, and in recent times centred mainly upon the maintenance of basic administration within their jurisdiction and the observance of bye-laws and other law and order instruments. By far the greatest concern, expenditure and administrative attention in each district went into the maintenance of this staff establishment, which commonly included hundreds of chiefs and other administrative positions at all levels (district, county, sub-county, parish). Invariably this made the district government the largest employer in the area, even if in recent years matters of recruitment and salary scales were handled not by local bodies but by sub-committees of the Uganda Public Service Commission (Since these sub-committees themselves were locally recruited, to the average citizen the distinction tended to be merely formal).

Over and above this administrative edifice stood the political leadership: the secretary-general, some other salaried but political officials functioning as department heads, and finally the district council. The secretaries-general and their political associates were invariably recruited from amongst the party or faction within a party which commanded a majority in the district council at the time of their appointment. (From 1966 till 1971 they were appointed by the central government from amongst the majority leadership in the council.) Apart from routine business, such as an annual budget session and some other required meetings concerned with the maintenance of the establishment, it is no exaggeration to say that this leadership's attention was most heavily preoccupied with questions as to which individuals were given what political appointments. Not surprisingly, these concerns were not necessarily exhibited in formal council meetings, but rather in caucus gatherings beforehand. If the leadership of a faction could be installed into office, chances for the followers to be rewarded with positions and sinecures would be considered greater. In addition, promotions and transfers were important tools available to the leadership of successful factions. As noted earlier, 'loyal' chiefs (and primary school teachers) could be rewarded by posting them to attractive areas, 'opposition' chiefs were liable to be assigned to out-of-the-way stations.

Factions competing for such prizes did not develop along random lines, but as we have seen could usually be distinguished on the basis of other criteria – party, ethnic, clan, religious, region, or some combination of these. Without doubt, in some instances long-standing enmity between groups was a contributing factor, transposed as it may have been to new forms of expression. We have seen the development of this in the particular case of Ankole. Nonetheless, other factors added to this propensity for political strife. One was that besides issues concerning the maintenance of the administrative district structures as such, there was not too much else to occupy the attention and interest of the district council and the other elements of the district political arena. Moreover, since these structures were elaborate, the interest in a share of the resources on the part of local groups was accordingly greater, the more so in the relative absence of alternative employment opportunities such as business. Thus, a paradoxical feature of district government in Uganda was that the councils could have provided a ready-made forum for the discussion of development priorities in the area but failed to be used for that purpose. There was no procedure set down to induce a dialogue on development issues between the specialist officers at the boma and the district's political representation on the council. In consequence, the experts remained devoid of relevant popular information while factional groups, for lack of issues outside their own immediate differences, turned to more entrenched positions against each other. Structurally, it would be difficult to conceive of conditions which would have been more supportive of factional politics than the ones embedded in the framework for local government operative in Uganda until 1971.

The tendencies that this set-up induced were largely borne out by the record of the Ankole district council, until 1967 the Eishengyero. During the last half decade of its existence, the council met only infrequently, at an average of about four meetings of a few days each year. Approval of the agenda by the Uganda Minister of Regional Administrations was required before a meeting could be held. During every session there was one budget meeting, which never led to major dialogue because expenditure was determined and controlled by the central government. There was doubtless bargaining and pressure upon the Uganda government to provide various services or to finance projects of the Ankole district administration[18], but this was usually conducted between departments; it is not certain that many councillors were aware of this financial nexus. Above all, council minutes showed major preoccupation with matters concerning its own composition and organisation, often formal issues through which ascendancy of one faction over others might be promoted. In addition, there were recurrent resolutions supporting or congratulating the central government on various moves or decisions – votes representing tokens of political strength and reaffirmations of allegiance. Very few items of the council's business were concerned with any development issues, as opposed to matters about the framework's maintenance and control. Naturally, the same focus determined the council's informal operations.

The question should thus be raised what pattern would have emerged if there had not been two but essentially one structure of government operations in Ankole, integrated into a single political process. Notwithstanding the dynamics of factional cleavages in the district and indeed a degree of inevitability of political factionalism, such an arrangement might well have had some effect in reducing the pervasiveness of conflict. Basically, this would have required a reappraisal of the relationship and division of tasks between the boma and the local government. We have noted the involvement of the expert officers at the boma, who in various capacities were charged with functions concerning the social and economic development of the district. Though they kept each other informed about the timing and organisation of their projects, none of their plans were channelled on to the local government arena for consultation or even discussion. At the same time the political leadership of Ankole was expected to lead in the promotion of social and economic welfare in the district. Yet, beyond stating general desirabilities and prophecies, there was little they could contribute in this regard as they lacked the logical structure for a realistic engagement in these spheres. Hence the tendency was to alternate between the extreme generalities characteristic of public speechmaking and the petty involvements of factional disputes. In the mid-1960s the local administrations of Uganda, Ankole not excepted, were criticised by central planning officers for their preoccupation with shopping list planning: when required to submit planning priorities which were meant to be integrated into the national five-year plan, most local authorities listed new office buildings, roads, schools, and numerous other items without consideration for the requisite mobilisation of resources. In the structural set-up within which these orientations were articulated, however, it was difficult to see how they might have arrived at different kinds of proposals.

This situation might have changed if the relationship between the boma and the Ankole government had involved more than merely supervision and control. If development plans and projects designed at the boma had been forwarded for discussion within the district political arena, both sides would have stood to gain – and to lose relatively little. The planning officers might have gained what is a critical condition for effective implementation, namely local understanding and interest in what their plans and projects were about. This condition relates closely to the need to include channels for interest-expression in the design of political-adminstrative structures. Its rationale is that development programmes and policies cannot just be made *for* people, but will have to involve the people concerned if they are to have a chance of success. Without that, if people are not involved and do not derive a sense that the project they are in is theirs, the chances are they will also not be interested and that plans handed down from central agencies will remain sterile. Even if time-consuming and otherwise difficult, popular participation, including recognition of popular interests, should have been considered a necessary component in the process by which development priorities were formulated. Moreover, without such popular involvement it is generally difficult to see how officials of central government departments could have known what was best for people in a particular local area; they largely lacked the popular information which might make technical plans and priorities more realistic from a local point of view. Particularly, it seemed hard for the officials concerned (who as a matter of policy were all non-Banyankore and usually did not speak the local language) to become alerted to specific local conditions, political and other, which need to be anticipated in the design of projects if they are to get a generally positive reception. The individual freehold project and the Ankole ranching scheme are cases in point of such failures.

On the local government and politics side such a changed relationship might similarly have made a difference – even if only a modest one. As in all situations where resources are scarce, it was quite logical for each of the factions concerned to raise their competitive claims for benefits at the level where they seemed most effective. Again, the institutional framework underlying these actions was one that appeared to compel almost any group in office, irrespective of composition and background, to adopt roughly similar kinds of strategies and tactics. While it would have been hardly realistic to try and alter the interests involved, what might have been varied was the range of issues over which local groups would challenge one another. More specifically, the interests at stake might have been expanded so that instead of a nearly exclusive focus on distributive competition a greater preoccupation with alternative, developmental policies and perspectives for the district at large might have emerged. In part, such different task-orientations were dependent on the kind of structural arrangements – virtually the only variable, and manipulable, element in the framework. A changed focus in the political arena could have followed: to engage political groups into debating alternative development projections may shift attention and conflict towards matters outside the arena itself and turn it into a more valuable instrument for the determination and realisation of development objectives.

That suitable channels for interest expression were limited was largely a result of the kind of political frameworks that have been handed down over time, not only in Ankole, but in Uganda and even in Africa more generally.[19] The general tendency has been for viability structures concentrating on law and order, either of a centralised or a decentralised variety, to be continued – with accretions added to them more through a process of cellular growth than as a result of conscious planning. There does not seem to have been a compelling reason why this should have remained the predominant pattern. Changed institutional frameworks with a specific orientation on developmental requirements, it appears, would have constituted an improvement. But, perhaps, they have failed to be adopted for lack of appeal in terms of, precisely, the interest processes they might modify. Questions about 'constraints' and institutional relevance, it turns out, appear to have a rhetorical quality.

ANKOLE KINGSHIP IN RETROSPECT

Having looked back at some of the determinants and effects of Ankole's 'new' institutions, we should finally reconsider the developments experienced by one of its oldest, i.e. the kingship. We have seen that the Ankole kingship basically lost its distinctive functions and encountered formidable obstacles in developing new ones. There have been good grounds to argue that in the process the institution had become redundant and in the end could be easily pushed aside. Let us now ask, then, what lessons, if any, we might learn from the experience: is such a process 'retrogressive', to be regarded with concern and consternation; should it be viewed as 'modernisation' or 'progress' – or as what indeed?

In the voluminous but short-lived literature on 'political develop-ment', institutionalisation was frequently put forward as a strategy, and as a yardstick for evaluation. 'Structures' were to transform themselves into 'institutions'; where such processes would obtain 'political development' was said to be forthcoming. Often the same imperative was implied in certain themes of anthropology, as well as of public administration and political sociology.[20] Perhaps most emphatic of all, practitioners of the sub-field labelled 'organisational development' would maintain that to institutionalise – i.e. to strengthen organisational structures against 'turbulent' environments – is a *sine qua non*.

Now, it goes without saying that institutionalisation is something quite different from institutional decline and redundancy. Quite clearly these two notions are diametrically opposed. But precisely because they are so, it should logically follow that if a positive value is attached to institutionalisation, then institutional decline should be negatively assessed.

Is it in this way, then, that we should judge the decline and eclipse of Ankole kingship? Much of the evidence goes to suggest so. We have seen the major colonial transformations to which the institution was subject and we have noted the unspectacular exit of the monarchy at the time of its abolition. Clearly, the transformations it was faced with were manifold, drastic, and largely concurrent, and it is indeed difficult to see how any institution whose role was so evidently rooted in a different historical context could have overcome them. Neither the expansion of scale of Ankole nor the kingdom's incorporation into Uganda were particularly conducive to a continued meaningful role of the kingship or to a successful search for new relevance. The same was true, as indeed we have seen, for the redefinition of the socio-political context of the Obugabe – the reduction of Bahinda influence and the increasingly tenuous Bairu-Bahima division. Perhaps most clearly of all, the organisational role (or lack of it) which the Omugabe was given to play in the colonial framework was ridden with ambiguities and manifestly failed to provide or allow for a meaningful involvement. Thus the lack of reaction at the abolition of Ankole kingship did not seem very surprising; it rather tended to confirm and exemplify the extent of unrelatedness that had grown between the kingship and Ankole society.

A case might thus well be made for the argument that the Ankole kingship had become a redundant institution, whose discontinuation made no particular difference to the socio-political framework and process of Ankole. If we do this, it will be evident that the argument must hinge largely, though not exclusively, on the accuracy of the lukewarm reactions evidenced at the time of the monarchy's abolition. This must be so because in the case of institutions which are largely expected to command popular allegiances (such as religious institutions and other symbolic structures) a test of institutional redundancy should particularly lie in the nature of the orientation which their presumed 'clienteles' exhibit towards them. Lack of power *per se* is therefore not necessarily a criterion of such redundancy. Clearly, as long as an institution has a certain influence, no matter how one evaluates this impact, it cannot be described as 'redundant'. Power and influence may be viewed or experienced in either positive or negative terms, but to talk of institutional redundancy only makes sense if such influence is by and large lacking in either way. It is suggested, therefore, that an institution is redundant if it no longer serves a meaningful purpose within its socio-political context – in other words, if its presence or absence makes no difference to the overall social and political process.[27]

In the case of symbolic institutions such as the Ankole monarchy – and it is hard to see that any other role could be claimed for the Obugabe in its terminal years – their relevance or redundancy would thus need to be an expression of the extent to which people are knowledgeable of, identifying with, or indifferent towards these institutions, or else would plainly reject their role or existence. In this sense, then, institutional redundancy comes in as a variant, and a measure of assessment, of institutional decline. It does not essentially matter in this respect that there are normally only few issues on which an entire society unequivocally shares the same views. Anything like 'complete' redundancy is indeed an abstraction which in reality will be found in exceptional cases only; institutional redundancy in terms of popular allegiances, in other words, means no more – nor less – than that in some predominant measure that quality seems applicable. Again, however, in 1967 there was nothing to indicate that this was not the case with regard to Ankole kingship.

On the above basis we would indeed come to qualify the Ankole kingship as a redundant institution. But is that all? Beyond – or before – making such a qualification, which as understood is particularly reflective of the 1967 situation, we will need to consider two further aspects of the matter. The first requires that we look at the institution's role during the transformation of Ankole's socio-political context, not so much for the way in which these transitions impinged upon its own performance, but rather to see what its presence did (or did not do) to facilitate or otherwise affect the processes of change to which the society was subject. The second point is closely related and asks whether or not institutional decline and redundancy in this particular case may have correlated with, or resulted from, processes of growth or development in other directions.

As regards the first of these queries, on the basis of notions of political development which rest on criteria of institutionalisation it can be argued that Ankole kingship was an institution in 'decay'. In the same vein some would consider it an example of political regression, not development. Strictly speaking, if the interest is purely in the fortunes of a specific institution, such a view cannot be disputed. Obviously, Ankole kingship did not 'develop' in the present century. By some of the standards we have noted above, Ankole kingship definitely was not a case of political development, it lacked the conditions for an effective search of new goals, it did not exhibit an increase in functional complexity, and its longevity in the end was thwarted.[21]

Again, however, the question remains how useful it is to employ such a yardstick.[22] The functions of the Ankole monarchy were eroded when a different and more inclusive organisational framework was imposed upon the society. Basically, there was no compelling requirement for a role of kingship in that framework. But since there happened to be a monarchy in Ankole, its retention suggested itself at least on the ground that a premature decapitation might generate popular reactions which could hamper the development of an effective administration. In point of fact, while the monarchy was made to shed its functions one by one, its continuation during the establishment of colonial political and administrative structures probably helped obviate an abrupt legitimacy crisis. Its own problems and ambiguities were no less severe when serving that purpose, however; indeed these problems were rendered all the more acute by the process of self-liquidation to which the kingship found itself subjected. The main significance of the Ankole monarchy was that it acted as a shell for transformation. It helped to define the cognitive map of many members of Ankole society at a time when major transitions were under way. As these transformations were reaching completion, the shell could be finally thrown away.

Thus it appears that the Ankole monarchy was 'useful' in a way while losing its functions, or in a sense relevant while growing redundant. Indeed the connection perhaps was even more immediate: its growing redundancy may well have been a 'relevant' factor in the light of the widening Bairu-Bahima division, preventing the occurence of more direct political confrontation between the two groups. But did the kingship's decline also correlate with 'growth' or 'development' in any other ways? Again, this must be a matter of judgment and criteria, which in fact throws up one or two issues which seem to remain when reviewing the monarchy's fortunes over the present century. If we are merely to look for features of growth, such as the expansion, proliferation and increasing diversity of administrative and political structures, roles and regulations, then by all means the tendency in Ankole has been an 'upward' one over the years. Thus, if we left it there, we might not just see a correlation of phenomena of administrative growth and the eclipse of the Ankole kingship, but it could be argued that the monarchy's decline was a result and an accelerator of these institutional changes on a wider scale. In this sense, then, the role of the Ankole kingship, even as a declining institution, could conceivably be related to 'growth' – of a kind. The example would underscore that limited utility is to be gained by analysing institutions in isolation for assessing 'political development', and suggest that the elimination of a superfluous institution may itself be regarded as an instance of such development. In its broadest sense, the case would illustrate a universal phenomenon, namely, that growth processes throw up redundancy.

Still, two caveats remain when drawing these conclusions, and they are of no small importance. One was already alluded to and indeed was to be anticipated in the first place. The other as we will see evolved from a somewhat unexpected development and in fact was not without an element of surprise. Both raise open, though for that matter no less fundamental questions. Let us consider each briefly.

As regards the first of these issues, one of the points of this study essentially has been that the colonial framework imposed upon Ankole society pushed out the monarchy as a relevant institution. In the structure for colonial control and transformation which permeated the society, little room was left for the kingship. Its social context, moreover, was drastically changed as political divisions tended to further reduce its role. Consequently, the institution became increasingly superfluous and irrelevant. After Uganda's independence these tendencies did not change but instead were drawn to their logical conclusion.

Now, without belabouring the obvious, it should be quite clear that the redundancy of Ankole's kingship was determined by the colonial framework and indeed came to constitute institutional irrelevance in terms of that framework. Quite specifically, therefore, the monarchy's decline was contextually determined. As noted also, the colonial framework embodied growth of some kind – the nature of which needs no more to be detailed here. But it would be difficult to consider such growth development in any stricter sense. Colonial welfare and benefits to incorporated populations in most instances came as by-products of other objectives, political as well as economic ones. It was these which were paramount and followed from the dictates of metropolitan policies; colonial operations were simply not primarily motivated by concern with the interests of annexed societies.

While clearly this must be borne in mind when regarding the nature of the framework which eroded the Ankole monarchy, there is also another aspect to consider. As we have seen, the legacy of institutional structures in many ex-colonial societies, including that of Ankole, is such that increasingly the arrangements of these superstructures themselves are being regarded as a major constraint on development efforts. Put starkly, many inherited structures appear not so much irrelevant but disfunctional instruments in terms of the declared purposes of development policies. Still, it was largely through the establishment and proliferation of such structures that an institution such as the Ankole monarchy came to lose its essential meaning and purpose. Though this does not alter the kingship's decline and increasing lack of relevance, it is nonetheless difficult to regard it as an example of obsolescence at the hands of patterns of 'progress'. Rather, a summing up might be that a once functional institution was eroded by disfunctional arrangements – Gresham's law applied to politics.

Lastly, a rather unexpected development as mentioned threw up a second caveat, which from another angle again raises the question of institutional relevance. It will be recalled that in January 1971, a few years after the abolition of monarchical institutions in Uganda, an army coup overthrew the Obote government and put General Amin in power. During the first few months of his presidency the General evidently faced a need to cultivate sources of support in addition to the backing of the soldiers who had helped put him in power. Spending little time in the office, for a considerable period he extensively toured the country, addressing public gatherings and engaging in discussions with 'Elders' (a newly coined category of hand-picked notables assumed to represent public opinion in each district) about the problems which concerned them. Many of the policy statements which thus emerged seemed to assume that Uganda's problems had been largely caused by the previous regime: on issue after issue where the Obote government had said 'yes', Amin's government would say 'no' (or *vice versa*) in an attempt to establish its credibility.

One step for which Obote's government was of course vividly remembered was its abolition of the monarchies. From the outset, however, this happened to be a matter for which the new regime did not want to change the beacons. One of the '18 points' the soldiers had submitted upon their January 1971 takeover was that Uganda was to remain a republic. Nonetheless, there continued to be strong feelings about the matter among the neo-traditional Buganda elite, a category which was of no small concern to Amin in his efforts to gain popularity and support. The Buganda elite had felt hurt through the loss of status and influence they had suffered during the Obote years, so much of which had seemed symbolised by the Kabaka's deposition. At the same time, to Amin they appeared as a powerful force to count with.

Once installed, one of Amin's first moves did a great deal to get the Baganda on his side: he had the body of Sir Edward Mutesa, the late Kabaka deposed by the Obote government, flown over from London. and given a State funeral in Uganda. Also, the Kabaka's relatives received various kinds of compensations and at not a few public occasions a deliberate limelight was put on them, particularly on Ronald Mutebi, the late Kabaka's son. Gestures of a somewhat similar conciliatory nature were also made towards the ex-rulers of the other abolished kingdoms of Uganda, whom Amin used to meet from time to time during the first half year or so of his government. The political climate seemed to be changing and to open up for a reconciliation with (neo-)traditional leadership.

Then, the inevitable question was raised. The Baganda 'Elders', stimulated no small amount by Amin's policies of reversal, asked for the restoration of the Kabakaship. When first commenting on the request, the General did not flatly say 'no'. Possibly anticipating a promise of political goodwill, he instead congratulated the Baganda Elders for their frankness and responded that the issue was a very important one which required careful study of all aspects, especially costs. Also, he added, opinions from all the districts of Uganda would have to be made clear on the matter before it could be further considered.[23]

With this the Baganda began to see a possibility of their case being won. The new government appeared ready to reconsider the question of kingship. The main thing necessary seemed to be for the right kind of representations to be put forward. If all groups respectful of tradition could be mobilised, monarchies would be restored to their true standing.

Uganda for a short spell thereafter experienced one of its most lively and interesting discussions. The government had called for public debate on the question of restoration. In response, during August and September, 1971, memorandum after memorandum was produced and submitted to the General by the Elders of each district. Virtually every conceivable argument pro or contra was presented. As it happened, however, the pro's emanated almost exclusively from the Baganda quarters. For lack of consensus or even a beginning of majority opinion, therefore, the issue soon dwindled as rapidly as it had arisen.

Part of this episode's interest for a retrospective look at Ankole kingship lies nonetheless in the arguments which were advanced on the possible restoration of monarchical institutions. As can be seen from their memorandum,[24] the Ankole representatives among other things stressed the need to curb factionalism, costs, unwanted exaltations, and divided loyalties in opposing such restoration. Significantly, some of these arguments had earlier been heard at the time of the abolition of the kingships.

At the same time the Ankole memorandum also derived a special significance from the cross-section of political leadership which endorsed it. In the light of the prolonged rivalry for influence which had been taking place in the district political arena, it was quite remarkable that leaders of Bahima and Bairu, of Protestants, Catholics and Muslims, and even of the factions which formerly were opposed within the Uganda People's Congress, for once appeared jointly as the signatories to a statement pleading against the restoration of kingship.

Still, the Ankole memorandum's greatest significance lay perhaps not in its argumentation or even its endorsement, but in the fact that the representatives who submitted it to General Amin included

Ankole's ex-Omugabe, Gasyonga II. This rather unique fact – an ex-king requesting the non-restoration of kingship – appears important no matter which of two possible motivations might have been at play: whether it was Gasyonga's own will and initiative to be included in the party, or whether others had pressed him to lend his name to it. In either case, what mattered was the effort made to legitimise the continued abolition of Ankole kingship by enlisting the ex-monarch's support for it. The effort seemed but to point to one last question: was the Ankole kingship yet not without a relevance?

Memorandum by the Elders of Ankole to the President, General Idi Amin Dada, on the Restoration of Kingdoms*

'We, the representatives of the Elders of Ankole gathered in Mbarara on Monday 23rd August, 1971 wish to congratulate Your Excellency and the men of the Uganda Armed Forces on the successful take over of Government on 25th January, 1971, and also on the manner in which Your Excellency has conducted the affairs of this country since you assumed its leadership as President of the Second Republic of Uganda.

'The people of Ankole, and indeed the whole of Uganda look forward to your continued leadership so that this country may take its proper place among other progressive and peaceful nations of the world.

'Your Excellency, permit us also to take this opportunity on behalf of the people of Ankole to thank you for the honour you did us and the love you showed us by visiting our District only a few days ago. Your visit which had been long and anxiously awaited was hailed by thousands of people in Ankole, as it enabled you to see for yourself the undoubted support that Your Excellency commands in the District.

'Your Excellency, during your visit you talked to the people in the language they understand, you listened to their problems and requests with all your patience and you brought them nearer to you than any other leader has ever done. For this and for many other things you have done, we thank you most sincerely.

'Your Excellency, may we thank you also for the good will you have shown towards the former rulers of this country since the Military take-over of Government – the return of the remains of the late Sir Edward Mutesa, the honour and respect which you and your

*Source: *Uganda News*, Ministry of Information and Broadcasting, Kampala, Uganda. 24th August, 1971.

Government paid at the funeral of the late Sir Tito Winy, the restoration of property to Prince Kaboyo and the assistance you have continued to render to Sir Charles Gasyonga.

'Your Excellency, the Elders of Ankole feel that this is a period when your Government is busily engaged in the programme of reconstruction and re-organization of the affairs of the Nation; a period when no energies and efforts should be lost in building Uganda as a strong united country and also a period when all of us living in Uganda must look forward and not backwards.

'Your Excellency, the Elders of Ankole feel that while there may be merit in re-examining some of the past deeds of the former President Milton Obote and his Government, your Government should not be rushed into taking decisions on matters which may distract your attention from, and frustrate your efforts in Nation building.

'Your Excellency, in our view, the question concerning the restoration of Kingdoms is one of those crucial matters which we feel should not be raised or even discussed in the Second Republic of Uganda, because of the following reasons:—

'(a) It is your declared Policy that all political activities are suspended at the present time. The restoration of Kingdoms would most likely revive political divisions and factionalism contrary to the declared policy of Government. It is our view that if Uganda is to develop as a strong United Sovereign Nation, any divisive tendencies must not be allowed to emerge.

'(b) The country at the moment faces a very heavy deficit, the country's financial position cannot therefore sustain any expenditure connected with the restoration of Kingdoms. In addition Kingship imposes all sorts of indirect taxations, all of which are undesirable.

'(c) Present circumstances demand that all our efforts and resources in the Second Republic of Uganda should be concentrated on the economic and social reforms of the country for the benefit of many, instead of being used to enhance the prestige of a few individuals.

'(d) The people in Kingdoms Districts have in the past shown a tendency of divided loyalty between their former Rulers and the Central Government. For the Military Government to consolidate its position and to carry out its programme of re-organization unimpeded a situation which tends to create divided loyalty among the people must be avoided at all costs.

'(e) The 18 points declared by the soldiers on the take over of Government included the statement that Uganda will continue to be a Republic. This was further repeated at the State House, Entebbe, where the representatives of the Royal families were present. It would be going back on the soldiers' word if we started talking about the restoration of Kingdoms. Government must not give in to pressure of this kind.

'Your Excellency, we say these things not with any malice, but we strongly feel that if we are to march forward to our stated goal of freedom and progress we must break with the past where this stands in our way and therefore our views must be accepted in this spirit.

'In conclusion Your Excellency, we reiterate on behalf of the people of Ankole our full support to you and your Government. The people of Ankole are behind you in what you are doing and have every confidence that you will successfully accomplish the great task that you have set out to do for God and our Country.'

The memorandum was signed by the following people:
Z. C. K. Mungonya (Chairman); B. K. Bataringaya (Secretary); Canon Y. Buningwire (Member); P. K. Garubungo (Member); E. C. Cook (Member); C. B. Katiti (Member); A. Mulumba (Member); Y. Makuku (Member); W. Mukaira (Member); E. T. Kihika (Member); T. K. Kururagire (Member); N. K. Bananuka (Member); Sheik A. Kadunyu (Member); Haji Abbas Kayemba (Member); E. Rutehenda (Member); and J. B. K. Bwetere (Member).

Notes

NOTES TO CHAPTER 1: 'LOCAL POLITICS IN UGANDA'

1 Cf. Raymond Apthorpe, 'Does Tribalism Really Matter?', *Transition* 37, and P. H. Gulliver (ed.), *Tradition and Transition in East Africa* (London 1969), Introduction.
2 Cf. M. M. Edel, *The Chiga of Western Uganda* (New York 1957), p. 24.
3 Gulliver, *op. cit.*
4 *Uganda Census 1959*, African Population (Uganda Protectorate, Ministry of Economic Affairs, Statistics Branch), p. 18.
5 Joseph H. Greenberg, 'Africa as a Linguistic Area', in William R. Bascom and Melville J. Herskovits (eds), *Continuity and Change in African Cultures* (Chicago 1962, Phoenix Edition).
6 Uganda Government, Department of Information, Annual Reports.
7 These figures are based on the 1959 Uganda Census. The present situation would show substantial increases.
8 Cf. Pierre Van den Berghe, 'European Languages and Black Mandarins', *Transition* 34, pp. 19-23.
9 Milton A. Obote, 'Language and National Identification', *East Africa Journal* (April 1967), pp. 3-6. The Amin Government has announced its interest to select one of the Ugandan languages as a national language.
10 Uganda Protectorate, *Development of Kiswahili as an Educational and Administrative Language in the Uganda Protectorate* (Entebbe 1928).
11 Obote, *op. cit.*
12 J. H. Speke, *Journal of the Discovery of the Source of the Nile* (London 1863).
13 Cf. Audrey I. Richards (ed.), *East African Chiefs* (London 1959), p. 358, and Lloyd A. Fallers (ed.), *The King's Men* (London 1964), p. 11.
14 Joan Vincent, *African Elite: The Big Men of a Small Town* (New York and London 1971), *passim*.
15 C. C. Wrigley, 'The Changing Economic Structure of Buganda', in L. A. Fallers (ed.), *The King's Men*, p. 31; A. B. Mukwaya, *Land Tenure in Buganda* (Kampala 1953).
16 Ankole was one of these areas.
17 Serious frictions occurred particularly in the Eastern Region and in Kigezi District. In Ankole, as we will see, the role of the Baganda chiefs should be considered within the context of the Bahima political hegemony in the district.
18 For a discussion of the Dundas reforms, see D. Apter, *The Political Kingdom in Uganda* (Princeton 1961), pp. 211-212 and pp. 224-226.

19 The main instrument was the *Administration (Western Kingdoms and Busoga) Act* (1963), codifying the position which had come to exist on the basis of renegotiated *Agreements* with the Western Kingdoms.

20 On the Buganda issue before independence, see Apter, *The Political Kingdom in Uganda* and Fallers, *The King's Men*. On the Rwenzururu movement, see Martin R. Doornbos, 'Kumanyana and Rwenzururu: Two Responses to Ethnic Inequality', in Robert I. Rotberg and Ali A. Mazrui (eds.), *Protest and Power in Black Africa* (New York 1970), pp. 1109-1130.

21 D. A. Low, *Political Parties in Uganda 1949-62* (London 1963), p. 14.

22 These arrangements were largely based on the recommendations of the Munster Commission; see Uganda Protectorate, *Report of the Uganda Relationships Commission 1961* (Entebbe 1961).

23 The major documents of this process include: *African Local Government Ordinance* (1949); *District Administration (District Councils) Ordinance* (1955); *Local Administration Ordinance* (1952); *Administration (Western Kingdoms and Busoga) Act* (1963); the renegotiated *Agreements* with the Kingdoms of Buganda, Ankole, Toro and Bunyoro (appended as *Schedules* to the *Independence Constitution of Uganda*); *Report of an Inquiry into African Local Government in the Protectorate of Uganda* (Wallis Report) (1953); *Report of the Constitutional Committee* (Wild Report) (1959); *Report of The Uganda Relationships Commission* (Munster Report) (1961); *Report of the Uganda Independence Conference* (1962).

24 For the development of party politics in Uganda, see Apter, *The Political Kingdom in Uganda*; Low, *Political Parties in Uganda 1949-62* (London 1963); and F. B. Welbourn, *Religion and Politics in Uganda 1952-1962* (Nairobi 1965).

25 An additional inducement for the desire to have constitutional heads was that these office-holders, next to the rulers of the kingdoms, could be put up as candidates for Presidential elections.

26 On Acholi divisions, see Colin Leys, *Politicians and Policies: An Essay on Politics in Acholi, Uganda, 1962-1965* (Nairobi 1967), chapters 2 and 4; on Sebei, James Graham, 'Two Case Studies in Fragmentation: Bwamba/Busongora and Sebei', unpublished MS, African Studies Programme, Makerere University College, Kampala, 1966; on Bukedi and Bugisu, Uganda Protectorate, *Report of the Commission of Inquiry into the Disturbances in Certain Areas of the Bukedi and Bugisu Districts of the Eastern Province during the month of January, 1960* (Entebbe 1960).

27 In Ankole, keen awareness of the potential implications of suffrage extension was demonstrated in an attempt to draw boundaries of electoral constituencies so that the minority Bahima would gain a relative overrepresentation.

28 Cf. Uganda Protectorate, *Exchange of Despatches between His Excellency the Governor and Secretary of State for the Colonies concerning the creation of Sebei District* (Entebbe 1962); and Uganda Government, *Report of the Commission of Inquiry into the Recent Disturbances among the Baamba and Bakonjo People of Toro* (Entebbe 1962).

NOTES TO CHAPTER 2: 'STATE AND SOCIETY IN PRE-COLONIAL NKORE'

1 The name Ankole is a mixed Luganda-English corruption of Nkore. In the discussion that follows 'Nkore' refers to the 19th century kingdom, 'Ankole' to the enlarged post-1900 kingdom-district and 'Ankole area' to the historical region comprising Nkore and its surrounding areas.

2 The main societies adjacent to Nkore are named here as they were just prior to the colonial intervention.

3 G. N. Uzoigwe, 'Pre-colonial Markets in Bunyoro-Kitara', *Comparative Studies in Society and History*, vol. 24, no. 4, 1972, pp. 441-445.

4 J. B. Webster (ed.), *Uganda Before 1900*, vol. 1 (Nairobi 1973), Introduction.

5 See Brian K. Taylor, *The Western Lacustrine Bantu* (London 1962); Audrey I. Richards (ed.), *East African Chiefs* (London 1959).

6 Uganda Protectorate, *Report on the Runyankore-Rukiga Orthographic Conference*, Government Printer, 1956.

7 Z. C. K. Mungonya, 'The Bacwezi in Ankole', *Uganda Journal*, vol. 22, no. 1, 1958; and C. C. Wrigley, 'Some Thoughts on the Bacwezi', *Uganda Journal*, vol. 22, no. 1, 1958. Some mythological parallels can be found even further afield, cf. Luc de Heusch, *Le Roi Ivre ou l'origine de l'Etat* (Paris 1972).

8 H. F. Morris, *A History of Ankole* (Kampala 1962), p. 6. Even in Ankole there are further variations to the tale. A distinctly Bairu version is related in P. J. Gorju, *Entre le Victoria, l'Albert et l'Edouard* (Rennes 1920), pp. 279-281.

9 For an interesting speculation about the relationship between ecology, crops and the development of political organisation in parts of the interlacustrine area, see Conrad P. Kottak, 'Ecological Variables in the Origin and Evolution of African States: the Buganda Example', *Comparative Studies in Society and History*, vol. 14, no. 3, 1972.

10 D. J. Stenning, 'Salvation in Ankole', in M. Fortes and G. Dieterlen (eds.), *African Systems of Thought* (London 1965), p. 268.

11 G. N. Uzoigwe, *op. cit.*, pp. 444-447.

12 M. T. Mushanga, 'The Clan System among the Banyankore', *Uganda Journal*, vol. 34, no. 1, 1970, pp. 29-33.

13 In Ankole, for instance, this appears to have been true for the Abasingo clan; cf. S. R. Karugire, *A History of the Kingdom of Nkore in Western Uganda to 1896* (Oxford 1971), p. 51.

14 The primary example of a three-tiered pattern of ethnic stratification was Rwanda, where Batusi, Bahutu and the tiny minority of Batwa were ranked in an order of decreasing prominence. See Jacques J. Maquet, *The Premise of Inequality* (London 1961).

15 Maquet, *ibid.*; René Lemarchand, *Rwanda and Burundi* (London 1970).

16 The break-away of Toro from Bunyoro-Kitara and Toro's own vulnerability to centripetal forces – especially in Busongora, Kitagwenda and Kibale – illustrated this tendency.

17 All major historical sources thus far have been concentrated on Nkore: John Roscoe, *The Banyankole* (Cambridge 1923); K. Oberg, 'The Kingdom of Ankole in Uganda', in Meyer Fortes and E. E. Evans-Pritchard (eds.), *African Political Systems* (London 1940); A. G. Katate and L. Kamugungunu, *Abagabe b'Ankole*, Ekitabo 1 and 2 (Kampala 1955); Morris, *op. cit.*; Karugire, *op. cit.*

18 Cf. D. J. Stenning, 'The Nyankole', in Audrey I. Richards (ed.), *East African Chiefs*, p. 154.

19 For an interpretation of historical change in the Nkore kingdom, see Karugire, *op. cit.*

20 E.g. Stenning, 'The Nyankole', p. 153.

21 In the present century Bairu have acquired increasing numbers of cattle and as early as 1938 they owned almost as many head as the Bahima did. See W. L. S. Mackintosh, *Some notes on the Bahima and the Cattle Industry in Ankole* (Mbarara

1938). Today, the total Bairu ownership of cattle almost certainly surpasses that of the Bahima. In 1970 Ankole's cattle population was 508,724 head, on the basis of which the district ranked third in Uganda (after Teso and Karamoja); the Uganda total was 4,280,455. (Republic of Uganda, Statistics Division, Ministry of Planning and Economic Development, *1971 Statistical Abstract*, Government Printer (Entebbe 1971), p. 55.)

22 Recent census figures, indicating a total population of 861,145 have not distinguished between Ankole's ethnic groups (*1971 Statistical Abstract*, p. 10). But it can be estimated that the Bairu account for about 90% of the population, the remainder being made up by Bahima and relatively recent immigrant groups, especially Bakiga from the neighbouring Kigezi district. Mushanga, (*op. cit.*, p. 29) estimates the Bairu to constitute 92-96% of the total, the remainder being Bahima. Stenning more or less similarly estimates the proportions of Bairu and Bahima to be 'about nine to one'. (D. J. Stenning, 'Salvation in Ankole', p. 258). Lukyn-Williams, however, estimated the proportions to be 14 to 1. (F Lukyn-Williams, 'Blood-brotherhood in Ankole (Omukago)', *Uganda Journal*, vol. 2, no. 1, 1934, p. 34.)

23 Still, Johnston in 1902 cites information suggesting that 'the Hima population and their stock of cattle at the present day [are] not more than a third of what they were fourteen years ago'. (Sir Harry Johnston, *The Uganda Protectorate*, vol. 2 (London 1902), p. 626.)

24 J. H. Speke, *Journal of the Discovery of the Source of the Nile* (London 1863), p. 246.

25 Inevitably, the discussion has led to various speculations as to the presumed area of origin of the Bahima. Whereas it has usually been assumed that Bairu were indigenous to the area, an astounding perplexity of origins has been attributed to the Bahima, most often Ethiopia and Somalia, but also ancient Egypt as well as ancient Israel. See J. F. Cunningham, *Uganda and its People* (London 1905), x-xi; Sir Harry Johnston, *The Uganda Protectorate*, vol. 1 (London 1902), p. 210; Robert P. Ashe, *Two Kings of Uganda* (London 1889), pp. 337-338. Sir Albert R. Cook summarises a good deal of the early opinion on the Bahima by stating that 'everyone has remarked their extraordinary likeness to the old Egyptian mummies', and Alfred R. Tucker describes the typical Muhima as 'a man the very image, you would say, of Ramses II'. (Sir Albert R. Cook, *Uganda Memories (1897-1940)* (Kampala 1945), p. 118; Alfred R. Tucker, *Eighteen Years in Uganda and East Africa* (London 1911), p. 272.) Recently, the debate has shifted to biochemical arguments, although it seems, not yet with conclusive proof. See Merrick Posnansky, 'Kingship, Archeology and Historical Myth', *Uganda Journal*, vol. 30, no. 1, 1966, pp. 6-7 for a dismissal of theories of extraneous origin because of lack of archeological evidence, and the alternative hypothesis that Bairu and Bahima may have originated from the same stock but developed different physiques as a result of contrasting diets; and G. C. Cook, 'Tribal Incidence of Lactose Deficiency in Uganda', *The Lancet,* April 2, 1966, pp. 725-730 for an analysis of different lactose resistances which reaffirms the suggestion of 'original' differences between Bairu and Bahima. See also below, p. 33.

26 Kottak, *op. cit.*, pp. 352-353. He pointedly adds: 'Perhaps scholars have assumed, having witnessed so many examples of European conquest and colonialism in non-European areas, that this is the only, or the principal way, in which a societal form can be changed'.

27 F. Lukyn-Williams, 'The Inauguration of the Omugabe of Ankole to Office', *Uganda Journal*, vol. 4, no. 4, 1937, p. 309. See also Karugire, *op. cit.*, p. 97.

28 As is illustrated by the Nkore mythical charter, cited above. (p. 20).

29 The term 'Bahima state' was used by Oberg (*op. cit.*, p. 128). While Oberg's account of the traditional system needs qualification, there are good grounds to borrow the notion of a 'Bahima state' as a shorthand designation of the Nkore political structure. See below, especially pp. 47-50.

30 In the light of speculations about ethnic 'origins' the common clan system of Bairu of Bahima is intriguing. Assuming different origins, in Ankole today two explanations are offered. One, mostly advanced by Bahima, holds that the incoming Bahima 'reorganised' the Bairu into 'followings' that still account for the present common clan membership.

Another, more distinctly Bairu interpretation, suggests that the 'invading' Bahima found an existing (Bairu) clan organisation, which they found suitable as a means of control and for purposes of acculturation. The latter view can be related to Lukyn-Williams' observation that 'there is little doubt that we have in Ankole . . . an example, by no means unknown throughout the world, of a conquering race adopting the language and customs of the conquered, while at the same time keeping themselves separate'. (Lukyn-Williams, *op. cit.*, pp. 33-34). In the absence of conclusive evidence on the origins of Bairu and Bahima both explanations are highly speculative and seem primarily political rationalisations.

31 Mushanga, *op. cit.*

32 Today the exceptions cited are rather of educated Bairu men marrying educated Bahima girls.

33 Oberg, *op. cit.*, p. 134.

34 *Ibid.*, p. 130.

35 Stenning, 'The Nyankole', p. 169.

36 Karugire, *op. cit.*, p. 50. Earlier, Morris had written of the Bairu and Bahima in class terms; cf. H. F. Morris, *The Heroic Recitations of the Bahima of Ankole* (Oxford 1964), p. 9.

37 Karugire, *op. cit.*, pp. 38, 40, 41.

38 *Ibid.*, p. 66.

39 For example, it is difficult to reconcile 'the vital point that the Omugabe was the greatest single source of wealth – cattle – for the Bairu as well as for the Bahima' and the observation that 'the Bairu and the Bahima rendered him . . . services for which they were similarly rewarded' (*ibid.*, p. 53) on the one hand, with the author's statement that 'the legal and security system was heavily weighted in favour of the class that possessed the capital, and that class was composed of the Bahima', and his further categorisation that 'it was a class system . . . in which the Bairu were of lower social standing than the Bahima, (p. 66), on the other. The latter, again, is difficult to match with the observation that 'these terms – Bairu and Bahima – came into use as descriptions of areas of economic activities or occupations' and 'acquired the superior and inferior overtones which their use evokes today from cross-currents [in contemporary Ankole politics]' (p. 71). Similar ambiguities concern the extent of socio-economic interdependence between Bairu and Bahima, which is emphasised in places (e.g. p. 38) and de-emphasised in others (e.g. p. 67).

40 This procedure is adopted for heuristic purposes mainly. Without implying, at this stage, that Nkore *was* two societies, a discussion and reconstruction of the pre-colonial social structure will be facilitated by starting out from a consideration of the most extreme possibility, that of a dichotomy between two 'societies'. Also, we will be better able, initially, to relate and grasp aspects of social stratification through a discussion of 'society' than might be possible through the use of other

concepts. The reconstruction attempted here finally leads us to speak of 'two more or less separate communities' in respect of the Bairu and Bahima of Nkore.

41 Cf. Marc J. Swartz (ed.), *Local-Level Politics* (Chicago 1968), Introduction; F. G. Bailey, *Stratagems and Spoils, a Social Anthropology of Politics* (Oxford 1970), p. 16, p. 135.

42 To pose instead the question in terms of one or two 'tribes' in Nkore would only add confusion due to various ambiguities of that term. Nonetheless, that the point is alive may be illustrated by the question once asked at a meeting in 1967 by the President of the Ntare History Society – a student organisation at Mbarara dedicated to the study of Ankole history and society – whether Bairu and Bahima ought to be called one or two tribes.

43 While the historical occurrence of stratification has often been questioned with reference to various parts of Africa, rather the opposite has been true for most of the interlacustrine region.

44 See e.g. the collection of essays in André Béteille (ed.), *Social Inequality* (Harmondsworth 1969).

45 The 'good land'.

46 Cf. Fredrik Barth (ed.), *Ethnic Groups and Boundaries, The Social Organization of Culture Differences* (Bergen-Oslo and London 1969), Introduction, p. 11.

47 *Willis Journal*, vol. 1, unpublished (January 1, 1901), p. 106. (A copy of this journal is available in the library of Makerere University, Kampala.)

48 A. Mutashwera, Personal communication.

49 Roscoe, *The Banyankole*.

50 Roscoe (*ibid.*, p. 78) wrote: 'There were many degrees of service from the bought slaves up to the messengers of the Mugabe:

Muhuku — a bought slave who might be used for menial tasks.

Mwambale [*sic*] — servants in personal attendance on their masters.

Mwiru [*sic*] — peasants who cultivated and were to a certain extent independent, though under pastoral masters.

Musumba [*sic*] — herdsmen who milked and were of the pastoral class.

Bagalagwa — personal servants of the Mugabe who, after they finished their term of service, were given cows and land.

Banyiginya — the highest class. These were princes, but the Mugabe might use them as special messengers for confidential work.'

51 Not withstanding his general conclusion, Karugire makes a similar point; *op. cit.* pp. 56 and 57.

52 Cf. Stenning, 'The Nyankole', p.147. A recent bio-medical theory suggests that different lactose proportions within Bahima and Bairu make it physically as difficult for the latter to take milk as it is for Bahima to go without it. (Cf G. C. Cook, 'Tribal Incidence of Lactose Deficiency in Uganda', *loc. cit.*) As noted above, consideration of dietary differences relates to archeological speculation about the origins of Bahima and Bairu. Assuming that lactose discrepancies take many centuries of evolution to be developed, the discrepancies suggest that Bairu and Bahima have different origins, thus confirming the hypothesis that Bahima migrated into the Ankole area some five hundred years ago.

On the other hand, assuming greater flexibility and adaptability of lactose resistance, the suggestion that Bahima and Bairu represent two groups 'recently' split from what was originally one stock might deserve more serious attention. (Posnansky, 'Kingship, Archeology and Historical Myth', *op. cit.*) What remains in any event unanswered, however, is how different diets would not only affect stature but also specific facial features. Recognition of the latter is implied in a popular observation in Ankole that 'Europeans have the nose of Bahima but the teeth of Bairu'.

53 Lord Hailey notes that 'The Hima Aristocracy of the Interlacustrine kingdoms were accustomed to obtain their vegetable food by barter or tribute from their subjects'. Lord Hailey, *An African Survey* (Revised Edition, London 1957), p. 36. It should be pointed out, however, that whatever it was they obtained by barter or tribute, it was little vegetable food.

54 Karugire, *op. cit.*, p. 70f. The 'malcontents' included 'those Bairu who felt they were denied a fair chance of advancement [and felt] resentful against an 'unfair' system which, according to their history lessons, dated from the remote period of history when their 'own people' were conquered by a race which they were taught was superior to theirs' and also especially those Bahima 'who were rated as failures by all normal standards [but] could hardly fail to draw a certain kind of pride from belonging to a 'superior' race in comparison to the 'upstarts' – the wealthy Bairu'.

55 Karugire, *op. cit.*, Appendix B (Biographical Details of Informants), pp. 263-268.

56 We are reminded on this point of Kottak's warning, cited above (p. 26).

57 E.g. 'The Bahima are a more moral people than the surrounding negroes . . . They are domineering in attitude towards subject races, and are a very proud people, but are generally courteous towards Europeans, with whom they claim a certain kinship in origin. They are usually very honest and truthful. . . . The men of Hima blood are born gentlemen . . . .' (Sir Harry Johnston, *op cit.*, p. 630.)

58 Morris' observation that 'the Bairu . . . were in a position somewhat comparable to the villein of medieval Europe. They were by no means without rights, but they had to render services to their Bahima masters . . .' may illustrate the point, though elsewhere Morris expresses himself more guardedly. H.F. Morris, *The Heroic Recitations of the Bahima of Ankole*, p. 1.

59 The term was applied to Rwanda in the title of Maquet's book; Maquet, *op cit.*

60 *Morris, op. cit.*, p. 1. With reference to Nyabushozi, Karugire writes that a handful of cultivators 'lived near the kraals of the pastoralists, cultivating short-term crops such as vegetables and sweet potatoes which they supplemented with dairy products from the kraals. They were always ready to move at short notice, either following their pastoralist neighbours or changing to more suitable areas to engage in settled agriculture' (Karugire, *op. cit.*, p. 35). One must presume that Karugire's denial of these arrangements a few pages later is meant to refer to other areas of Nkore: 'if the Bairu moved whenever the Bahima moved, they could not have carried on settled agriculture as they did. Since this did not happen, it is difficult to see how . . . "feudal obligations" in terms of services rendered could have arisen.' (p. 40).

61 The simple but key fact that one word, 'Bairu', was used – and perhaps, due to limitations of vocabulary, may have *had* to be used – to refer at once to a small category of 'servants' and to the larger population of 'cultivators' unwittingly may have had far-reaching implications. In Somalia, a similar ambiguity in a not altogether dissimilar situation, namely in regard to the agriculturalist population between the Juba and Shebelle rivers on the one hand and a small group of bondsmen traditionally attached to the pastoralists on the other, caused Lewis to typographically distinguish between Sab for the former and *sab* for the latter. (I. M. Lewis, *A Pastoral Democracy* (London 1961), p. 14.) When failing to make such a distinction, both observers and, today, Bairu or Bahima 'participants' may generalise from either one connotation or the other and thus arrive at a radically

changed historical perspectives.

In this connection an intriguing but now virtually unanswerable question is whether around the turn of the century, there were any *alternatives* of terminology in regard to the Nkore agricultural population. In that case, a different 'choice' of terms might well have subsequently induced different perceptions of the social structure. This would have been a possibility if the agriculturists in, say, Rwampara or Shema, had they been more directly involved in the identification of social categories reported in early literature, would not have called themselves 'Bairu' but, for example, Banyarwampara or Banyashema, or perhaps would have advanced yet another typology.

62 Cf. Karugire, *op. cit.*, p. 39, p. 64. In a situation such as that of the Bairu, it is not altogether clear exactly what external threats gave 'protection' a content beyond, perhaps, tacit agreement by those in power not to raid. At times, nonetheless, a certain arbitrariness may not have been altogether absent, as seems implied in Bairu anecdotes about Bahima who came searching for sweet bananas: Bairu would lead them through their gardens, denying they had any such bananas, which their Bahima visitors, unable to tell one tree from another, found difficult to check.

63 In practice Bahima have long remained disinterested in marketing cattle; only in the past decade or two have increasing numbers of Bahima given the cash value of their cattle more serious consideration.

64 Stenning, *op. cit.*, p. 152.

65 Cf. Karugire, *op. cit.*, p. 115.

66 Stenning, *op. cit.*, p. 153.

67 Karugire, *op. cit.*, p. 66.

68 Cf. Oberg, *op. cit.*, pp. 130-131.

69 Stenning, 'Salvation in Ankole', p. 259.

70 Cf. Lemarchand, *op. cit.*, pp. 36-41.

71 Cf. Mackintosh, *op. cit.*, p. 20; Oberg, *op. cit.*, pp. 129-130.

72 Roscoe, *op. cit.*, p. 1.

73 As noted, the name 'Bakiga' as a general 'ethnic' categorisation appears as novel as may have been the case with 'Bairu'. Cf. M. M. Edel, *The Chiga of Western Uganda* (New York 1957), p. 24.

74 H. B. Thomas and Robert Scott, *Uganda* (London 1935), p. 93. As they further point out, 'In Bunyoro, on the other hand, the pastures lay at a distance from the best agricultural areas, which are grouped closely together, and the control of the Bantu population was not, therefore, compatible with migratory habits'.

75 The term 'freemen', used by Oberg (*op. cit.*, pp. 128-136), does not seem inappropriate if the wider context in which they acted is kept in mind. Cf. also Jacques J. Maquet, 'Institutionalisation féodale des relations de dépendence dans quatre cultures interlacustres', paper presented at the *Colloque du Groupe de Recherches en Anthropologie et Sociologie Politique* (Paris 1968).

76 Barth, *op. cit.*, p. 19.

77 *Ibid.*, p. 20.

78 Cf. Oberg, *op. cit.*, p. 131; Stenning, *op. cit.*, p. 153.

79 Again it must be stressed that it is beyond the scope of this study to differentiate between the Nkore political organisation of one period from the next. Thus, it may well be that the Omugabe was gradually moving to a more powerful position, as happened in Buganda (see Martin Southwold, *Bureaucracy and Chiefship in Buganda*, East African Studies, No. 14 (Kampala 1961)), or else that his

position was growing weaker, but our information does not enable us to validate either hypothesis.

80 See the insightful discussion of Peter C. Lloyd, 'The Political Structure of African Kingdoms: An Exploratory Model', in M. Banton (ed.), *Political Systems and the Distribution of Power* (London 1965), pp. 63-112.

81 A notable exception, however, is Karugire, who on the subject of Nkore kingship gives a well-balanced analysis, the general lines of which are consistent with our present interpretation. Karugire, *op. cit.*

82 Roscoe, *op. cit.*, p. 12.

83 *Ibid.*, p. 36.

84 W. L. S. Mackintosh, *op. cit.*, p. 13.

85 Oberg, *op. cit.*, pp. 136, 137.

86 Ntare School History Society, *The Governmental Institutions in Ankole before the British Rule,* mimeo (Mbarara n.d., 1965), p. 1.

87 J. Vansina, 'A Comparison of African Kingdoms', *Africa*, vol. 32, no. 4, 1962, p. 332.

88 The implied analogy is to a characteristic Bahima skill, namely the stretching of a cow's hide.

89 H. F. Morris (ed.), *The Heroic Recitations*, p. 1. Cf. also Oberg, *op. cit.*, p. 136. According to some Banyankore, the present spelling of the word 'Omugabe' carries Luganda influences. Although the term does have historical roots, in past times the king was more commonly addressed as 'Omukama'. In the earlier colonial period, the British referred to him as 'Kabaka', which was their favourite term for traditional rulers in Uganda. The term 'Omugabe' appears to have become more prevalent since roughly the 1930's.

90 Lukyn-Williams, 'Inauguration of the Omugabe', p. 312.

91 The paradox this points to was noted in Robert H. Lowie, *Social Organization* (London 1950), pp. 344-345. See also Roscoe, *op. cit.*, p. 51.

92 Cf. Karugire, *op. cit.*, pp. 105-106.

93 Cf. Oberg, *op. cit.*, p. 134.

94 E. G. Tucker, *op. cit.*, p. 272.

95 *Willis Journal*, vol. 2, p. 228.

96 Roscoe, *op. cit.*, pp. 15-16.

97 Taylor, *op. cit.*, pp. 35, 62.

98 Roscoe, *op. cit.*, p.14.

99 Stenning, 'The Nyankole', p. 157.

100 Transcript of a discussion with the Omugabe and senior princes of Ankole, 27th September, 1966, recorded by Mr. Gersham Nshemereirwe. The point was made by Mr. Samwiri Rwabushongo.

101 *Ibid.*

102 The selection of a Muhima of a non-royal clan appears to have been the general rule. Nuwa Mbaguta, who was Enganzi at the establishment of British rule, was a member of the royal clan of another kingdom, Mpororo. Muhigi, the Enganzi of Ntare V, was a Mwiru, although of a clan which was gradually moving to higher social status, the Basingo.

103 Stenning, *op. cit.*, p. 157.

104 Roscoe, *op. cit.*, p. 95.

105 Mackintosh, *op. cit.*, p. 12.

106 Oberg, *op. cit.*, p. 129; Maquet, 'Institutionalisation féodale', p. 2.

107 Roscoe, *op. cit.*, pp. 15-16.

108 Stenning, *op. cit.*, p. 152.

109 *Willis Journal*, vol. 2, pp. 290-291.
110 Oberg, *op. cit.*, pp. 133-134.

NOTES TO CHAPTER 3: 'COLONIAL INCORPORATION
AND CONTROL INCENTIVES'

1 This quality seems aptly illustrated by some of the counsel contained in the *Notes for Officers appointed to Uganda*, published by the Crown Agents for the colonies (London, 1934): 'In Entebbe, Kampala and Jinja and the larger centres the population and facilities permit of most English games being pursued. Golf, cricket, tennis, soccer and occasionally rugger are played, and in the majority of out-stations there are tennis-courts and rough golf courses. If, however, in bush stations these facilities are entirely lacking, regular exercise should always be taken, such as a brisk walk or a stroll with a shot gun'. (p. 19)

2 Uganda Protectorate, *Native Administration* (Entebbe, 1939), p. 4. With its implied 'receptivity' of colonial rule, this statement does not quite describe the process as it took place in Ankole. Though in no way of the magnitude of the physical violence used in the subjugation of Bunyoro, a few instances of physical conquest occurred in Ankole, mainly involving some of the areas which were subjugated and incorporated into the expanded district. Cf. Tarsis B. Kabwegyere, 'The Dynamics of Colonial Violence: The Inductive System in Uganda', *The Journal of Peace Research*, vol. 9, no. 4, 1972.

3 *Native Administration*, p. 5.

4 *Ankole Agreement*, 1901, para. 3.

5 *Willis Journal*, vol. 2, pp. 227-229.

6 Cf. *Daudi Ndibarema vs. Enganzi of Ankole,* Her Majesty's Court of Appeal for Eastern Africa, Civil Appeal No. 78 of 1959.

7 The precolonial position has been summarised as follows in *East African Chiefs*: '1. Isingiro, the old Kaaro-Karungi, i.e. the nucleus of the kingdom of Nkore; 2. Shema, formerly part of the kingdom of Mpororo; 3. Rwampara, formerly part of the kingdom of Mpororo; 4. Nyabushozi, taken by conquest at the expense of Bunyoro; 5. Kashari, ditto; 6. Mitoma, ditto. To this core, the British added on their assumption of power: 7. Igara, a kingdom of similar status to Nkore until the mid-nineteenth century, when it became its tributary. This relationship was formalised by the British; 8. Buhweju, a kingdom that came into the sphere of influence of Nkore in the eighteenth century; 9. Bunyaruguru, an offshoot of the kingdom of Mpororo.' A. I. Richards (ed.), *East African Chiefs* (London 1959), pp. 156-157. For a more detailed account of the expansion of the kingdom, see H. F. Morris, 'The Making of Ankole', *Uganda Journal*, vol. 21, no. 1, 1957, pp. 204-7, and Morris, *A History of Ankole* (Kampala 1962).

8 It was also stipulated, however, that these ten divisions did 'not include the whole area of the district of Ankole, but [that] those portions of the district which border more closely on the Congo Free State and German Territory will be subject to the same regulations as those set forth in this Agreement, and will for the present be administered by the principal European official placed in civil charge of the Ankole district, until such time as the chiefs thereof voluntarily place themselves under the suzerainty of Kahia' (*Ankole Agreement*, para. 2). Kahia is an earlier spelling of Kahaya, the Omugabe of Ankole.

9 Morris, *A History of Ankole*, p. 43.

10 E.g., 'Kabula and Mawogola counties should return to Ankole' (translated title), *Agetereine*, vol. 4, no. 9 (April 27, 1962) p. 7.

11 See below, pp. 70-73.
12 See H. F. Morris, 'The Kingdom of Mpororo', *Uganda Journal*, vol. 19, no. 2, 1955, pp. 204-207 and Morris, *A History of Ankole*, pp. 17-22.
13 F. Lukyn Williams, 'Nuwa Mbaguta, Nganzi of Ankole', *Uganda Journal*, vol. 10, no. 2, 1946, pp. 196-208.
14 The Enganzi was the above mentioned Muhigi (Ch. 2, n. 102). It should be noted, however, that the memory of past Abagabe appears to have fluctuated. Roscoe writes that when he first visited Ankole '. . . it was impossible to obtain from the people any information as to the names of their previous rulers.' In part, this fluctuation seemed to be explained to him by the fact that 'contact with other tribes, especially with the Baganda and the Bakitara, aroused a desire to have a genealogy of the royal family, and a list of kings was prepared for the purpose.' See Roscoe, *The Banyankole*, p. 34.
15 H. F. Morris, *A History of Ankole*, p. 35.
16 A useful introduction to the puzzle is H. F. Morris, 'The Murder of H. St. Galt', *Uganda Journal*, vol. 24, no. 1, 1960, pp. 1-15. Despite minute inquiries, the background to this incident has long remained a mystery. In recent years, the view has been circulated that the murder was a Bahinda plot to thwart Mbaguta's popularity with the British. The alleged murderer was a Mushambo who was himself found killed immediately following the Galt murder. Whether there was indeed an attempt to implicate Mbaguta by construing an incident for which the onus would come to lay on the Bashambo remains unproved. Its result, at any rate, was a strengthening of Mbaguta's position.
17 'Obugabe' is the Runyankore word for Ankole kingship.
18 According to Low, the chief concerned, Duhara of Rwampara, was a Mwiru who had been installed shortly before the signing of the Agreement at British instigation. Local opinions in Ankole dispute this, holding that no Mwiru was party to the Agreement. D. A. Low, 'The Establishment of British Administration: Two Examples from Uganda, 1900-1901,' EAISR Conference Paper, 1956, p. 3.
19 *System of Chieftainships of Ankole*, Government Press, Uganda, 1907.
20 *Ibid.*, p. 1.
21 *Ibid.*, p. 5.
22 Apart from some immigrants, Babito (presumably of Nilotic origins) included the ruling dynasty of the incorporated Buhweju kingdom.
23 This absorption has been closely related to 'external' marriages. Both Bairu and Bahima have frequently married immigrants to Ankole, more often indeed than they married each other. Commonly assimilation of the new members into Ankole society has followed readily. However, this assimilation was largely effected within, and thus supportive of, Ankole's ethnic divisions, a tendency which seemed partly due to the existence of roughly parallel status distinctions in Ankole and its adjacent societies. For example, while Batusi tended to merge with the Bahima substratum, Bahutu were assimilated with the Bairu. Also, Babito (supposedly of Nilotic origin) and high-status Bahororo and Banyakaragwe tended to integrate with the Bahima, whereas Bakiga, Bakonzo and other 'lower' status groups associated with the Bairu.

In recent times, possibilities of differential assimilation have reappeared. Large numbers of Bakiga settlers who have come to Ankole may in time be expected to identify most closely with the Bairu population. In contrast, the influx of Batusi refugees from Rwanda in early 1960's was welcomed for some time by the Bahima as a means of bolstering their numbers. By the same logic, Bairu opposed such absorption and instead argued in favour of spreading the Banyarwanda over the various regions of Uganda. (Cf. *Ankole Government Memorandum to the O.A.U. Commission on Refugees*, Mbarara, 1964.)

24 Baganda have been an exception to the tendency of two-pronged assimilation. Over the years many Baganda have come to Ankole, but relatively few have come to be identified as Banyankore. The explanation of this contrast with other groups may partly be that the Baganda could not as readily be identified with either low or high statuses and thus fitted less easily into the Ankole divisions. Also, they came in rather large numbers and in a variety of capacities which perhaps made assimilation less likely, even over several generations. The first Baganda came as religious refugees in the 19th century; their reasons for coming lay in Buganda, not in Ankole. Subsequently, many Baganda came as chiefs and as traders, both of which were occupations which created some social distance. The distinctiveness of Luganda as compared to some other immigrant languages, plus a certain sense of chauvinism in being the most 'advanced' among Uganda's population groups during colonialism may have further prevented their full integration into Ankole society.

Assimilative borrowing and adaptations have rather been in the opposite direction. As noted in Chapter I, Baganda chiefs set patterns of authority and behaviour which many Banyankore aspirants tended to follow. They emulated Kiganda dress, eating habits and demeanours and until recently the Ankole chiefs were styled by official titles adopted from Buganda. The county chiefs, for instance, were titled Kahima, Kitunzi, Kangaho, Pokino, Kaigo, Mukwenda, Sekibobo, Katambara, Kashwiju and Mugyema, each of which had a specific meaning in the Buganda context though not in Ankole.

In other ways, too, Baganda were instrumental in introducing change. Plantains, now quite characteristic of the Ankole landscape, were adopted from Buganda, similarly to the husbandry of chicken and other small animals for consumption. Also, cotton and coffee cultivation had been undertaken by Baganda before it was introduced to Ankole. Finally, Baganda chiefs acted as proselytising agents for the Protestant Native Anglican Church.

25 This task is somewhat complicated due to amalgamations of administrative divisions, especially at the sub-county level.

26 Cited in a letter from the Enganzi to the District Commissioner, 1 June 1942, no. 7. This was in response to a request for information from the DC, dated 27 May, 1942, who asked, 'Please let me have a list of saza and gombolola chiefs (titles only) who are of (a) pure Hima stock (b) partly Hima (c) Bairu.' This communication indicates an emergent concern on the part of protectorate officials with the ethnic composition of the chiefly ranks in Ankole.

27 Cf. Chapter 2, pp. 32-33 and footnote 61, p. 40.

28 The distinction was the one developed in M. Fortes and E. E. Evans-Pritchard (eds.), *African Political Systems* (London 1940).

29 Sir Harry Johnston, *The Uganda Protectorate*, vol. 2, p. 630. There was one exception to this tendency, though the view concerned was as manifestly unfounded as the praise bestowed upon the Bahima. Before coming to Ankole, Willis reflected 'What one hears of the natives, who are Bahima by race [*sic*], is not to their credit: they seem to be an idle and untrustworthy people; one hears the same report from all sources. So we shall need much prayer.' *Willis Journal*, vol. 1, p. 101.

30 Cf. Chapter 2, pp. 27-51.

31 In the 1930's these powers were virtually institutionalised. A frequent entry under 'Reasons for selection' on forms then used in connection with the appointment and

dismissal of chiefs read 'Recommended by Omugabe and his advisers.' These recommendations were discussed and formulated in meetings of the county chiefs and the Omugabe, in which Mbaguta played a key role.

32 The concept of 'franchise' may help to solve an apparent contradiction between external control and colonial authoritarianism on the one hand and the existence of extensive chiefly powers on the other. Colonial domination in many parts of the world was maintained, and perhaps largely had the impact it had, through a certain 'formula' for government and administration. While its execution was laid in the hands of local individuals and groups, strict adherence to the formula was continuously demanded. Among other things, this gave the system its near-universalistic quality and made the pattern of organisation roughly comparable to that of, e.g., the Roman Catholic church or some multinational corporations.

33 *Ankole Agreement,* para. 7.

34 *Ibid.*

35 Letter from the Acting Collector, Mbarara Collectorate, to the Sub-Commissioner, Western Province, 8th April, 1907.

36 As cited in a letter from the District Commissioner, Ankole, to the Provincial Commissioner, Western Province, 10th March, 1923.

37 Entries in District Commissioner's Baraza Book, Ankole. This material as well as the documentation referred to below, is available in the archives of the District Commissioner's Office, Mbarara.

38 Baraza held on 18/12/29, District Commissioner's Baraza Book, Ankole.

39 This posture was of critical significance in generating Bairu grievances with the system. To many Bairu, Bahima attitudes of arrogance towards them were more objectionable than their preponderance in official posts.

40 The following comment by Johnston might be noted here, notwithstanding the generally low reliability of this author and his erroneous understanding of 'mixed Bairu clans' and their designations: 'The word "Bairo" is apparently the Hima designation of those whom the proud Hamitic invaders regard as their slaves. . . . Amongst themselves the Bairo, who are divided into numerous clans, take the names of Basita, Ngando, Basambo, Baitera, Bayondo, Abagaihe, Bawago, Bashikoto, Balisi, Bachawa, and Barendi, though all these clans have now become so mixed as to be fused generally under the common race-name of Bairo'. Johnston, *op. cit.,* p. 607.

41 The establishment of schools and churches was often a concurrent undertaking. Nonetheless, the generalization is sometimes advanced in Ankole that in the early colonial period Protestants began with schools and Roman Catholics with churches.

42 In addition a Muslim minority developed largely through the proselytising efforts of Baganda traders. However, this conversion was not only religious but in most cases also involved a change of 'ethnic' identity. Most Baganda traders who came to Ankole were Muslims, and, though they were limited through a lack of funds and schooling facilities as compared to the Protestant and Catholic missions, for many years they were able to sustain a steady proselytisation into Islam. Islam and Baganda were closely identified, which meant that almost all Banyankore who became Muslims also 'became' Baganda: once they embraced the faith, they adopted Kiganda names, dress and even speech. Today the number of Muslims in Ankole is well over 10,000, but only a few hundred adhere to Islam while identifying as Banyankore.

43 *The System of Chieftainship of Ankole* in 1907 differentiated between chiefs on the basis of the size of their cattle ownership (in addition to their ethnicity). Thus,

most chiefs were listed as owning a few dozen or even a few hundred head of cattle; several had over a thousand head. In contrast, for example, one of the key classifications in the 1955 survey on which *East African Chiefs* was based, ranked the Ankole chiefs in terms of the number of years of educational experience. While most had two or more years of primary education, several had secondary school qualifications.

44 Based on an analysis of the Register of Mbarara High School by Richard Kaijuka in collaboration with the author.

45 Cf. Karugire, *A History of the Kingdom of Nkore in Western Uganda to 1896*, p. 41.

46 D. J. Stenning, 'Preliminary Observations on the Balokole Movement Particularly among Bahima in Ankole District,' *EAISR Conference Paper*, January, 1958.

47 See Chapter 4, p. 157.

48 For an articulation of this perspective, cf. the admonitions contained in the Omugabe's address to the Bahima of Nyabushozi, pp. 104-105 below.

49 Yet, the security derived from this base was vulnerable to some erosion, and might in fact cause the Bahima to lose their lead, as a result of the pastoralists' non-involvement in the cash economy. (E.g., for years administrative efforts to stimulate a ghee (butter) industry among the Bahima failed due to their disclination to sell this product.) Awareness of a possible encroachment on their economic advantages perhaps was indicated by the Bahima elite's reproaches of Bairu who in the late 1920's undertook to sell milk in Mbarara.

50 Cf. Richards (ed.), *East African Chiefs*, p. 171, and Chapter 4, pp. 123-124.

51 The hierarchy of the Anglican Church in Ankole, like that of the government, became dominated by Bahima.

52 See Chapter 4, pp. 130-131 and pp. 146-148.

53 *East African Chiefs*, pp. 171-173.

54 In the end, non-intervention would actually produce political pay-offs. When Bairu protest was articulated and began to gain momentum, the colonial government could make a shift of support and pose as the champion of Bairu aspirations, thus commanding their popularity. The credibility of such change of position was enhanced by the extent to which the theory of 'traditional' Bahima overrule had become accepted.

55 Chapter 2, pp. 51-60.

56 Uganda Protectorate, *Native Administration*, p. 4.

57 He was not told then, however, that he was 'king'. Roscoe wrote in his preface: 'I have found it advisable in this case to retain the native title of *Mugabe* for the king in deference to the wishes of the officers at work in the country, who dislike the title of king being used for rulers of small African states.' Roscoe, *The Banyankole*, v.

58 With one exception, i.e. Buhweju county, the provision in the Ankole Agreement that the principal chiefs were entitled to nominate their successors had soon fallen into oblivion. As we have seen, after the erosion of the Bahinda elite a cooptative element was nonetheless retained and the Bahima establishment had a considerable influence on the appointments that were made.

59 A note in the margin of the minutes of the meeting of saza chiefs held on 19 May, 1938.

60 Letter from the Sub-Commissioner, Western Province, to the Chief Secretary, Uganda Protectorate, on 20th March, 1907. It may be noted that Kahaya was indeed ostensibly treated as a schoolboy, by administrative officers, missionaries and other Europeans alike. Some of this transpires in the following comment: 'As for the King, he has almost to be kept away from the house by main force. I almost think he would like to take up his permanent abode down here. Twice a day he likes

to come down, and will not take the broadest hint to go. He is exactly a child, and one must of necessity act accordingly, and tell him when to go, and make him to do it. But there is no question about his friendliness, only it is not conducive to much work.' (*Willis Journal*, vol. 2, p. 328.) The exchange of courtesies with the Omugabe corresponded with these attitudes. It also was somewhat incongruous: '[There arrived some] young heifers from the King, one for each of us. When you think that the price of a cow, sold by government is 50 rupees, and that there is a proverb 'What does not kill the Muhima will not separate him from his cow', so keen are the Bahima on their cows, this means a good present. Mbaguta, not to be outdone, sent down a fine cow and a calf for Savile and the following morning sent me a beautiful cow, both these last being of the hornless kind, which they say are the best of all. Finally he sent us down a really magnificent ram. We did not know really what to give in return as our needs are so very different from theirs, and what is useful to us is no good at all to them. However, they are very keen on European boxes: so we got two wooden boxes, painted them red, wrote KAHAYA and MBAGUTA respectively on them, and sent them up. We also gave each a bottle of Eau de Cologne'. (*Willis Journal*, vol. 2, p. 252.)

61 Letter from the Sub-Commissioner, Western Province, to the Acting Collector, Mbarara Collectorate, 20th March, 1907.
62 Letter from the Acting Collector, Mbarara Collectorate, to the Sub-Commissioner, Western Province, 5th March, 1907.
63 Letter from the District Commissioner, Ankole, to E. S. Kahaya, Omugabe, 17th September, 1921.
64 Letter from the Provincial Commissioner, Western Province, to the Omugabe of Ankole, 27th October, 1927.
65 Report of the District Commissioner, Ankole, on his visit to the Omugabe, 17th March, 1933.
66 Letter from the District Commissioner, Ankole, to E. S. Kahaya, M.B.E., Omugabe w'Ankole, 10th December, 1933.
67 Letter from the Provincial Commissioner, Western Province, to Omugabe of Ankole, 1st February, 1926.
68 Letter from Provincial Commissioner, Western Province, to Officer-in-Charge, Mbarara, 11th April, 1927.
69 Katikiro and Sekibobo are Luganda-derived titles for the Enganzi and the county chief of Mitoma respectively. The term Katikiro was dropped in the 1930s in favour of 'Enganzi'.
70 Letter from the Omugabe to the District Commissioner, Ankole, 7th November, 1927.
71 Precis of the Omugabe's Speech to the Bahima at Nyabushozi, 15th February, 1940.
72 Letter from the Omugabe to the District Commissioner, Ankole, 29th January, 1940.
73 Letter from the Omugabe to the Governor of Uganda, 24th November 1944.
74 The meaning of S.A.A.F. is not clear from the record. Possibly it refers to the South African Air Force.
75 See the respective District Reports for those years.
76 Cook, *Uganda Memories*, p. 118. Willis' first encounter with Kahaya induced him to adopt somewhat similar notions: 'The King is a young fellow, very much like a great overgrown boy, well over six feet in height and big in every way: huge long flabby hands and enormous slabs of feet – a terrible and significant warning against drinking much milk!' (*Willis Journal*, vol. 1, p. 109.) An early

anthropological explorer, Cunningham, even took the liberty to take the measurements of Kahaya, which he recorded as follows:

'Height, standing in thin sandals	6 ft	$+6\frac{1}{2}$ inch
Chest, under coat	4	$\frac{1}{2}$
Neck	1	$4\frac{1}{2}$
Wrist	0	8
Waist, outside garments	5	3
Buttocks	5	$7\frac{1}{2}$
Ankle (just above)	1	0
Calf	1	$1\frac{1}{4}$
Foot (length of)	1	$1\frac{1}{4}$
Weight	301 lb., or $21\frac{1}{2}$ stone'	

Cunningham commented that 'It will be seen from the measurements that, literally, the King of Ankole is a powerful man. He is just twenty years of age, weighs 301 lb. and stands 6 ft $6\frac{1}{2}$ inch in height. He is erect, but, as might be expected, not very active. When he travels, he is carried in a large basket slung on poles by a team of the strongest men amongst his following. The team is grouped in fours, and each four carriers take the poles in turn, resting them on their shoulders. On a good road they can travel at a rate of four or five miles an hour.' J. F. Cunningham, *Uganda and its people* (London 1905), pp. 20-21.

77 As if to confirm this, paragraph 182 of the Ankole District Annual Report, 1935, states: 'While it cannot be said that [the Omugabe] has given any constructive assistance during the year, it must, on the other hand, be admitted that he has not been the cause of creating any unsurmountable difficulties.'

78 Uganda Protectorate, *Native Administration*, p. 4.

79 E.g. 'a change in any one part of the culture will be accompanied by changes in other parts, and . . . only by relating any planned detail of change to the central values of the culture is it possible to provide for the repercussions which will occur in other aspects of life.' Margaret Mead (ed.), *Cultural Patterns and Technical Change* (Paris 1953), p. 10.

80 Though the case of Buganda is not discussed in this study, it is instructive to note that Buganda's more homogeneous population structure, its greater concentration of powers within the office of the Kabaka, as well as the 'contract' nature of the relationship between the British and the Buganda establishment, in Buganda led to markedly different patterns of transformation from those of the Ankole experience.

NOTES TO CHAPTER 4:'PROTEST AND ACCOMMODATION
  IN ANKOLE POLITICS'

1 The senior chiefs, especially the county chiefs, for a long time continued to occupy a conspicuous position in Ankole society. At least until political parties appeared, chieftainships tended locally to be regarded as a form of 'political' representation. This may help to explain the keen interest exhibited in Ankole regarding the ethnic distribution of these posts. Of late, the county chieftainships still carried a great deal of prestige, although the main burden of the administrative work had increasingly been placed upon the sub-county chiefs.

2 In the essay from which these paragraphs are adapted, I described protest as a concomitant of the process of 'modernization'. This was perhaps rather less than critical acceptance of this magic word on my part. The article is

'Kumanyana and Rwenzururu: Two responses to Ethnic Inequality', in Robert I. Rotberg and Ali A. Mazrui (eds.), *Protest and Power in Black Africa* (New York, 1970), p. 1089.

3 Since the early 1940's the proportions of senior chieftainships held by Bahima and Bairu continued to change slowly. By 1955, there was still the same division at the level of the county chiefs as there had been in 1942 (cf. Chapter 3), namely seven Bahima county chiefs, two Bairu and one Muganda. In 1960, Baganda chiefs no longer functioned at the county level, and the ten posts were then held by six Bahima and four Bairu. In 1965, the position had become 5 : 5, and by 1967 Bairu had ascended to two more county chieftainships. Meanwhile, in or about 1955, approximately one-third of a total of some fifty chiefs at the sub-county level were Bahima,[a] whereas in more recent years the ethnic distribution among these ranks was as follows:[b]

	1961	1963	1966
Bahima	14	17	9
Bairu	35	37	37
Baganda	3	2	3
	—	—	—
	52	56	49

[a] Stenning, 'The Nyankole', p. 173.
[b] This table is based on the Establishment lists of pensionable officers and employees of the Ankole Kingdom Government for the respective years. The variations in the totals are due to vacant positions.

4 Meanwhile, Bairu ascendancy to administrative positions partly coincided with, and was a function of, expansion and differentiation of the Ankole administrative framework. Similar to the senior chieftainships, for a long time the central positions within the Ankole Government administration were primarily occupied by Bahima. (Only few Baganda have held central administrative posts in Ankole). From early in the century till the early 1950's, the core of the Ankole establishment was limited and consisted mainly of the offices of the Omugabe, the Engazi, the Omubiki (Treasurer), the Omuramuzi (Chief Judge), and somewhat later the Kihimba (Administrative Secretary). For most of the time Bairu were excluded from these posts – those of the Omubiki and Omuramuzi were held by Bahima even until the late 1960's. During the 1950's and 1960's, however, various other functions were added to this nucleus – a development which perhaps was hard to foresee at the time of initial Bairu protest. Most of these new posts were taken up by Bairu and a cursory idea of the changing ethnic distribution of the positions at the Ankole district headquarters can be gathered from the fact that in 1961 Bahima held ten such positions out of a total of thirty-one (three being occupied by Baganda, the remainder by Bairu), whereas in 1963 the number held by Bahima was six and in 1966 three. (Source: Establishment Lists, Ankole Kingdom Government).

5 By marriage Mungonya was related to Bahima circles. Since his term the office of Enganzi was continuously held by Bairu, although it was only in 1955 that the principle was more definitely established with the nomination of Mr. Kesi Nganwa. Both successions to office have come to be regarded as major landmarks of Bairu emancipation and advancement.

6 These were the ten county chieftainships, initially about an equal number of senior posts at Kamukuzi, the local government headquarters, and lastly about fifty sub-county chiefs.

7 It should be noted that during the first three decades of this century the chiefs who

were found guilty of such breaches of jurisdiction were not only Bahima but included a substantial number of Baganda. However, far from unifying the indigenous population in opposition, as happened in neighbouring Kigezi, it seems that the Bairu of Ankole have regarded the role of the Baganda chiefs as being basically supportive of the Bahima superstructure.

8 Stenning, 'The Nyankole', p. 171.

9 Some distinctions between Rwanda and Ankole in regard to the potential for revolutionary tendencies are made in my paper, 'Protest Movements in Western Uganda: Some Parallels and Contrasts', *Kroniek van Afrika*, 1970/3. For a comparison of ethnic relationships in traditional Rwanda and Ankole, see Jacques Maquet, 'Institutionalisation féodale des rélations de dépendance dans quatre cultures interlacustres', *Colloque du Group de Recherche en Anthropologie et Sociologie Politique* (Paris 1968) pp. 10-13.

10 After 1955, changes in the religious background of the higher ranks of chiefs are indicated in the following table – based on the Ankole Kingdom Government's Establishment Lists – which comprises county and sub-county chiefs:

	1961	1963	1966
Protestants	50	52	34
Roman Catholics	12	14	9

The 1966 figure included 2 Catholic county chiefs, as against one in 1963. In Ankole, the increase at this level tended to be looked upon as a strengthening of the Catholic representation in government. However, this perception appears to have obscured the apparent decline of the Catholic element among the two higher ranks taken together.

For senior officers other than chiefs, the religious distribution during the same interval was roughly as follows:

	1961	1963	1966
Protestants	27	27	27
Roman Catholics	4	4	2

The tentative nature of this table must be kept in mind, especially in view of alterations to the administrative structure during this particular period. Nonetheless, it suggests a further weakening of the Catholic component; generally, data on the religious background of chiefs and other principal officers in the Ankole administration up till 1966 continued to show a considerable over-representation of Protestants. If these data are an insufficient basis to conclude that an actual regression took place in the proportion of posts held by Catholics, they nonetheless warrant the deduction that little change was initiated since 1955 to modify their under-representation in official positions.

11 *Uganda News*, No. 4220/1972.

12 D. J. Stenning, 'Coral Tree Hill' (preliminary field report of land tenure enquiry in West Ankole District), EAISR Conference Paper, mimeo, 1958.

13 A different arrangement which has nevertheless been the object of similar kinds of economic and political pressure, is the Ankole Ranching Scheme. See Martin R. Doornbos and Michael F. Lofchie, 'Ranching and Scheming: A Case Study of the Ankole Ranching Scheme', in Michael F. Lofchie (ed.), *The State of the Nations: Constraints on Development in Independent Africa* (Berkeley and Los Angeles 1971).

14 For the pre-1900 period, cf. Chapter 2, pp. 56-57.

15 Apthorpe finally attributes such confusions to what he has termed the 'ownership-fixation' at the basis of many land policies and arrangements. Cf. Raymond Apthorpe, 'Land Law and Land Policy in Eastern Africa', Makerere University, Kampala, mimeo, 1968.

16 Chapter 3, p. 81.
17 Beverley Brock, 'Customary Land Tenure, "Individualisation" and Agricultural Development', Rural Development Research Paper, No. 65, Makerere University, Kampala, mimeo, 1968.
18 Chapter 3, p. 85.
19 Lord William Bentinck, 'The Speech on November 8, 1829', cited in Ramkrishna Mukherjee, *The Dynamics of a Rural Society; A Study of the Economic Structure in Bengal Villages* (Berlin 1957), p. 32.
20 Uganda Protectorate, *Land Tenure in Uganda* (Entebbe 1957).
21 Ankole Government, Report, Commission of Enquiry into Ankole Mailo Land, Mbarara, mimeo, 1965; and Ankole Government, White Paper on Report of Commission of Enquiry into Ankole Mailo Land, Mbarara, mimeo, 1965.
22 Uganda Protectorate, *Land Tenure Proposals* (Entebbe 1955).
23 Uganda Protectorate, *Report of the Commissioner Appointed to Inquire into the Operation of the Land Tenure Scheme in Ankole* (Entebbe 1962), p. 4.
24 Among other things, it called for the application of the adjudication rules by official notice to a particular district, followed by the declaration by the District Commissioner of a parish to be adjudication area, then the election of an adjudication committee composed of between fifteen and twenty-five adult male taxpayers of the area, the surveying of the land by air photography and the erection of beacons to be photographed, the application by any occupant of land to be registered as a freehold proprietor, the issuance of an official adjudication notice to be publicly displayed for thirty days, a meeting of the adjudication committee to which representations can be made and objections raised, the preparation by the committee of a certificate giving all details of the land concerned for use by the District Commissioner, the public display of this certificate for another thirty days and reference of the case to the court if anyone wished to appeal against the proposed issuance of title, the signing of the certificate by the D.C. and again its subsequent public display giving the name of the recognised owner, the application by the owner for a freehold title, and the issuance of such title after his payment of the fees. (*Ibid.*, pp. 9-11).
25 These changes will be discussed in the next section.
26 Brock, 'Customary Land Tenure', pp. 11-12.
27 Uganda Protectorate, *Report on the Land Tenure Scheme in Ankole*, p. 17.
28 *Ibid.*, pp. 11-13.
29 .Doornbos and Lofchie, 'Ranching and Scheming'. The Ankole Ranching Scheme involved a $4,000,000 project jointly sponsored by USAID and the Uganda government, to establish commercial cattle ranches in Ankole. Political pressure resulted in the majority of these ranches being allocated to members of the Ankole establishment.
30 An alternative strategy, namely an attempt to delineate constituency boundaries on the basis of spatial divisions, not population density, misfired as a result of a ruling of the Uganda High Court (*Attorney-General vs. Godfrey Katondwaki*, High Court of Uganda, Civil Case No. 619 of 1962).
31 As a recent report graphically described the rationale, 'The Bahima were always worried about Bairu Protestants whom they believed were working to remove kingship in Ankole and therefore take away power from the hands of the Bahima. This led to Bahima forming an alliance with the Bairu Catholics who also did not like Bairu Protestants, and these two therefore joined DP when it was introduced in Ankole in 1959.' Uganda Government, Report of the Committee of Inquiry into Ankole District Council and District Administration Affairs, mimeo, 1969.

32　*Ibid.*
33　See my 'Kumanyana and Rwenzururu'.
34　Article 118 (1) of the 1967 *Constitution of the Republic of Uganda* reads: 'The institution of King or Ruler of a Kingdom or Constitutional Head of a District, by whatever name called, existing immediately before the commencement of this Constitution under the law then in force, is hereby abolished'.
35　Cf. Audrey Richards (ed.), *East African Chiefs* (London 1959), pp. 357-358.
36　*The People*, 17 June 1967.
37　See letters to the editor in *The People* and *Uganda Argus*, June through September, 1967. For an early expression of the monarchist minority viewpoint consult the article 'Banyankore do not support the new Constitution' (translated title), *Sekanyola*, 10 May, 1966.
38　For instance, after a visit to Rwanda, the Omugabe stressed the unity he expected of the Banyankore in the following terms: 'In Ruanda, there are three types of people, namely Bahutu, Batutsi and the Batwa. They work together in cooperation and . . . their motto is 'omuguha gw'enyabushatu' (a rope with three strands) representing these classes of people in Ruanda. You will agree with me that no country should expect progress if there is lack of cooperation and disunity. Division and hatred engineered by subversive elements in a country exhibit a gloomy picture and their ends are fatal. I should like you to be 'Omuguha gw'enyabushatu'. That is when we shall achieve Ankole's will as a nation. (From the 'Speech by Rubambansi the Omugabe at the Opening Ceremony of the Eishengyero of Ankole', 17th January, 1956.)
39　Letter from Provincial Commissioner, Western Province, to District Commissioner, Ankole, 23 July, 1951.
40　Minute 3 of the Eishengyero, May, 1953.
41　Minute 46 of the Eishengyero, May, 1953.
42　Minute 70 of the Eishengyero, 1954.
43　Minute 24 of the Eishengyero, 1957. In recent times, though, the Omugabe was more than once left out from public functions, as some political leaders from Ankole wanted to avoid identification with what they felt was the symbol of Bahima overrule.
44　Minute 25 of the Eishengyero, 1957. The idea was copied from Buganda, where the presentation of chiefs to the Kabaka was known as *Okweyanza*.
45　Minute 67 of the Eishengyero, 1961.
46　See Schedule 2 of the *Constitution of Uganda*, 1962.
47　*Agetereine*, 14th September, 1962.
48　*Uganda Argus*, 31st August, 1962.
49　*Ibid.*
50　The Agreement had been worked out in consultation with the Governor by a Constitutional Committee consisting of Ankole representatives. There had only been two points of difference which needed to be referred to the Colonial Secretary for settlement. One of these was whether or not the Ankole Ministers were to enjoy individual or collective responsibility, the other concerned the number of guns to be fired for the Omugabe on ceremonial occasions. On the first issue, the final decision was that they were individually responsible, which meant they were essentially department heads. On the number of guns 'the Committee demanded fifteen while the Governor was only prepared to grant nine.' (*Uganda Argus*, 8th March, 1962.) In the end, he got nine.
51　News release, Enganzi of Ankole, undated (August, 1962).
52　Criminal Revision, No. 30 of 1962 of the Kashari County Court of Ankole.

53 Open letter from Enganzi to Governor of Uganda, 10th August, 1962.
54 *Uganda Argus,* 9th February, 1962.
55 'Official Statement by the Enganzi; Warning to K.Y. Infiltration in Ankole', 14th September, 1965, mimeo.
56 'Speech by Owekitinisa the Enganzi on the 20th Coronation Anniversary of Rubambansi the Omugabe of Ankole, Sir Charles Godfrey Gasyonga II', 27th September, 1965, mimeo.
57 'Speech by Ow'Ekitinisa the Enganzi on the Opening of the First Eishengyero of Ankole', 21st April, 1966, mimeo.

NOTES TO CHAPTER 5: 'ETHNICITY AND KINGSHIP AS POLITICAL FACTORS'

1 Cf. Raymond Apthorpe, 'Does Tribalism Really Matter?' *Transition*, 37.
2 Some of the next few paragraphs are adapted from my article 'Some Conceptual Problems concerning Ethnicity in Integration Analysis,' *Civilisations*, vol. 22, no. 2, 1972.
3 Clifford Geertz, 'The Integrative Revolution; Primordial Sentiments and Civil Politics in the New States', in Clifford Geertz (ed.), *Old Societies and New States* (New York, 1963), p. 109.
4 Lucian W. Pye, *Aspects of Political Development* (Boston 1966), p. 63. Though suggestive, it seems doubtful whether the concept of 'identity crisis', originally constructed with reference to individual life experiences, can adequately be transposed to the level of nationalities. For the original concept see Erik H. Erikson, *Young Man Luther* (New York 1958), p. 254.
5 P. H. Gulliver (ed.), *Tradition and Transition in East Africa* (London 1969), p. 1.
6 One curious result of these warnings was that, at times, people began to introduce themselves as 'I am a Ugandan from the Ankole District in the Western Region'.
7 Cf. A. L. Epstein, *Politics in an African Urban Community* (Manchester 1958), p. 231. A contrary argument is advanced in Ali Mazrui's essay, 'Pluralism and National Integration', in Leo Kuper and M. G. Smith (eds.), *Pluralism in Africa* (Berkeley and Los Angeles 1969), pp. 333-350.
8 Less than full assimilation is evident from the case of American Blacks and repeatedly from an ethnic backlash from white groups.
9 Lipset's *The First New Nation* failed to recognise the difference in this respect between the American experience and that of the new states. S. M. Lipset, *The First New Nation* (New York 1963). Cf. the critique of H. M. Jolles in *Mens en Maatschappij*, vol. 39, no. 3, 1964, pp. 188-192.
10 S. N. Eisenstadt, 'The Process of Absorption of New Immigrants in Israel', *Human Relations*, V, 1952, pp. 223-246.
11 Indeed, in a sample survey of self-identifications conducted in Ankole between 1965 and 1968 among several hundred adults, no conflicts along these lines – let alone any 'identity crises' – were found. Though identifications as Banyankore were remarkably pronounced, these were not perceived as conflicting with respondents' statuses, and identifications, as Ugandans. The results of this study are reported in Marshall H. Segall, Martin R. Doornbos, and Clive Davis, *Political Identity: A Case Study from Uganda* (Syracuse, 1976).
12 *Ibid.*
13 Cf. Lucy Mair, 'Busoga Local Government', *Journal of Commonwealth Political Studies*, vol. 5, no. 2, 1967, p. 91.

14 Such a focus is by no means novel, but it remains to be more fully applied to the framework of regional government in development situations. David Truman was one of the first authors to analyse this relationship in depth for the United States, where it was found that pressure groups direct their efforts to the state legislatures for some purposes, to the federal level for others, in each case dependent upon which government branches exercise the kind of powers which most directly affect the goals of interested constituent groups (David B. Truman, *The Governmental Process* (New York 1953), pp. 321-350).

For Britain S. E. Finer showed the logic of pressure group activity being concentrated upon the bureaucracy rather than parliament since, as he saw it, in most cases room for the modification of British legislation is severely curtailed once the legislation has passed the preparatory stage at the hands of the bureaucracy (S. E. Finer, *Anonymous Empire* (London, 1963) pp. 18-27).

15 A contrast in this regard to the pattern in Ghana is discussed in my article, 'Some Structural Aspects of Regional Government in Uganda and Ghana,' *Journal of Administration Overseas*, vol. 12, no. 2, 1973. The present paragraphs are adapted from this article.

16 For further background see K. J. Davey, 'Local Bureaucrats and Politicians in East Africa', *Journal of Administration Overseas*, vol. 10, no. 4, 1971, pp. 268-279.

17 *Boma* is the Swahili for fort and is the word used in anglophone East and Central Africa for the building where district headquarters are based.

18 Cf. Colin Leys, *Politicians and Policies* (Nairobi 1967).

19 Cf. David E. Apter and Martin R. Doornbos, 'Development and the Political Process: A Plan for a Constitution', in A. R. Desai (ed.), *Essays on Modernization of Underdeveloped Societies*, vol. 1 (Bombay 1971).

20 The Institution Building school or movement is of particular interest in this regard. For an introduction, see Joseph W. Eaton (ed.), *Institution Building and Development, From Concept to Application* (Beverly Hills/London 1972). The contributions of Esman might be noted, though, for their recognition of the need for social relevance of institutions. See e.g. Milton J. Esman and Fred C. Bruhns, 'Institution Building in National Development: An Approach to Induced Social Change in Transitional Societies', in Holis W. Peter (ed.), *Comparative Theories of Social Change* (Ann Arbor 1966).

21 Cf. Samuel P. Huntington, 'Political Development and Political Decay', *World Politics*, vol. 17, no. 3, 1965, pp. 386-430.

22 Cf. my article 'Political Development: The Search for Criteria', *Development and Change*, vol. 1, no. 1, 1969-1970.

23 *Uganda News*, no 3569/71, 6th August, 1971.

24 See Appendix I.

Bibliography

Agetereine, Runyankore paper, fortnightly, Mbarara.
Ankole District Administration
  Annual District Reports.
  District Commissioner's Baraza Books.
  Official correspondence and other archival material.
Ankole Government
  Eishengyero minutes.
  Ankole Kingdom Government Establishment lists (1961, 1963, 1966).
  Ankole Government Memorandum to the O.A.U. Commission on Refugees (Mbarara 1964).
  Report of the Ankole Kingdom Customary Law Committee (Mbarara 1964).
  Report, Commission of Enquiry into Ankole Mailo Land, mimeo (Mbarara 1965).
  Ankole Government White Paper on Report of Commission of Enquiry into Ankole
    Mailo Land, mimeo (Mbarara 1965).
  Official correspondence and other archival material.
Apter, David E., *The Political Kingdom in Uganda: A Study in Bureaucratic Nationalism*
  (Princeton 1961).
Apter, David and Doornbos, Martin R., 'Development and the Political Process: A
  Plan for a Constitution', in A. R. Desai (ed.), *Essays on Modernization of
  Underdeveloped Societies*, vol. 1 (Bombay 1971).
Apthorpe, Raymond, 'Does Tribalism Really Matter?', *Transition* 37.
——, 'Land Law and Land Policy in Eastern Africa', mimeo, Makerere University
  (Kampala 1968).
Ashe, Robert P., *Two Kings of Uganda* (London 1889).
Bailey, F. G., *Stratagems and Spoils, A Social Anthropology of Politics* (Oxford 1970).
Barth, Fredrik (ed.), *Ethnic Groups and Boundaries, The Social Organization of Culture
  Differences* (Bergen-Oslo and London 1969).
Beattie, John, *Bunyoro, An African Kingdom* (New York 1960).
Béteille, André (ed.), *Social Inequality* (Harmondsworth 1969).
Brock, Beverley, 'Customary Land Tenure, "Individualization" and Agricultural
  Development', Rural Development Research Paper, no. 65, Makerere University
  (Kampala 1968).
Cook, Sir Albert A., *Uganda Memories (1897-1940)*, (Kampala 1945).
Cook, G. C., 'Tribal Incidence of Lactose Deficiency in Uganda', *The Lancet*, April 2,
  1966.
Crown Agents for the Colonies, *Notes for Officers Appointed to Uganda* (London 1934).
Cunningham, J. F., *Uganda and its People* (London 1905).
Dahrendorf, Ralf., *Class and Class Conflict in Industrial Society* (London 1959).
Davey, K. J., 'Local Bureaucrats and Politicians in East Africa', *Journal of
  Administration Overseas*, vol. 10, no. 4, 1971.

Doornbos, Martin R., 'Political Development: The Search for Criteria', *Development and Change*, vol. 1, no. 1, 1969.

——, 'Kumanyana and Rwenzururu: Two Responses to Ethnic Inequality', in Robert I. Rotberg and Ali A. Mazrui (eds.), *Protest and Power in Black Africa* (New York 1970).

——, 'Protest Movements in Western Uganda: Some Parallels and Contrasts', *Kroniek van Afrika*, 1970, 3.

——, 'Images and Reality of Stratification in Pre-colonial Nkore', *Canadian Journal of African Studies*, vol. 7, no. 3, 1973.

——, 'Some Structural Aspects of Regional Government in Uganda and Ghana', *Journal of Administration Overseas*, vol. 12, no. 2, 1973.

——, 'Some Conceptual Problems concerning Ethnicity in Integration Analysis', *Civilisations*, vol. 22, no. 2, 1972.

——, *Regalia Galore: the decline and eclipse of Ankole kingship* (Nairobi 1975).

——, 'Land Tenure and Political Conflict in Ankole, Uganda', *Journal of Development Studies*, vol. 12, no. 1, 1975.

——, 'Ethnicity, Christianity and the Development of Social Stratification in Colonial Ankole, Uganda', *International Journal of African Historical Studies*, vol. 9, no 4, 1976.

——, 'Ankole', in René Lemarchand (ed.), *African Kingships in Perspective* (London 1977).

——, and Michael F. Lofchie, 'Ranching and Scheming: A Case Study of the Ankole Ranching Scheme', in Michael F. Lofchie (ed.), *The State of the Nations: Constraints on Development in Independent Africa* (Berkeley and Los Angeles 1971).

Eaton, Joseph W. (ed.), *Institution Building and Development, from Concept to Application* (Beverly Hills and London 1972).

Eisenstadt, S. N., 'The Process of Absorption of New Immigrants in Israel', *Human Relations*, V, 1952.

Edel, M. M., *The Chiga of Western Uganda* (New York 1957).

Epstein, A. L., *Politics in an African Urban Community* (Manchester 1958).

Erikson, Erik H., *Young Man Luther* (New York 1958).

Esman, Milton J. and Bruhns, Fred C., 'Institution Building in National Development: An Approach to Induced Social Change in Transitional Societies', in Hollis W. Peter (ed.), *Comparative Theories of Social Change* (Ann Arbor 1966).

Fallers, L., 'The Predicament of the Modern African Chief', *American Anthropologist*, vol. 57, no. 2, 1955.

Fallers, L. A. (ed.), *The King's Men* (London 1964).

Finer, S. E., *The Anonymous Empire* (London 1963).

Fortes, M. and Evans-Pritchard, E. E. (eds.), *African Political Systems* (London 1940).

Geertz, Clifford, 'The Integrative Revolution: Primordial Sentiments and Civil Politics in the New States', in Geertz (ed.), *Old Societies and New States* (New York 1963).

Gorju, P. J., *Entre le Victoria, l'Albert et l'Edouard* (Rennes 1920).

Graham, James, 'Two Case Studies in Fragmentation: Bwamba/Busongora and Sebei', unpublished Ms., African Studies Program, Makerere University College (Kampala 1966).

Greenberg, Joseph H., 'Africa as a Linguistic Area', in William R. Bascom and Melville J. Herskovits (eds.), *Continuity and Change in African Cultures* (Chicago 1961).

Gulliver, P. H. (ed.), *Tradition and Transition in East Africa* (London 1969).

Hailey, Lord, *An African Survey*, Revised Edition (London 1957).

Heusch, Luc de, *Le Roi Ivre ou l'origine de l'Etat* (Paris 1972).

Huntington, Samuel P., 'Political Development and Political Decay', *World Politics*, vol. 17, no. 3, 1965.

Johnston, Sir Harry, *The Uganda Protectorate*, vols. 1 and 2 (London 1902).

Kabwegyere, Tarsis B., 'The Dynamics of Colonial Violence: The Inductive System in Uganda', *The Journal of Peace Research*, vol. 9, no. 4, 1972.

Karugire, S. R., *A History of the Kingdom of Nkore in Western Uganda to 1896* (Oxford 1971).

Katate, A. G. and Kamugungunu, L., *Abagabe b'Ankole*, Ekitabo I and II (Kampala 1955).

Kottak, Conrad P., 'Ecological Variables in the Origin and Evolution of African States: the Buganda Example', *Comparative Studies in Society and History*, vol. 14, no. 3, 1972.

Leach, E. R., *Political Systems of Highland Burma* (London 1954).

Lemarchand, René, *Rwanda and Burundi* (London 1970).

——, 'Power and Stratification in Rwanda: A Reconsideration', *Cahiers d'Etudes Africaines*, vol. 6, no. 4, 1966.

Lewis, I. M., *A Pastoral Democracy* (London 1961).

Leys, Colin, *Politicians and Policies: An Essay on Politics in Acholi, Uganda, 1962-1965* (Nairobi 1967).

Lipset, S. M., *The First New Nation* (New York 1963).

Lloyd, Peter C., 'The Political Structure of African Kingdoms: An Exploratory Model', in M. Banton (ed.), *Political Systems and the Distribution of Power* (London 1965).

Low, D. A., *Political Parties in Uganda 1949-62* (London 1963).

——, 'The Establishment of British Administration: Two Examples from Uganda, 1900-1901', EAISR Conference Paper (Kampala 1956).

Lowie, Robert H., *Social Organization* (London 1950).

Lukyn Williams, F., 'The Inauguration of the Omugabe of Ankole to Office', *Uganda Journal*, vol. 4, no. 4, 1937.

——, 'Blood Brotherhood in Ankole (Omukago)', *Uganda Journal*, vol. 2, no. 1, 1934.

——, 'Nuwa Mbaguta, Nganzi of Ankole', *Uganda Journal*, vol. 10. no. 2, 1946.

Mackintosh, W. L. S., *Some Notes on the Bahima and the Cattle Industry in Ankole* (Mbarara 1938).

Mair, Lucy, 'Busoga Local Government', *Journal of Commonwealth Political Studies*, vol. 5, no. 2, 1967.

Maquet, Jacques J., *The Premise of Inequality* (London 1961).

——, 'Institutionalisation Féodale des relations de dépendence dans quatre cultures interlacustrines', *Colloque du Groupe de Recherches en Anthropologie et Sociologie Politique*, mimeo, (Paris 1968).

Mazrui, Ali A., 'Pluralism and National Integration', in Leo Kuper and M. G. Smith (eds.), *Pluralism in Africa* (Berkeley and Los Angeles 1969).

Mead, Margaret (ed.), *Cultural Patterns and Technical Change* (Paris 1953).

Morris, H. F., *A History of Ankole* (Kampala 1962).

——, (ed.), *The Heroic Recitations of the Bahima of Ankole* (Oxford 1964).

——, 'The Making of Ankole', *Uganda Journal*, vol. 21, no. 1, 1957.

——, 'The Kingdom of Mpororo', *Uganda Journal*, vol. 19, no. 2, 1955.

——, 'The Murder of H. St. Galt', *Uganda Journal*, vol. 24, no. 1, 1960.

Mukherjee, Ramkrishna, *The Dynamics of a Rural Society: A Study of the Economic Structure in Bengal Villages* (Berlin 1957).

Mungonya, Z. C. K., 'The Bacwezi in Ankole,' *Uganda Journal*, vol. 22, no. 1, 1958.

Mushanga, M. T., 'The Clan System among the Banyankore', *Uganda Journal*, vol. 34, no. 1, 1970.

Ntare School History Society, 'The Governmental Institutions in Ankole before the British Rule,' mimeo (Mbarara, n.d, 1965).

Oberg, K., 'The Kingdom of Ankole in Uganda', in M. Fortes and E. E. Evans-Pritchard (eds.), *African Political Systems* (London 1940).

Obote, Milton A., 'Language and National Identification', *East Africa Journal,* April, 1967.

Posnansky, Merrick, 'Kingship, Archeology and Historical Myth', *Uganda Journal,* vol. 30, no. 1, 1966.

Pye, Lucian W., *Aspects of Political Development* (Boston 1966).

Richards, Audrey I. (ed.), *East African Chiefs* (London 1959).

Roscoe, John, *The Banyankole* (Cambridge 1923).

Segall, Marshall H., Doornbos, Martin R., and Davis, Clive, *Political Identity: A Case Study from Uganda* (Syracuse, 1976).

Sekanyola, Luganda paper, Kampala.

Southwold, Martin, *Bureaucracy and Chiefship in Buganda,* East African Studies, no 14, (Kampala 1961).

Speke, J. H., *Journal of the Discovery of the Source of the Nile* (London 1863).

Stenning, D. J., 'Preliminary Observations on the Balokole Movement Particularly among Bahima in Ankole District', *EAISR Conference Paper* (Kampala 1958).

———, 'Salvation in Ankole', in M. Fortes and G. Dieterlen (eds.), *African Systems of Thought* (London 1965).

———, 'The Nyankole', in Audrey I. Richards (ed.), *East African Chiefs* (London 1959).

Swartz, Marc J. (ed.), *Local-Level Politics* (Chicago 1968).

Taylor, Brian K., *The Western Lacustrine Bantu* (London 1962).

The People, Weekly (changed later into a daily paper), Kampala.

Thomas, H. B. and Robert Scott, *Uganda* (London 1935).

Truman, David B., *The Governmental Process* (New York 1953).

Tucker, Alfred R., *Eighteen Years in Uganda and East Africa* (London 1911).

Uganda Argus, daily paper, Kampala.

Uganda Government, *Constitution of Uganda,* 1962.

———, *Report of the Commission of Inquiry into the Recent Disturbances among the Baamba and Bakonjo People of Toro* (Entebbe 1962).

———, *Administration (Western Kingdoms and Bugosa) Act,* 1963.

———, *Constitution of the Republic of Uganda,* 1967.

———, Report of the Committee of Inquiry into Ankole District Council and District Administration Affairs, mimeo, 1969.

———, *Statistical Abstract,* 1971.

———, Department of Information, *Annual Reports.*

Uganda News, Ministry of Information and Broadcasting, Kampala, Uganda.

Uganda Protectorate, *Ankole Agreement, 1901.*

———, *System of Chieftainships of Ankole,* 1907.

———, *Development of Kiswahili as an Educational and Administrative Language in the Uganda Protectorate* (Entebbe 1928).

———, *Native Administration* (Entebbe 1939).

———, *Local Administration Ordinance,* 1952.

———, *Report of an Inquiry into African Local Government in the Protectorate of Uganda* (Wallis Report), 1953.

———, *District Administration (District Councils) Ordinance,* 1955.

———, *Land Tenure Proposals* (Entebbe 1955).

———, *Report on the Runyankore-Rukiga Orthographic Conference,* 1956.

———, *Land Tenure in Uganda* (Entebbe 1957).

———, *African Local Government Ordinance*, 1959.

———, *Report of the Constitutional Committee* (Wild Report), 1959.

———, *Report of the Uganda Relationships Commission* (Munster Report), 1961.

———, *Exchange of Despatches between His Excellency the Governor and Secretary of State for the Colonies concerning the Creation of Sebei District* (Entebbe 1962).

———, *Report of the Commissioner Appointed to Inquire into the Operation of the Land Tenure Scheme in Ankole* (Entebbe 1962).

———, *Report of the Uganda Independence Conference*, 1962.

Uzoigwe, G. N., 'Pre-colonial Markets in Bunyoro-Kitara', *Comparative Studies in Society and History*, vol. 24, no. 4, 1972.

Van den Berghe, Pierre, 'European Languages and Black Mandarins', *Transition*, 34.

Vansina, J., 'A Comparison of African Kingdoms', *Africa*, vol. 32, no. 4, 1962.

Vincent, Joan, *African Elite: The Big Men of a Small Town* (New York and London, 1971).

Webster, J. E. (ed.), *Uganda Before 1900*, vol. 1 (Nairobi 1973).

Welbourn, F. B., *Religion and Politics in Uganda 1952-1962* (Nairobi 1965).

Willis, J., *Willis Journal*, vols. 1 and 2, unpublished. Makerere University Library, Kampala.

Wrigley, C. G., 'The Changing Economic Structure of Buganda', in L. A. Fallers (ed.), *The King's Men* (London 1964).

———, 'Some Thoughts on the Bacwezi', *Uganda Journal*, vol. 22, no. 1, 1958.

Index